Fogg, Erik
Wedged : how you became
a tool of the partisan p
[2015]
33305234517377
CU   08/31/16

D1504803

WEDGED

ERIK **FOGG** & NATHANIEL **GREENE**

Copyright 2015 by Erik Fogg and Nathaniel Greene.

Published by MidTide Media

All rights reserved.

Printed in the United States of America.

No part of this book may be reproduced in any manner whatsoever without written permission except in the case of brief quotations embodied in critical articles and reviews. For information, address MidTide Media, 123 Pleasant St, Suite 300, Marblehead, MA 01945.

MidTide Media books are available at special discounts for bulk purchases in the US by corporations, institutions, and other organizations. For more information, please contact MidTide Media at the above address.

Editorial Production by Molly Rubenstein

Copyediting by Katy Gero

Book Design by Stephanie Tyll

Graphical Design by Stella Komninou Arakelian

Cover Art by Emily Alexander

ISBN (paperback): 978-0-9898654-4-9

ISBN (eBook): 978-0-9898654-5-6

TABLE OF CONTENTS

INTRODUCTION:
HOW AMERICAN POLITICAL DIALOGUE FELL APART

"Let us not seek the Republican answer or the Democratic answer, but the right answer. Let us not seek to fix the blame for the past. Let us accept our own responsibility for the future."

-John F Kennedy, 35th President of the United States

Think of an issue that one might encounter in regular discussions about policy and politics in an advanced democratic society, such as tax rates or the number of legal migrants that the country should accept in a given year.

You would probably expect the distribution of opinion to follow something like a bell curve (or the "normal" curve) along the left-right political spectrum.[1] Most people would likely have an array of opinions with a lot of overlap and some variation; on

---

1   We do not strictly mean the mathematical definition of the normal or Poisson distribution, but simply one in which there is a lump in the middle that trails off as it reaches the left and right edges of the graph.

the left and right extremes of the political spectrum, we would see small numbers of people with hard-line political opinions.[2]

In most advanced democracies, including the United States, polling on specific policy measures tends to reflect this curve. Most Americans inhabit a "middle ground" of ideas while a few have hard-line views to the left or right of this group. This is even true with highly emotional issues of conscience: for instance, when you ask a randomized group of Americans to tell you up to how many weeks pregnant should abortion be available, you see this pattern:[3]

OPINIONS ON ABORTION AT 20 VS 24 WEEKS

The US Supreme Court has said abortion is legal without restriction in about the first 24 weeks of pregnancy. Some states have passed laws reducing this to 20 weeks.

If it has to be one or the other, would you rather have abortions legal without restriction up to 20 weeks, or up to 24 weeks?

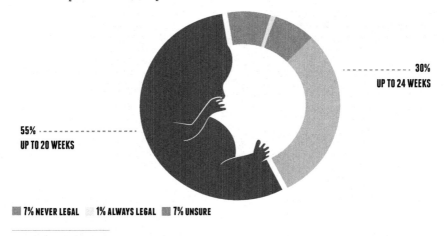

30%
UP TO 24 WEEKS

55%
UP TO 20 WEEKS

■ **7% NEVER LEGAL**　　**1% ALWAYS LEGAL**　■ **7% UNSURE**

QUINNIPIAC UNIVERSITY POLL - July 28-31, 2013. N=1,468 registered voters nationwide

4

2　　We model a person's political disposition as being a loose sum of their political positions. If one's political positions are consistently on a far end of a spectrum, they are "partisan" or "extreme."

3　　Note the framing here: we do not use a poll asking people about whether they are pro-life or pro-choice. Because such terms are highly politicized (as we'll discuss later), they provoke people into taking extreme positions. If we control the framing to be about policy questions, we can get more accurate representations of Americans' policy preferences, rather than their tribal identities.

4　　*Quinnipac University Poll*, July 28-31, 2013. Pollingreport.com http://www.pollingreport.com/abortion.htm, accessed 8/15/2015

On most political issues, we observe a general trend of a large group in the middle with a relatively small fringe element across a grey scale of policy options. This makes intuitive sense.

GREENE - FOGG CURVE

Spectrum of opinions vs national political engagement on a given issue

■ Distribution of Political Opinions

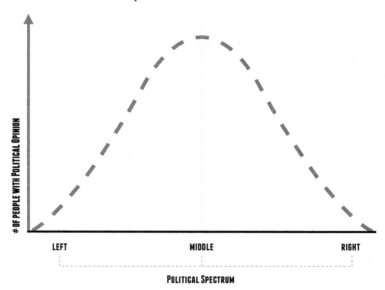

If 90% of Americans preferred three brands of ice cream, you might expect those three brands to dominate the shelves of the ice-cream aisle in most grocery stores. Similarly, it stands to reason that you would see the activity of the political industry -- campaigning, lawmaking, media coverage, and public consumption -- match the distribution of public opinion on these issues. We would expect most politicians and political media to be discussing the views of this middle ground, with little attention paid to the fringes. We would expect our own in-person and online discussions to follow the same pattern, with those at the extremes having relatively little voice.

You may have noticed that the actual engagement level at different policy positions does not follow this distribution. In modern American politics, it looks like this:

GREENE - FOGG CURVE

Spectrum of opinions vs national political engagement on a given issue

■ Distribution of National Engagement

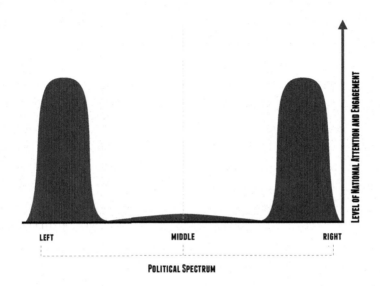

Most of the national attention and dialogue is devoted to hard-line and uncompromising left- and right-wing positions, even though they make up a proportionally small portion of popular opinion. A small group in the middle objects to this binary framing of American politics, but it has relatively little political power and its proposed solutions do not yet appear strong enough to bridge the divide.

GREENE - FOGG CURVE

Spectrum of opinions vs national political engagement on a given issue

◼ Distribution of Political Opinions ◼ Distribution of National Engagement

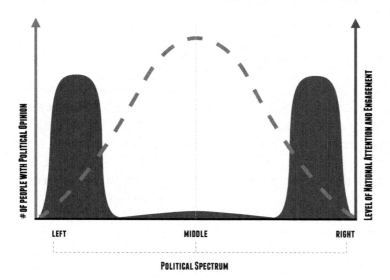

We observe that the middle ground has become silent and disengaged. Those who lean slightly to the left or right have been politically co-opted, so that their voices power the extremes. They have been "magnetized" to support one partisan camp or the other.

This dynamic has become all too familiar in the United States. The political system appears to consist of two camps of people standing on two very tall platforms with a wide chasm between them, yelling at each other. They consider each other enemies, threatening the nation's well-being. These two dominant political groups are so far apart that there is little chance of them influencing each other. The national dialogue becomes a war between them and politics grinds to a standstill. Congress sits in perpetual gridlock, neither passing productive legislation nor accurately representing the policy views of most Americans.

Americans recognize that there is a serious problem with the political system. 72% of Americans are dissatisfied with the direction of the country,[5] and **for the first time in the modern United States, the government itself is seen as the single biggest problem facing the nation.**[6] The leading driver of this dissatisfaction? Gridlock.[7]

HOW DID WE GET HERE?

If one looks back to the 1980s and 1990s, one sees a very different political reality in the United States. One saw presidencies like those of Ronald Reagan, George H.W. Bush, and Bill Clinton, during which politicians in Washington were able to reach across the aisle, make deals, find common ground, and get things done. The parties themselves contained more ideological diversity; there were liberal Republicans and conservative Democrats and many moderates in each party[8] pushing towards productive compromise. Legislators formed temporary coalitions on different pieces of legislation, as representatives pursued the nuanced and diverse interests of their constituencies.

We saw an electorate that could agree on what to do to help the country and two parties that--while they postured and disagreed--worked together to accomplish what they believed was right.

What changed?

Let's imagine that you're a politician. To be elected to office you have to win the general election, but first you have to win your primary.

---

5   *Gallup poll*, August 5-9. http://www.gallup.com/poll/1669/general-mood-country.aspx, accessed 10/9/2015

6   *Gallup.* "Cluster of Concerns Vie for Top U.S. Problem in 2014." Gallup.com, www.gallup.com/poll/180398/cluster-concerns-vie-top-problem-2014.aspx, accessed 9/14/2015

7   Of those that responded that they are dissatisfied with Congress (78% of all polled), they were asked why. 59% cited gridlock and inaction as the top reason. Lydia Saad, Gallup. "Gridlock is top reason Americans are critical of Congress." 6/12/2013, http://www.gallup.com/poll/163031/gridlock-top-reason-americans-critical-congress.aspx, accessed 10/30/2015.

8   *Pew Research.* "Political Polarization in the American Public." http://www.people-press.org/2014/06/12/political-polarization-in-the-american-public/, accessed 10/28/2015

It is important to recognize that, for most people, the more extreme their opinion, the more time and money they are willing to put into something. For example, if you couldn't care less if you had an iPhone or Android, you'll just buy a phone when you need one, with the features and price that you like best. But if you're an iPhone fanatic, you'll camp out overnight to be among the first to have them. The same is true in politics. The fanatics are those who are most likely to vote, contribute, volunteer, and promote candidates.

This means that to win the primary, candidates actually need to be more politically extreme than the average party viewpoint in order to appeal to those party extremists, who are most motivated to expend energy supporting them.

In recent decades, marketing and campaigning have become more sophisticated. Politicians and political media gained access to useful data about their target audiences through the rise of the internet, high-frequency polling, and sophisticated analytics tools. Marketers gained access to developments in human psychology and statistical analysis. Consultants joined campaigns and news marketing teams in droves.[9] Party-related activists grew more prevalent and increasingly sophisticated in their capacity to rally voters.[10]

Through this evolution, politicians and media companies learned that nothing would more effectively and reliably drive Americans to tune in and vote than emotionally sensationalizing the political issues that the country faces. In effect, they learned that the easiest method of getting attention and getting elected is to pit us against one another.

We call this manufactured emotional divide "the wedge" in American politics, and the tactics used to create it, "wedging." These tactics focus largely on exploiting "wedge issues" that incite strong emotions in each end of the political spectrum.

---

9   Douglas Lanthrop. The Campaign Continues: How Political Consultants and Campaign Tactics Affect Public Policy. Praeger Publishers: Westport, CT, 2003.

10   Geoffrey C. Layman, et al. "Party Polarization in American Politics: Characteristics, Causes, and Consequences." Annual Review of Political Science. 2006, issue 9, pages 83-110.

Over the past 20 years, wedging tactics have grown increasingly effective and sophisticated. These tactics play on humans' natural emotional tribal tendencies, driving partisan Americans to propagate this cycle themselves by accepting that politics is about defeating an enemy. They have driven antipathy deeply into the political culture of this country.

THE WEDGE

By leading us down this path, politicians have introduced a dangerous disease into the American political system.

Wedging tactics are self-perpetuating. Like a virus, counter-productive antagonistic framing and tribalism spread throughout the players in the system.

It starts when politicians resort to emotionally manipulative strategies in their campaigns. Effective campaigners brand their opponents as badly intentioned and the opposition's policies as dangerous, threatening the values of the target electorate.

This rhetoric reinforces the suspicions of voters and other lawmakers who already have partisan leanings. Successfully riled up, they become angrier and more afraid of defeat and are inspired to take action: they pontificate on Facebook, they demonstrate, they vote, they give money. The media jumps on board, creating reliable viewers and readers by stoking those emotions.

More moderate voices become frustrated by the extremism and either leave the parties to become

> In politics, a wedge issue is a social issue, often of a divisive or controversial nature, which splits apart a population or political group. Wedging can be done intentionally (designed to split an opposing party) or unintentionally, when energizing a political base (polarizing a population into political extremes). Typically, wedge issues have a cultural or populist theme, relating to matters such as crime, national security, morality, religion, sexuality, gender, or race.

Independents or simply shut down and disengage from politics altogether, leaving behind shrinking parties increasingly dominated by extreme partisans. Because of the US primary system, that leaves only the hardliners to select the candidates that the dominant two parties send to the general election.

Simply demanding that politicians "stop" won't fix this. The incentives are stacked against reason and moderation: those politicians who wedge best win elections. Selective pressures push candidates to develop and refine their emotionally manipulative tactics each election to stay ahead of their opponents. Those who try to remain "above the fray" end up becoming irrelevant.

And so the large middle ground is hollowed out. Many Americans that lean slightly left or right migrate towards the fringe: their opinions do not become more extreme, but in an effort to remain politically relevant, they throw their lot in with these powerful political extremes, defending the positions of the loudest in order to maintain a perceived need for solidarity. Those that don't choose a side disengage and withdraw from the discussion out of frustration and exhaustion. Both behaviors power these partisan camps and what results is a positive feedback loop in which a small, polarized fringe wields ever-greater power in the American political system.

It becomes clear that the American political process is breaking down. The cause is not the typically-cited problem of partisanship: there are good arguments that partisanship and disagreement can be highly productive for a democracy.[11] The dysfunction of American politics is driven by the wedging techniques that have empowered the fringes and destroyed the majority middle ground.

As the middle ground dissolves, day-to-day political dialogue among the public grows increasingly unproductive and unpleasant. For those of you brave (or foolish) enough to engage

---

11   Arguments include each party challenging the other's statements and facts to "keep them honest," voters having greater choice, and solutions being forged from different ideas. Some good further reading is available from The Atlantic's 2008 article, "The Case for Partisanship." http://www.theatlantic.com/magazine/archive/2008/04/the-case-for-partisanship/306700/, accessed 10/9/2015

in political discussion, you may have noticed some odd arche-
types emerge.

GREENE - FOGG CURVE

Spectrum of opinions vs national political engagement on a given issue

■ Distribution of Political Opinions ■ Distribution of National Engagement

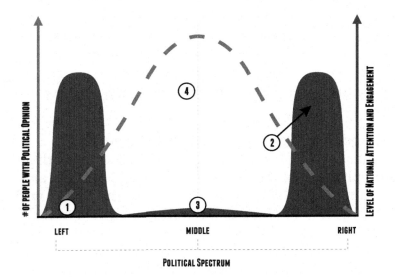

1. **The True Believers:** This comparatively small group of
   extremists sits at either end of the bell curve. They are
   fully committed to fighting a great ideological battle
   to defeat their counterparts on the other side of the
   spectrum. Their devotion means there is no room for curiosity or exploration of political ideas: you are either with
   them or against them.

2. **The Hijacked:** You will find some people who have been
   co-opted: their beliefs are nuanced, but they have thrown
   their lot in with party hard-liners rather than become
   irrelevant. They know they are not "pure to the cause,"
   but fear rejection from the group if they deviate from
   the party-line. When challenged, they might dig in and
   shut down conversation with an angry retreat to a safe
   "one liner." Their energy adds to the power of the True
   Believers.

3. **The Disengaged:** Many Americans will now declare that "one does not talk about politics in polite company." This largest group is so disengaged that they simply won't listen anymore. They will proudly declare that they "stay out of politics." They make up much of the middle of the spectrum that has evaporated.

4. **The Lost:** Left in the middle are some confused people that wonder why the world went mad. They make general statements like "we should just get together and work this out," or "if only a more reasonable candidate was out there."

Meaningful policy discussions are dead. The national dialogue has been left to fringe elements furiously agreeing with themselves, some confused and angry people who are caught up in party loyalty, and a vacuum between. Today, John F. Kennedy would have probably just run a tech startup. Millennials, often criticized for not engaging in politics, might just be wise enough to realize that engaging in modern US politics is currently largely a waste of time.

The result of all of this is a shift over time to become more politically extreme. It is a natural outcome of a two party system with a winner-takes-all electoral structure. It has strong mechanisms in place that are powerful and will continue to reinforce the situation.

THE FALSE CHASM

Most people that observe this process believe its cause is a growing divide in values in the United States: there is a culture war in which one America pits itself against another.

We believe that the notion of "two Americas" is false and that the culture war is largely fabricated, that modern polarization is driven not by divergent values but by manipulation. We claim instead that, at its core, there is one America. As a nation, we share a wide and thorough swath of intractable values that bind us and - for better or worse - separate us from many of our peer nations.

This does not mean that we won't, or shouldn't, disagree. We each bring our unique experience and background to the table when we are solving the problem of how to make things better. Such differences can be incredibly valuable in groups that choose to work together: from the Continental Congress to Lincoln's Team of Rivals, fierce disagreement has led to incredible progress.

But the wedge drives us beyond disagreement and into blind war. If we do nothing, it will get worse. We are playing our parts in the destructive cycle by allowing ourselves to be manipulated. The American public will need to change in order to overcome the wedge and heal the partisan divide.

This isn't easy. As humans, we're programmed to identify with and defend our tribe -- for millennia, that was the best way to avoid getting killed or eaten or dying from starvation. And evidence suggests that no matter how capable our brains are of great curiosity and critical thinking in abstract problem-solving or even personal decision-making, *it's the tribal identification and defense mechanisms, an entirely different part of our brain, that engages when we think about politics.*[12] This makes us highly vulnerable to wedging.

STRATEGIES FOR EXTRACTING THE WEDGE

Most Americans recognize that political dysfunction is a major problem in the United States and some have proposed solutions to it, with various levels of sophistication. Consider these five approaches:

Capitulate

The most superficial level of trying to solve the problem involves each partisan side insisting that the other side should be "more bipartisan." We can imagine one saying, "American partisanship is a serious problem: if only the other side wasn't so

---

12   Joshua Greene's Moral Tribes, Drew Westen's The Political Brain, Jonathan Haidt's The Righteous Mind, Jesse Prinz's The Emotional Construction of Morals, Jason Weeden & Robert Kurzban's The Hidden Agenda of the Political Mind, and many other good books have been written on the topic.

unreasonable, it would be fine." But for people that believe this, "we should be more bipartisan" most often equates to "the other side should just agree with me." The partisan camps within this group get into heated arguments, share political memes and inflammatory articles, and try to "shut down" the alleged foolishness of the other side. Peace comes after victory.

Such attempts to crush the opposition have dominated political dialogue in the past 20 years and have driven the wedge deeper into American politics.

Cut the child in half

When it becomes clear that total victory won't happen, a desire to compromise is floated. "We need to work together and compromise," or "we need to meet in the middle." This strategy is tantamount to demanding that both sides betray half of their perceived ideals. Politicians that want to "compromise away" their party positions are at risk of being dislodged in a primary challenge.[13]

Talk to an empty room

If the current crop of politicians are not able to compromise, then perhaps we can simply find new politicians that are "reasonable" or "moderate," some argue. This approach views the problem of hyper-partisanship as a fairly arbitrary decision by legislators to be partisan. If we just changed the people in office, it would be fine.

But such novel politicians show up to an empty room: without the emotional appeal of candidates armed with wedging tactics, nobody in the primaries will be inspired to support them. In theory this approach has much merit, but it is unlikely to work anytime soon.[14]

---

13   See Robert G. Boatright, Getting Primaried: The Changing Politics of Congressional Primary Challenges.

14   Perhaps the best example of this effort is in creating "open primaries," in which unaffiliated and/or other-party voters can vote within a party's primary. Such an effort allows candidates to court the middle ground outside of the party base, but it falls short in part due to ongoing low turnout in primaries from Independent voters.

Unilateral disarmament

Once one recognizes the power of the wedging strategy, one might believe that the disillusioned American voter will demand that politicians stop using it. Perhaps a clean campaign pledge would lessen the effect of wedging.. A unilateral disarmament would take place, and "reasonable" politics would come back.

But this ignores the political incentives at work. Because wedging strategies win elections, those that unilaterally disarm will lose and be washed out of politics, so the promise is lost as soon as the election occurs.

Our Solution: Build the middle ground

If we want the graph of national political engagement to reflect the bell curve of real American political positions, if we want to elect politicians that actually represent the views of the elec- torate, then we need to re-engage those who have dropped out of the conversation. Wedging tactics silence the middle ground. But they are also the most powerful way to compete for political influence and market share -- we can't simply wish them away. To reverse their effects, we need to take away their power.

We accomplish this by crafting an environment in which wedging is no longer effective. Success requires the creation of a climate where people react with disgust to the tactic being used on them and reject the false black-or-white framing of different political issues; a culture that rejects the false split-identity and re-centers itself on the core values that Americans share.

This is our mission with Wedged: to begin building the middle ground, reversing the trend of polarization in the United States by helping Americans become less susceptible to wedging. We want people who read Wedged to respond differently to wedging tactics. We want them to be primed to say, "hang on a minute," when wedging tactics are used on them, and consider alterna- tive ways to think about problems that aren't sensationalized extremes.

We start by helping people understand how they are being manipulated and how their power is being co-opted. In **Part 1**, we offer a clinical analysis of the wedge: how it evolved, how it functions, and what it looks like when you see it in your everyday life.

The next step is to start practicing a different way of looking at things. In **Part 2**, we carefully examine a series of wedge issues, introducing data from a variety of sources and challenging the way these issues have been framed for us by politicians, the media, and likely our friends and family.

In **Part 3**, we show how wedge issues can lose their power over the public.

In **Part 4**, we begin the discussion of how to actively fight the wedge in our day-to-day lives, both in ourselves and with our friends.

This is not intended to be a passive experience for you and it may not be an entirely comfortable one. We are likely to introduce data or analyses that contradict your firmly held beliefs. We do not ask that you blindly believe us but we do ask that you engage with us. Recognize any partisan fist-pumping reflexes in your response and decide if they are actually in tune with what you really believe on some specific issues. This is an exercise meant to increase your own political effectiveness: get as much out of it as you can.

We wrote this book because we believe that Americans are capable of overcoming the poison and dysfunction in our current political system. We believe that Americans are motivated to do so and have both the smarts and grit necessary. When Americans are aware of the roots behind the toxic state of modern politics, and aware of the wedging tactics being used all around them, they'll be armed to fight it. With this, we can turn the tides and redirect our lawmakers to the challenging and important work of arguing productively and forging solutions together.

There are a lot of people that believe American politics is doomed and our efforts are futile. But there is a path to changing it. This book is the very nascent beginning of the steps it will take to destroy wedging tactics. The rest is up to us.

PART I
THE WEDGE IN AMERICAN POLITICS

CHAPTER ONE:
THE DIRE STATE OF AMERICAN POLITICAL DYSFUNCTION

"In the areas of marriage, race, victimhood: if it hurts America, it helps the Democratic Party." [1]

> -Dennis Prager, conservative columnist and political commentator

"Civilization as we know it would be in jeopardy if Republicans win the senate." [2]

> -Nancy Pelosi, house minority leader

THE BREAKDOWN

The apparent political polarization of the United States has been increasing over the past twenty years and has now reached

---

1   Dennis Praeger, *National Review.* "What's Bad for America is Good for Democrats." http://www.nationalreview.com/article/391277/whats-bad-america-good-democrats-dennis-prager, accessed 10/28/2015

2   Brett LoGiurato, *Business Insider.* "NANCY PELOSI: 'Civilization As We Know It Would Be In Jeopardy' If The GOP Wins The Senate." http://www.businessinsider.com/nancy-pelosi-civilization-jeopardy-gop-senate-win-2014-9, accessed 10/28/2015

a state of crisis. Many of the most basic and important functions of congress are dangerously neglected. The core priorities of Americans are not being addressed. Special interest groups are driving policy debates in the absence of productive input from American citizens.[3] News media and politicians running for office are deliberately simplifying and sensationalizing the framing of political issues, taking advantage of human psychology in order to build and maintain attention and support.

This environment is driving Americans from the two-party system: registered Independents have hit a record high of 43% of voters.[4] Members of this growing group have become exhausted by the current state of politics and are dropping out nearly entirely. Highly-involved partisan extremes, despite representing a small and shrinking part of the electorate, have become the dominant force in the system.

During the George W. Bush and Barack Obama presidencies, the Democratic and Republican parties began to move away from each other. Since 1987, when the nonpartisan polling think-tank Pew Research started measuring it, agreement on policy steps has never been lower and the gap between Democratic and Republican policy stances has never been wider. [5]

3   Martin Gilens and Benjamin I. Page. "Testing Theories of American Politics: Elites, Interest Groups, and Average Citizens." *American Political Science Association*, 12:3, Nov 2014. http://scholar.princeton.edu/sites/default/files/mgilens/files/gilens_and_page_2014_-testing_theories_of_american_politics.doc.pdf, accessed 10/28/2015

4   Jeffrey M. Jones, *Gallup*. "In U.S., New Record 43% Are Political Independents." 1/7/2015. http://www.gallup.com/poll/180440/new-record-political-independents.aspx, accessed 10/28/2015

5   *Pew Research*. "Political Polarization in the American Public." http://www.people-press.org/2014/06/12/political-polarization-in-the-american-public/, accessed 10/28/2015

Democrats and Republicans More Ideologically Divided than in the Past

Distribution of Democrats and Republicans on a 10-item scale of political values

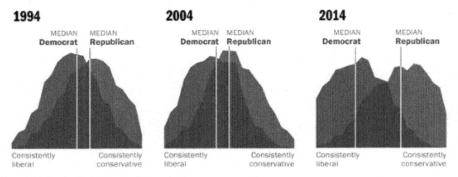

Source: 2014 Political Polarization in the American Public
Notes: Ideological consistency based on a scale of 10 political values questions (see Appendix A). The blue area in this chart represents the ideological distribution of Democrats; the red area of Republicans. The overlap of these two distributions is shaded purple. Republicans include Republican-leaning independents. Democrats include Democratic-leaning independents (see Appendix B).

PEW RESEARCH CENTER

In this graphic we see graphs that represent the ideological "spread," from liberal to conservative, of the Republican and Democratic parties. In 1994, we can see that many Republicans were somewhat liberal, and many Democrats were somewhat conservative. The median Republican and Democrat were fairly moderate. By 2004, we see fewer liberal Republicans and fewer conservative Democrats. By 2014, Democrats became much more liberal and Republicans much more conservative. The median party members are less moderate and there are far more hard-liners in each party.

Because they know that wedging wins, politicians are now less willing and able to work across the aisle and forge nonpartisan solutions than they used to be. An article from the journal Public Library of Science shows decisively that over the past 30 years, Republicans and Democrats in the House have worked together less and less.[6]

---

6   Clio Andris, et al. "The Rise of Partisanship and Super-Cooperators in the US House of
     Representatives." http://journals.plos.org/plosone/article?id=10.1371/journal.pone.0123507,
     accessed 10/28/2015

This graphic represents the tendency of members of the House of Representatives to vote either similarly or dissimilarly since 1949. Each dot represents a member of the House during a two-year period; dots to the right are Republicans and dots to the left are Democrats. The distance of each dot to another represents how similarly they voted: if two dots are touching, they vote the same all the time, and if they're far apart, they almost never vote the same.

If we look to the plots of the 1950s through the 1980s, we see Congresses with two major features. First, within each party votes are widely spread out, and second, it was commonplace for votes from members of the two parties to overlap. In the late 1980s, we see the centers of the two parties move farther apart and "tighten," voting as a block more often.[7] Fewer individuals of either party vote anything like individuals of the other. It looks like cell division: in the 1950s, one legislative body, made up of different materials; by the 2000s, two distinct and opposing bodies.

Much of this former legislative "closeness" was driven by temporary bipartisan coalitions that formed to champion different bills on issues like economics, defense, poverty and crime.

These days it is dangerous to be seen working with the opposition. Disagreeing on an issue like abortion means that it's impossible to work together on anything, lest we be seen as betraying the line we've drawn in the ground.

With few exceptions, the new rule of politics is this: if the blue team is voting for something, the red team will vote against it on principle, and vice-versa.[8] This leads to two dangerous outcomes: first, Congress is largely gridlocked and unable to pass a great deal of important legislation. Second, the legislation that does get passed depends entirely on the input from, and majority of, one party.[9]

---

7   The timing of this legislative mitosis suggests that the primary driver of polarization was not the 1960s party realignment (in which the southern states ended a tendency to elect Democrats to office and instead became a more Republican region) or "Southern Strategy." For 20 years after this realignment, the parties still worked together and partisan antipathy was limited.

8   A potential objection to our case is that one may argue that one of the parties is "more at fault" than the other, or that one party uses wedging tactics more than another. We argue that whether this is true is not important: blaming one party neither explains the root cause (which is based in political incentives) nor leads to a solution (which involves each of us understanding and fighting against these tactics when they're used).

9   An interesting implication of this second problem is that politics becomes "volatile:" a bill may be passed by one party, but when that party loses power to the other, the bill is highly vulnerable to be repealed quickly.

The Disease is in Us

"Good Lord, what madness rules in brainsick men

When for so slight and frivolous a cause

Such factious emulations shall arise!"

> -Henry VI, from William Shakespeare's "Henry VI," Act 4, Scene 1

It is not just in professional politics that we see this divide. We, the people, are experiencing a growing emotional disgust with the opposition. More than ever, we see our political opponents as threats to the very core well-being of the United States.[10] We have become each other's enemies.

---

10   *Pew Research*, "Political Polarization in the American Public." http://www.people-press. org/2014/06/12/political-polarization-in-the-american-public/, accessed 10/28/2015

INTER-PARTY ANTIPATHY AT NEW HIGHS

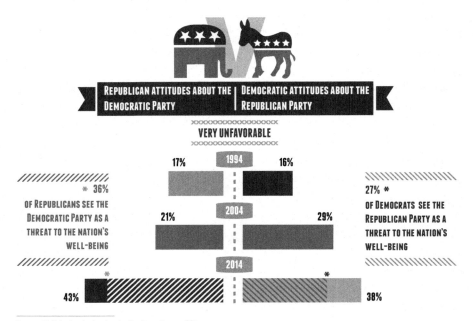

Source: Political polarization in the American public.
Notes: Questions about whether the Republican and Democratic Parties are a threat to the nation's well being asked only in 2014.
Republicans include Republican-leaning independents; Democrats include Democratic-leaning independents (see Appendix B).
PEW RESEARCH CENTER

As the parties have grown more polarized, they've also come to hate and fear each other. Between 1994 and 2004, more people in each party viewed the other party as "very unfavorable": fewer voters in each party had respect for the ideas of the other party.

By 2014, the number of party voters with very unfavorable views of the other party exploded, representing between one third and one half of each party. This growing rage was so stark that Pew Research actually changed the poll, adding a whole new category to capture the depth of antipathy. Over one quarter of Democrats and one third of Republicans declared that they viewed the other party as a **threat to the nation's well-being.** *Voters used to think the other party was* **wrong**, *and sometimes very wrong. Now, voters increasingly see the other party as* **bad for the nation**. *Party voters are downright terrified of the other party gaining power, lest it tear the country down.*

We may be tempted to believe that these larger proportions of angry voters in the parties come about simply because reasonable people are leaving the party. This may be in part true, but Pew made sure to include "leaning" independents – that is, independent voters that consistently vote for one party. The mindset of rage and fear has infected much of the country.

Almost one third of party-affiliated voters believe the other party is a danger to the nation. This feeling is reflected in, and stoked by, the rhetoric of politicians and media. But many Americans perpetuate it. In our homes, at our water coolers, in our bars, and in our dormitories, we've played right into it and created our own echo chambers of propaganda. We've lost the ability to respect – much less work with – those who we believe disagree with us and we actively inflate an apparent disagreement in policy to a disagreement of fundamental values.

PARTISANS KEEP FRIENDS THEY AGREE WITH

■ % Who say "Most close friends share my views on government and politics"
▨ % Who stopped talking to/being friends with someone because of politics

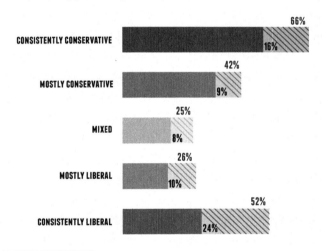

PEW RESEARCH CENTER – American Trends Panel (wave 1). Survey conducted March 10-April 2, 2014. Q44, Q46. Based on web respondents. Ideological consistency based on a scale of 10 political values questions (see About the Survey for more details).

Here we see that 16% of consistent conservatives and 24% of consistent liberals have admitted to taking people out of their lives that disagree on politics, where less partisan Americans do this far less often. These most partisan voters have developed so much anger over politics that they will eliminate friendships in order to avoid being exposed to the people who disagree with them.

Partisan Americans surround themselves with those that share their opinions and increasingly vilify those that hold other opinions. Almost half of self-identified consistent liberals and conservatives simply do not talk to people that disagree with them;[11] most surround themselves exclusively with people that agree with them fully.[12] Data from social media demonstrate that partisan thinkers vigorously eliminate connections with dissenting voices, essentially ensuring they will not be exposed to new ideas.[13] The more partisan the user, the more their social media exposure is focused only on what they already believe.[14]

11   *Pew Research.* "Political Polarization and Media Habits," 10/20/2014. "Striking Differences Between Liberals and Conservatives, But They Also Share Common Ground." http://www.journalism.org/2014/10/21/political-polarization-media-habits/pj_2014-10-21_media-polarization-26/, accessed 10/28/2015

12   *Pew Research.* "Political Polarization and Media Habits," 10/20/2014. "Consistent Conservative More Likely to Have Close Friends Who Share Their Political Views, But Consistent Liberals More Likely to Drop a Friend." http://www.journalism.org/2014/10/21/political-polarization-media-habits/pj_2014-10-21_media-polarization-03/, accessed 10/28/2015

13   *Pew Research.* "Political Polarization and Media Habits," 10/20/2014. "Whom Do You Talk With Most Often About Politics?" http://www.journalism.org/2014/10/21/political-polarization-media-habits/10-20-2014-2-31-55-pm/, accessed 10/28/2015

14   Eytan Bakshy, Solomon Messing, Lada Adamic. *Science* Vol. 348 no. 6239 pp. 1130-1132, 6/5/2015 "Exposure to Ideologically Diverse News and Opinion on Facebook." http://education.biu.ac.il/files/education/shared/science-2015-bakshy-1130-2.pdf, accessed 10/28/2015

PARTISANS BLOCK OTHERS ON SOCIAL MEDIA DUE TO POLITICS

% WHO FACEBOOK users in each group who have hidden, blocked, defriended or stopped following someone because they disagreed with a political post

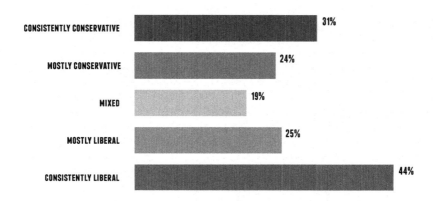

CONSISTENTLY CONSERVATIVE — 31%

MOSTLY CONSERVATIVE — 24%

MIXED — 19%

MOSTLY LIBERAL — 25%

CONSISTENTLY LIBERAL — 44%

PEW RESEARCH CENTER – American Trends Panel (wave 1). Survey conducted March 19-April 29, 2014. Q35. Based on web respondents who are Facebook users (N=2,153). Ideological consistency based on a scale of 10 political values questions (see About the Survey for more details).

Similar to their behavior with friends, the most partisan Americans will block disagreeing voices on social media more than those who are less partisan. Of Facebook users, 31% of consistent conservatives and 44% of consistent liberals do this.

Surrounded only by those that agree with us, we fail to expose ourselves to alternative ideas that could challenge our own. Instead, we simply receive confirmation after confirmation of our instinctive intuition that those who disagree with us are bad people.[15]

And it is the most partisan Americans that are most engaged and most likely to drive political discussions. This means their voices are heard more loudly than those of more moderate Americans. They get to set the tone for political discussion in the country.[16]

---

15   After sufficient ideological entrenchment, exposure to new facts actually "backfires" and causes people to dig in further. Joe Keohane, "How facts backfire: Researches discover a surprising threat to democracy: our brains." 7/11/2010. http://www.boston.com/boston-globe/ideas/articles/2010/07/11/how_facts_backfire/, accessed 11/3/2015.

16   *Pew Research.* "Political Polarization and Media Habits," 10/20/2014. "Consistent Conservatives, Liberals More Likely to Drive Political Discussions." http://www.journalism.org/2014/10/21/political-polarization-media-habits/pj_2014-10-21_media-polarization-31/, accessed 10/28/2015

As a reaction to this increasingly toxic political environment, less-partisan Americans disengage, participating in political dialogue far less often and enjoying it less when they do.[17]

PARTISANS MOST INFLUENTIAL IN DIALOGUE
% of respondents who are political discussion influentials

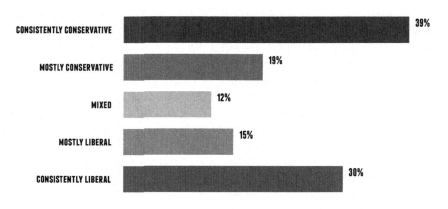

CONSISTENTLY CONSERVATIVE	39%
MOSTLY CONSERVATIVE	19%
MIXED	12%
MOSTLY LIBERAL	15%
CONSISTENTLY LIBERAL	30%

PEW RESEARCH CENTER – American Trends Panel (wave 1). Survey conducted March 19-April 29, 2014. Q.41, Q.47, Q.48. Based on web respondents. A respondent is considered a political discussion influential if they discuss politics at least a few times a week, report leading conservations about politics more than listening to them, and report having others come to them about political information more than going to others. Ideological consistency based on a scale of 10 political values questions (see About the Survey for more details).

This graphic shows that consistent partisans are more influential in political discussion. These "influentials" lead conversations about politics more than listening and have friends come to them for information about politics more than those friends go to others.

What this means: those that are most ideologically extreme and least likely to consider alternative views are the loudest, most active, and most influential in politics. The rest of us this get exposed to the most skewed, closed-minded ideas about politics.

For those moderates that do engage, the inter-party warfare around flashy, symbolic wedge issues exhausts and distracts us from attending to the challenges the country is facing that are actually most important to us. We are forced to focus on battle-fields on which we can declare victory, rather than opportunities

---

17   *Pew Research.* "Political Polarization and Media Habits," 10/20/2014. "Consistent Conservatives, Liberals Talk About Politics More, Enjoy It More." http://www.journalism. org/2014/10/21/political-polarization-media-habits/pj_2014-10-21_media-polarization-23/, accessed 10/28/2015

to make real progress. We are unable to disagree productively and work towards consensus and compromise. Many are unwilling to work together with political opponents we have decided are bad people.

ONE NATION, UNDER DISAGREEMENT

"Honest disagreement is often a good sign of progress."

-Mahatma Gandhi

Disagreement is an important and powerful tool in any decision-making situation. Groups get together to make decisions because the conversation around the different ideas brought to the table yields a better outcome. Indeed, by arguing about how to pursue our shared values, we often learn from each other and grow towards a better solution. By considering the points brought up in debate, Americans can choose what makes the most sense.

Wedging tactics are different: they are not meant to bring debatable points to the table, or bring analysis that can be challenged with facts. They're designed to appeal to identity, anger, and fear. They make us believe that the other side is an enemy that has to be defeated.

Because of decades of wedging, Americans believe that there is a culture war, that there are "two Americas" with distinctly different cultures and fundamentally incompatible values – conservative and liberal.

Values vs Methods

We believe that the notion of "two Americas" is false and that the culture war is fabricated. The widespread misconception of a nation split in two is the key premise that underlies mutual distrust between parties.

We claim instead that, at its core, there is one America. As a nation, we share a wide and thorough swath of intractable values that bind us and – for better or worse – separate us from many of our peer nations.

Uniquely American Values

American values are surprisingly homogeneous despite our great diversity as a country. This becomes apparent when we are compared to peer countries like Canada or those in the European Union: some of the values that Americans tend to agree on are not broadly shared by these peers. However often we may overlook it, these values make us uniquely American.

For example, Americans generally are much less willing to curb personal liberty for the group. This becomes clear in many cases: the vast majority of Americans believe law-abiding citizens should be allowed to have rifles and handguns[18] (though we agree on some restrictions like background checks) whereas in Europe, most countries require a citizen to obtain special authorization by the state before one can purchase them.[19]

In many European countries, speech and some other liberties are limited. Many countries do not allow Holocaust denial. Hijabs are banned in France. Minarets are banned in Switzerland. Police cameras line the streets of almost every major British city. The majority of Americans wouldn't seriously consider such restrictions.

Americans see welfare systems as a temporary safety net designed to help people get back to work.[20] The majority of Americans (from every party) believe in reducing or repealing the estate tax,[21] something that many Europeans find somewhat ridiculous.[22] Americans believe, more than almost any country in the world, that it's important to work hard to get ahead in life,

---

18   Gallup polls consistently showed 70%+ of Americans would not ban handguns. Most recent Oct 12-15, 2014. Pollingreport. http://www.pollingreport.com/guns.htm, accessed 9/16/2015

19   "European Union — Gun Facts, Figures and the Law." Gunpolicy.org. http://www.gunpolicy. org/firearms/region/european-union. The European Union also has restrictions on the number of firearms and amount of ammunition a citizen may obtain. Accessed 9/16/2015

20   Elizabeth Lower-Basch, "How Today's Safety Net Promotes Work – And How To Do More." *CLASP*, 7/23/2014. http://www.clasp.org/resources-and-publications/publication-1/ How-Todays-Safety-Net-Promotes-Work-And-How-To-Do-More-1.pdf, accessed 11/3/2015.

21   Kevin Drum, *Mother Jones*. "What's the Deal with the Estate Tax?" 12/15/2010. http://www. motherjones.com/kevin-drum/2010/12/whats-deal-estate-tax, accessed 9/16/2015

22   Roger Farmer, *The Guardian*. "Will Americans ever vote for a far-reaching wealth tax?" 10/20/2014. http://www.theguardian.com/business/economics-blog/2014/oct/20/wealth-tax-us-inequality-thomas-piketty, accessed 10/1/2015

and that merit, industrialism, and entrepreneurship should be rewarded.[23]

Perhaps the best example of a unique "Americanism" is that Americans consistently and nearly-universally hold that it is more important to provide equal economic opportunity than equal economic outcomes. 97% of Americans feel this way: far more than almost all other peer nations.[24]

80% of Americans believe that our history, culture, and Constitution "set us apart. "[25] Americans believe the US has a duty to lead (or help lead) the world and spread democracy.[26] Americans see themselves and their country as unique. This often irks or confuses American allies, who find these positions odd. We present these examples without judgment as to their accuracy or merit, but simply to illustrate some of the ways that American values and core beliefs stand out.

We believe most people would agree that there are even more core values that the vast majority of Americans share for the country. We've compiled a list below:

» Safety in our daily lives; the ability to live without undue fear of personal violence

» Safety from foreign threat

» The freedom to express our personal beliefs without fear of oppression

» Economic opportunity and the ability to work to earn a living

---

23   *Pew Research.* "Emerging and Developing Economies Much More Optimistic than Rich Countries about the Future." 10/9/2014. http://www.pewglobal.org/2014/10/09/emerging-and-developing-economies-much-more-optimistic-than-rich-countries-about-the-future/, accessed 8/27/2015

24   Benjamin I Page and Lawrence R Jacobs. *Class War? What Americans Really Think About Economic Inequality.* The University of Chicago Press, 2009

25   John A. Gans, Jr. *The Atlantic.* "American Exceptionalism and the Politics of Foreign Policy." 11/21/2011. http://www.theatlantic.com/international/archive/2011/11/american-exception-alism-and-the-politics-of-foreign-policy/248779/, accessed 9/16/2015

26   Andrew Kohut and Bruce Stokes, *Pew Research.* "The Problem of American Exceptionalism." 5/9/2006. http://www.pewresearch.org/2006/05/09/the-problem-of-american-exception-alism/, accessed 9/16/2015

» Access to a safety net to help us get back on our feet when hard times hit

» The ability to live free of unnecessary interference and make our own choices

» Justice for those who are wronged

» A healthy planet and environment

» Leaving the world a better place than it was when we were born into it

Did any of these make you twinge? For example: did you think that the first implied that we should enact stricter gun control? Does the second seem to you to imply that we should spend more on defense? Does the fourth sound like it implies more or less welfare?

These kinds of feelings are an indication of how wedging has infected all of us. It's hard to agree even with general values because we're worried someone will say "gotcha!" That worry makes us dig in and sometimes even support viewpoints we don't agree with.

Your instinct might have been to be skeptical about whether most of your opposition really believes some of these values. If so, quickly imagine someone you disagree with looking into the mirror and saying, "I really don't want..." any of the above. You don't have to believe that you would agree on all the details. You may even see that the extreme partisans on the other side act out of alignment with these shared values, or say things that seem to contradict these. There will always be a hard core of extremists that don't share our values, but they don't represent the majority of Americans.

Benefits of Different Methods

If we agree on values, there are many ways in which we can and should still disagree: we can have different understandings of the nature of a situation (like poverty or the state of US education); we can have different theories about how policy will affect a situation (will this government stimulus package increase job growth?); we can disagree on how best to trade off and balance our values (size of the tax burden vs. size of the social welfare system); we can disagree on the role government should play in a situation. A country of shared core values will still have different political groups that emerge, each with different ideas about how to advance and balance those core values.

Different people will approach a situation from different experiences and backgrounds, different access to facts, different assumptions, and different lenses for interpretation of the same facts. Such differences can be incredibly valuable in groups that choose to work together.

None of these disagreements actually represents a difference in core values, but we have been deliberately driven away from this understanding towards believing that differences in understanding of facts, or differences in preferred implementation, represent deep differences in values: we've been wedged.

CHAPTER TWO:
THE WEDGE: HOW IT WORKS

"It's an election year. We would prefer that voters didn't use common sense."

-Aaron Sorkin, The West Wing Script Book

If we are indeed one America with highly compatible goals and values for the country, why do we find ourselves at each other's throats? Why is it so difficult to work together with the smart folks across the aisle from us? Why has the US become so divided over the past 20 years?

In short, the American political industry uses emotional marketing and political tactics to manipulate American citizens into feeling anger, fear, and resentment. These emotions increase our identity with and loyalty to both political parties and news outlets, and increase our engagement and support.

WHY WE GET WEDGED: WEDGING WINS

"I think politicians know how to misrepresent data in order to support a political agenda. Politicians and the people that work for them – I should say – are expert at that."

> *-Seth Gordon, producer/director/screenwriter of fiction and documentaries*

This is not an unrecognized problem. Americans know polarization and sensationalism are hijacking the political process. Americans have become highly distrustful of both media[1] and politicians[2] for their participation in the process. But we know that strong incentives mean these tactics will continue to dominate, even when Americans are frustrated by them. And although we may complain, we are constantly rewarding politicians and the media for taking the low road: the more we are wedged into ideological extremes and animosity towards the opposition, the more likely we are to vote, donate money, and volunteer for campaigns.

---

1   Justin McCarthy, *Gallup*. "Trust in Mass Media Returns to All-Time Low." 9/17/2014. http://www.cnsnews.com/news/article/michael-w-chapman/gallup-60-americans-dont-trust-news-media, accessed 9/16/2015

2   Kevin Mathews, *truthout*. "Do You Trust the Government? 87% of Americans Don't." 8/16/2014. http://www.truth-out.org/news/item/25628-do-you-trust-the-government-87-of-americans-dont, accessed 9/15/2015

THE 'U-SHAPE' OF POLITICAL ACTIVISM:
HIGHER AT IDEOLOGICAL EXTREMES | LOWER IN THE CENTER

 Percent who always vote

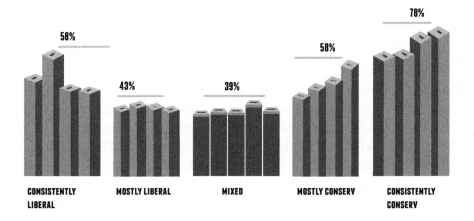

CONSISTENTLY LIBERAL	MOSTLY LIBERAL	MIXED	MOSTLY CONSERV	CONSISTENTLY CONSERV
58%	43%	39%	58%	78%

 Percent who contributed to a political candidate or group in the past two years

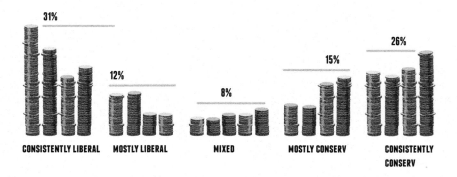

CONSISTENTLY LIBERAL	MOSTLY LIBERAL	MIXED	MOSTLY CONSERV	CONSISTENTLY CONSERV
31%	12%	8%	15%	26%

Source: 2014 Political Polarization in the American Public
Note: Bars represent the level of participation at each point on a 10 question scale of ideological consistency.
Figures are reported on the five ideological consistency groups used throughout the report (see Appendix A).
PEW RESEARCH CENTER

3

3   *Pew Research.* "Political Polarization in the American Public. Section 5: Political Engagement and Activism." 6/12/2014. http://www.people-press.org/2014/06/12/

It's clear from the above graph that if you want to win an election, the groups to target are the most polarized.

The more consistently ideological a voter is, the more they see the other side as an enemy.[4] By driving divisive and distracting wedge issues into the front of national political discourse, by convincing us that electoral defeat is existentially threatening to our tribe, politicians drive us to the ideological extremes, making us more reliable sources of votes and money.

Politicians who stick to their principles and don't make use of these manipulative tactics don't get elected. So how can we possibly expect a sea change to come from the politicians?

What About That Growing Group of Independents?

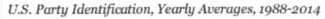

So why doesn't the burgeoning population of Independents entice politicians toward the center? There are certainly enough of them; Americans have been steadily fleeing the two-party system since 2004, reaching 43% of the electorate in 2014.

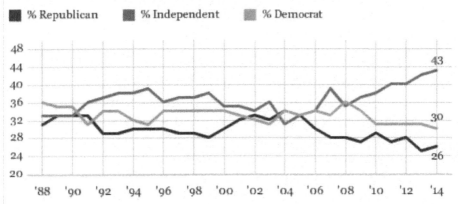

U.S. Party Identification, Yearly Averages, 1988-2014

■ % Republican   ■ % Independent   ■ % Democrat

Based on multiple day polls conducted by telephone

GALLUP

In this graph we see the proportion of Republican and Democratic voters beginning to decline in the mid-2000s,

---

section-5-political-engagement-and-activism/, accessed 8/1/2015.

4   Ibid.

accompanied by an increase in the number of Independent voters. The continuous seven-year growth in the number of Independents in the US is a new phenomenon.

You might think that 43% chunk of voters would be a tempting target. After all, this group is significantly larger than either the Republican or Democratic Party: why aren't politicians racing "towards the middle" in order to snap up their votes?

There are three reasons this doesn't happen:

1. Independent voters are just too disengaged for a single election to make a difference in their disposition. This group is the least likely to participate in the campaigns (either by voting, volunteering, or donating) and until there is a sustained shift in political culture, the effort required for going after this group is too high and the "payoff" too low compared to increasing turnout in one's base.

2. They are nearly as prone to partisanship as other voters: only 40% of Independents are self-styled moderates;[5] the rest are liberals and conservatives. This means that they don't represent any kind of unified, moderate bloc and don't naturally unite to vote for a moderate candidate.

3. Most importantly, the primary system means these Independents have all but neutralized themselves in the electoral system. In 32 of 50 American states, Independent voters cannot participate in the primary (or nomination) votes.[6] Politicians hoping to participate in the national or state election must win over the increasingly-insular, extreme party die-hards, and that means crafting themselves as extreme.

By removing themselves from the party system, registered Independents may be inadvertently making the problem worse

---

5   Lydia Saad, *Gallup.* "US Liberals at Record 24%, but Still Trail Conservatives." 1/9/2015. http://www.gallup.com/poll/180452/liberals-record-trail-conservatives.aspx, accessed 9/16/2015

6   Wikipedia. "Open primaries in the United States." http://en.wikipedia.org/wiki/Open_primaries_in_the_United_States, accessed 9/16/2015

by leaving only the most partisan voters in the primary elections. Politicians can't win by simply targeting the middle, which means there's no easy fix to the problem of having to target the extremes.

Some states (like California) are experimenting with open primaries, which may favor candidates who are able to appeal to a larger group than their partisan base. But entrenched political parties have incentives to block such reforms – ballot initiatives or referendums might be necessary to push these forward, and winning requires an engaged middle ground.

Media Incentives Work the Same Way

"What about the media?" we hear you ask. "Why would they contribute to the problem?" We'll turn the question back at you: if you're passionately left-wing or right-wing, are you going to read more Huffington Post or Fox News? In other words, are you going to seek news from a source you trust or one you distrust? Do you think the source you trust is more likely to support what you already believe or to challenge your viewpoint?

Just as votes are the primary selection mechanism for success or failure for politicians, consumers are the measure of success for news media. The news media that gets reliable viewers, listeners, readers, clickers, and sharers is the media that will profit and thus dominate the national dialogue.

Consistently-liberal Americans consume news mostly from CNN, NPR, and MSNBC (a combined 40% identify these as primary news sources), whereas consistently-conservative Americans consume mostly Fox News (47% identify these as primary news sources).[7] Fox News has the largest national revenue and profit, followed by CNN (plus affiliate Headline News or HLN), with MSNBC trailing in third.[8]

---

7   *Pew Research.* "Political Polarization & Media Habits: Striking Differences Between Liberals and Conservatives, But They Also Share Common Ground." 10/20/2014. http://www.journalism.org/2014/10/21/political-polarization-media-habits/10-20-2014-2-31-55-pm/, accessed 9/16/2015

8   *zap2it.* "Cable News: Fox News Most Profitable, Edging CNN & Headline News Combined, Far Ahead of MSNBC." 3/14/2010. http://tvbythenumbers.zap2it.com/2010/03/14/cable-news-fox-news-most-profitable-edging-cnn-headline-news-combined-far-ahead-of-msnbc/44944/, accessed 9/19/2015

It is difficult to measure media bias, but there are some news sources that are trusted by all major ideological groups in the United States, some that are distrusted by all, and some that are only trusted by one side of the partisan divide. It's likely that the sources most distrusted by one side and not the other will be the most biased.

It's not surprising then that the most popular news sources among consistent liberals and consistent conservatives[9] are highly distrusted by the opposite partisan groups for reporting bias.[10] University of Chicago professor Matthew Gentzkow also shows that media outlets with liberal or conservative readers and viewers tend to report with a liberal or conservative bias, and that cable and Internet news outlets have a stronger bias than more traditional news networks.[11] A study from UCLA used its own different methodology with similar results: they found that outlets like MSNBC and the New York Times have a liberal bias, and that Fox News has a conservative bias.[12] CNN and NPR leaned left of center, but not by as much.

9   *Pew Research.* "Political Polarization & Media Habits: Views of News Sources Among Those with Mostly Liberal Political Values." 10/20/2014. http://www.journalism.org/2014/10/21/political-polarization-media-habits/pj_2014-10-21_media-polarization-37/, accessed 9/19/2015

10   *Pew Research.* "Political Polarization & Media Habits: Trust Levels of News Sources by Ideological Group." 10/20/2014. http://www.journalism.org/2014/10/21/political-polarization-media-habits/pj_14-10-21_mediapolarization-01/, accessed 9/19/2015

11   Outlined by the Washington Post: Robert Samuelson. "Media bias explained in two studies."

12   Study led by UCLA political scientist Tim Groseclose, with Jeffrey Milyo of the University of Missouri. Meg Sullivan, UCLA Newsroom. "Media bias is real, finds UCLA political scientist." 12/14/2015. http://newsroom.ucla.edu/releases/Media-Bias-Is-Real-Finds-UCLA-6664, accessed 11/3/2015.

PARTISANS KEEP FEW CORE NEWS SOURCES

Consistent Conservatives   Consistent Liberals

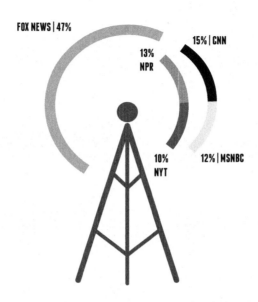

FOX NEWS | 47%

15% | CNN

13% NPR

10% NYT

12% | MSNBC

Pew Research asked voters where they were most likely to get their news. 47% of consistent conservatives get their news from Fox News, a source that is highly distrusted by liberals to be balanced and accurate. 50% of consistent liberals get their news from either CNN, NPR, MSNBC, or NYT: all four of these sources are highly distrusted by conservatives.

This suggests that those who strongly identify as liberals and conservatives most often get their news from sources that are biased and tell them stories that confirm what they already think.

Americans consume these news networks with greater consistency than they do networks that are more trusted by all ideological groups, such as the Wall Street Journal and the Economist.[13] As the viewerships of Fox and CNN grow,[14] those of the more

---

13   Ibid.

14   Dominic Patten, *Deadline*. "MSNBC Ratings Crater to All-Time Lows, Fox News Tops Q1 Results, CNN Up." 3/31/2015. http://deadline.com/2015/03/msnbc-ratings-all-time-low-fox-news-wins-cnn-1201402274, accessed 9/4/2015.

traditional (and less biased) national news networks ABC, NBC, and CBS have shrunk.[15]

TRADITIONAL NEWS RATINGS DROPPING
November-to-November average rating per night

■ ABC   ■ CBS   ■ NBC

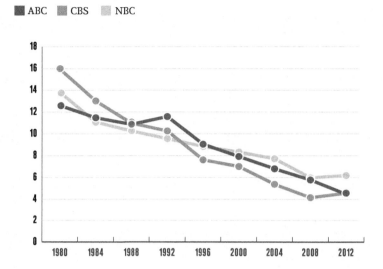

Source: Nielsen Media Research, used under license. Note: ratings taken for month of November.
PEW RESEARCH CENTER – 2013 STATE OF THE NEWS MEDIA

Winners in the market follow the money: the most popular news networks play to the emotions and biases of their partisan viewers because it brings them loyalty and revenue. So dominant media groups participate in the wedging of the American electorate just as much as politicians do.

Why Is Wedging Becoming More Powerful?

We know that wedging tactics are effective, but why have they become more powerful over time? We propose a possible narrative: a political "evolution," in both the Darwinian sense and that of Intelligent Design.

We of course don't mean that humans evolved genetically over the past 20 years, but that selective pressure is applied in

---

15   Emily Guskin, Mark Jurkowitz, and Amy Mitchell. The Pew Research Center's Project for
      Excellence in Journalism. "The State of the News Media 2013." http://www.stateofthemedia.
      org/2013/network-news-a-year-of-change-and-challenge-at-nbc/network-by-the-numbers/,
      accessed 9/4/2015.

politics, with elections serving as the selection mechanism: the politicians that employed the most successful election tactics rose to the top and enshrined those tactics. Those that used losing tactics were defeated. Rather than being purely random (in a Darwinian sense), the choice of tactics was driven by rigorous research and planning on the part of capable advisory staff. Different tactics for winning competed over decades of elections; the wedging tactic emerged victorious.

As polling methods became increasingly sophisticated, politicians learned which emotional messages had the biggest impact on donations and voter turnout – these messages later turned into the wedge issues we know today. Professor Douglas Lanthrop's 2003 book, *The Campaign Continues*,[16] rigorously outlines the rise of political consultants in the election and policy-making process. With more consultants and other experts at hand, these tactics improved.

As in any evolution, those who used these winning tactics survived and grew to dominate the political landscape.

Political hopefuls did not set out to polarize the nation. When politicians employ wedge issues in their campaigns, they do so simply in the hopes of winning the election: it's a professional tactic. But by marketing themselves

> To understand the game theory for politicians, let's imagine two political hopefuls in a party primary race, discussing abortion. One states that abortion is a highly complex question with nuanced perspectives and a biologically unclear definition of where life begins. The other states that it's a clear matter of rights and that those who disagree are knowingly and purposefully killing children or oppressing women. Who is more likely to generate excitement and win votes in an election where (during mid-terms) fewer than 15% or registered voters turn out to vote, of which most are party die-hards?

16   Douglas Lanthrop. *The Campaign Continues: How Political Consultants and Campaign Tactics Affect Public Policy*. Praeger Publishers: Westport, CT, 2003.

primarily to extremes in the political system, they hamper their own ability to work across the aisle and reduce their own legislative effectiveness.

WHAT ARE WEDGE ISSUES?

"In politics shared hatreds are almost always the basis of friendships."

> *-Alexis de Tocqueville, French enlightenment-era political thinker and historian*

Wedge issues are political issues used deliberately by politicians to mobilize their base through anger and fear, and by media outlets to capture devoted customers through the same emotions. The unintended and dangerous consequence is that reliance upon these issues "wedges" the electorate into two very different, distant, and emotional camps. But because the wedging tactic is effective in an individual election, it continues to be relied upon.

We define wedge issues as generally having a few particular characteristics. They're often highly emotional, difficult to debate with facts, and linked strongly to a sense of personal and group identity. Often, but not always, they're ultimately low on the list of voters' total priorities in government. Sometimes they're not even relevant to the job description of the politician using them to engage potential voters: for example, individual states have jurisdiction over abortion law, but national politicians use it as an issue to energize their base supporters.

Generally, think of wedge issues as those about which we'll spend a lot of time carrying banners and shouting at each other, but where slow or little progress towards consensus or solution is made.

Some good examples of wedge issues:

» Abortion & birth control

» Gay marriage

» Gun control

» Religious expression

» Moral "decay"/ behavior, pornography, etc.

The Wedge Paradox

Although wedge issues get a lot of our attention and emotion, they're not at the top of our minds when we are forced to choose our top priorities. For example, gay marriage/rights, abortion, and gun control each get between 0% and 1% of poll respondents saying they're the most important issue facing the country.[17]

When we are forced to really evaluate them, it is government dysfunction, economic growth, healthcare, unemployment, terrorism, and education that are our top priorities. It's not that the issues of gun violence and abortion aren't important – they're just not nearly as important to most Americans as other issues.

---

17 *Gallup.* "Most Important Problem." Poll Jul 8-12, 2015. http://www.gallup.com/poll/1675/most-important-problem.aspx, accessed 8/19/2015. A note here on methodology: it is certainly true that most Americans see many issues as important or highly important. Picking only the single most important is limiting. But most polls that attempt to determine what issues are very important to Americans tend to result in almost every listed issue being rated as important or very important by most people. Polls that force respondents to rank their priorities enables us to better understand what stands out from other issues, which gives us a better sense of relative priority. We use it to answer, "what issues are more important than other issues?"

MOST IMPORTANT PROBLEM FACING THE COUNTRY TODAY

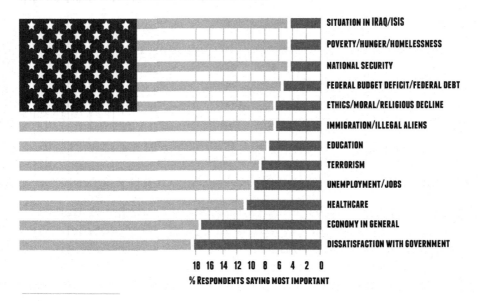

GALLUP | February 8-11, 2015

This poll asked Americans to rate their most important issue facing the country. Social issues like abortion, gay marriage, and gun control don't even show up. The exercise of ranking priorities is useful in showing what's most important without any of the bluster that makes many issues very emotional.

But wedge issues drive our party affiliation and get an incredible amount of attention. Slate conducted a wide study to find what got the most emotional attention on social media[18] and found that almost all the issues were related to identity politics – race, gender, sexuality, and religion/morality. Hundreds of protests, marches, and demonstrations over gay marriage and abortion occurred yearly in the US during the early 2010s.

A fascinating paradox emerges: when invited to rank their priorities, Americans state that these emotional wedge issues aren't the most important ones to tackle, but because these wedge issues rouse our emotions so effectively they receive a highly

---

18   Allison Benedikt, Chris Kirk, and Dan Kois, et al, *Slate*. "The Year of Outrage." 12/17/2014. http://www.slate.com/articles/life/culturebox/2014/12/the_year_of_outrage_2014_everything_you_were_angry_about_on_social_media.html, accessed 8/18/2015

disproportionate amount of our attention. It is simply easy to distract and engage us with a few simple emotional words. What groups in the US are we told want to:

- » See children die?
- » Wage a war on women or racial minorities?
- » Drive poverty?
- » Subvert the constitution?
- » Create a socialist super-state?
- » Cripple the future with debt?
- » Impose their religion (or lack thereof) on everyone?

How does this kind of issue-framing compare to the Federal Reserve interest rate, Social Security funding, and foreign trade agreements, in terms of ability to grab our attention?

HOW DO WE GET WEDGED?

"It is one thing to rouse the passions of people – and quite another to lead them."

> *-Ron Suskind, Pulitzer Prize winning American journalist and best-selling author*

Your Brain on Politics

There's a well-documented scientific reason for why our brains are so susceptible to these wedging tactics—why it can be so difficult to change our approach to politics and think about issues more calmly and thoroughly. A significant amount of literature[19] demonstrates that although in personal decisions or abstract problems our brains are often capable of great curiosity and critical thinking, when we think about politics a *completely different* part of the brain is engaged. This part of the brain has

---

19   Joshua Greene's *Moral Tribes*, Drew Westen's *The Political Brain*, Jonathan Haidt's *The Righteous Mind*, Jesse Prinz's *The Emotional Construction of Morals*, Jason Weeden & Robert Kurzban's *The Hidden Agenda of the Political Mind*, and many other good books have been written on the topic.

evolved for millennia to identify our tribe and "other" tribes, to support our tribe and defeat the others. This neurological evolution occurred during prehistory, in which survival depended on the ability of one's tribe to work together to acquire food and shelter, raise children, and defend against both wild animals and other tribes. Loyalty to the tribe was a successful survival tactic for early humans, so it has been hard-wired into our brains.

We can see the effects today of how humans can fanatically support one tribe and despise another: consider how upset people get over the victory or defeat of a local sports team – especially to an established rival. Fans will dress up in the colors and logos of their team, get into arguments with their rivals' supporters, and even sometimes go as far as physically abusing other fans, all because they are part of a "different tribe" in the primitive parts of our brains! In experiments where we are randomly assigned into different groups (based on things as arbitrary as eye color), we quickly become loyal to those groups and suspicious of other groups.[20]

In the modern world, where we are not at constant war with neighboring clans, our brains have made politics a primary battleground for this tribal thinking.

It can become part of our very identity to get caught up in supporting positions we don't believe in[21] for the sake of supporting the "tribe." Disagreeing with our friends feels threatening because *on some evolutionary level our brains actually believe that disagreeing with our tribe might threaten our chances of survival.* We take on simple "identifiers" that set ourselves apart from outside tribes in order to build a feeling of shared identity with our community. We find ourselves agreeing to things our friends say without questioning them too thoroughly, even peer-pressuring others in the tribe to fall in line. The critical reasoning parts of our brains then seek arguments to back up the gut instinct that the "others" are truly bad and wrong: we

---

20   Jane Elliott's experiment with 3rd graders that were split into blue and brown eyed groups showed how quickly humans form group loyalty and antipathy. See "Jane Elliott's Blue Eyes Brown Eyes Exercise." http://www.janeelliott.com/, accessed 11/3/2015.

21   Ann Friedman, *The American Prospect.* "All Politics is Identity Politics." 7/29/2010. http://prospect.org/article/all-politics-identity-politics-0, accessed 9/16/2015

pick out memes or articles on social media that support this hypothesis and share it with the rest of the tribe, in order to get the comforting and inspiring rush of belonging.

Politicians, political consultants, commentators, community organizers: the whole political industry knows this and those who get ahead take full advantage of it, knowingly triggering the tribal part of your brain instead of appealing to your reason. If you look closely, you'll realize that the vast majority of political messaging isn't meant to convince people to change their minds. Instead, it is geared towards displaying our tribal identity to others. It's just like wearing a sports jersey in public.

These are examples of where Americans have lined up into tribes that have strong cultural symbolism. Showing off these symbols to others is part of a self-reinforcement of one's identity with the tribe.

These tactics, when used effectively, make you think you hate the other tribe, even in cases where you have no substantial quarrel. But the prophecy is self-fulfilling: if both sides believe they are enemies, they become just that.

Issues are Crafted to Exploit Our Brains' Instincts

Understanding this aspect of human nature can help us understand what kinds of political issues are best designed to manipulate us and why those issues dominate national dialogue.

Political discourse is shaped largely by the issues highlighted by national media and politicians running for office. Because they are constantly competing for votes, dollars, and viewers, they focus on issues that emotionally inspire us to contribute those resources: wedge issues.

Seven common tactics are used in order to create, reinforce, and take advantage of a wedge issue. These tactics are used by politicians, media outlets, and ideologically extreme Americans to take control of the national dialogue.

1. **Inflated Issues.** The issue is made out to be world-stoppingly important: a matter of fundamental human rights, of our core values as Americans, of a very deep right-and-wrong. The stakes are made out to be very high, and any incremental movement or compromise is painted to be total loss on the issue, as it would create a slippery slope or domino effect towards defeat. Though we don't rank wedge issues as most important when forced to choose between them and other issues, they are made to feel highly important when we discuss them, and we are made to feel that we cannot give any ground, even on the parts of the issue we do not care as much about.

    Examples: Even though government functionality, the economy, and healthcare are the top priorities for Americans, it is most common to hear that disagreement issues like abortion and guns are those that will prevent someone from voting for a candidate. Abortion is a matter of murder vs.

the fundamental rights of women. Guns policy is a matter of inalienable constitutional freedoms vs. the lives of children.

2. **Tribe Rallies.** Simple arguments, bumper-sticker one-liners, and team identifiers dominate messaging. These are not intended to change the minds of others that disagree, but to create a sense of group identity among supporters. The issue is tied to the cultural identity of the demographic group that's being courted for the vote. This reinforces the emotional commitment of supporters and maintains social pressure not to break rank.

   Examples: Camps pick simple identifiers for themselves that don't allow for any nuance, like being "pro human rights" and "fighting oppression," or being "pro freedom" or advocating for "responsibility."

3. **Cherry-Picked Data.** Because complexity and nuance are a threat to a highly emotional narrative, wedging relies on the manipulation and careful selection of data to create so called "analyses" that support one side of the argument. Highly complex phenomena are broken down into simple graphs that claim to fully explain the problem with a single, simple variable. This provokes our natural confirmation bias and makes us more certain that anyone disagreeing with us is a fool.

   Examples: Events in the US are often compared to those in other countries, without controlling for the size of the American population. A correlation is presumed to be causation. Variables are deceptively defined and labeled. An event like a school shooting is used to show that we should ban all guns; a person stopping a robbery with a gun is used to show that we should all carry concealed weapons.

4. **Symbolic Battles.** Legislative or court battles over ultimately trivial, low-impact, or tangentially-related sub-issues are touted by supporters as great victories or grave defeats. Such battles reinforce a sense of progress, threat, and pride among supporters, and give politicians activity

that they can point to during campaign season when they have not made substantial progress in other fields.

Examples: The battle over whether abortion should be restricted to 20 or 24 weeks encapsulates only 1.2% of abortions, many of which are "health of the mother" exceptions, and would be allowed in either case.

5. **Enemy Groups.** The opposition to each camp's position on the issue is painted as stupid, evil, or both. They are made out to be enemies with bad intent that must be defeated and painted to share none of our core values to prevent the temptation to work towards consensus. This taps into our sense of righteousness, fear, and natural human tendency to be motivated by having an enemy to fight against. When the opposition is evil, one does not require curious investigation.

Examples: With gay marriage, the sides are painted as oppressing fundamental civil rights or attacking the moral foundations of our society. With economic inequality, the sides are painted as either corporate fat-cats stealing from hard-working Americans or government stealing from hard-working Americans to buy votes with welfare.

6. **Sensationalized Events.** Specific events in the news are pounced upon and editorialized in order to reinforce messaging. Each camp in a wedge issue wages a war of narrative, trying to successfully frame the event in the eyes of their camp as an example of the truth of their position. Though they are quickly forgotten, each event leads to a surge of energy and emotion for the camp. Rather than looking at a big picture, politicians and media can cherry-pick isolated events that stoke senses of fear, violation, and injustice.

Examples: Despite the small number of victims compared to other violence in the US, highly visible shootings (like those in schools) garner massive attention and cause each side of the guns issue to release a flurry of messaging. Every proposed change in taxes, no matter how small, sparks a fight. Amid the Confederate flag controversy, quite suddenly private individuals or institutions choosing to sell or not sell it, wave it or take it down, made enemies.

7. **Permanence.** Perhaps most importantly, the most successful wedge issues are those that are framed to be unresolvable. With demands that are intentionally vague and designed to not be fully addressed by new legislation, each camp is able to keep wedge issues at the forefront of the minds of their supporters.

   Examples: An issue like abortion will never be fully resolved unless there are zero abortions, or unless there are no barriers at all – between those two extremes, there is always room to fight. Taxes can be fought over endlessly unless the government is dissolved. Inequality can be fought over until everyone has the exact same amount of money. None of these will ever truly go away on its own.

As we saw earlier, the most politically engaged Americans see the opposition as a threat to the very nation. Politicians and media have created this sentiment by stoking the issues that are most emotional for us – these wedge issues. Politicians insist that if they are not elected, the enemy opposition will score a victory that cripples your side's stance on a wedge issue for good.

Consider for a moment the portrayal of some wedge issues that were emphasized in the recent election (or current one): which issues in media and political advertisements are being linked to group identity, high stakes, and emotions? Which issues make you most emotional? How are those issues portrayed or discussed? If your friends or community lean left or right, how do they talk about the stakes of the election with respect to these issues? How do they frame potential or actual defeat?

HOW TO KNOW YOU'RE BEING WEDGED

"The primary element of social control is the strategy of distraction which is to divert public attention from important issues and changes determined by the political and economic elites, by the technique of flood or flooding continuous distractions and insignificant information."

    -Noam Chomsky

Wedge issues are easy to spot in the wild if you know where you're looking.

When people start talking about wedge issues, they tend to get angry with their opponent or furiously agree with their confederate. They tend to use slogans and "bumper-sticker" points. Accusations fly, as if someone in the conversation is simply a bad person. We hear hyperbole and people trying to catch each other in rhetorical traps. Whatever the tactics, people start digging in and taking shots at each other, more to score points than to convince anyone of changing their minds. This fighting feeds our sense of justice or righteousness and the most emotionally engaged people feel a surge of adrenaline as they engage in a political throw-down with an audience watching. The True Believers at either end of the spectrum thrive in this environment, and their Hijacked allies awkwardly align themselves with these True Believers to avoid rejection.

The Socially Aware in the group become quiet: they believe there's nothing they can say to make the conversation better, so they hope that the conversation will peter out and move to more pleasant topics. They form a politics-free group that discusses sports, TV, vacation plans, and other less emotionally fraught topics.

On social media, wedge issues spawn ridiculous memes, captioned images of enemy politicians looking mean, or solitary and sensationalized stories with a strong emotional appeal to righteousness. The anger that spikes in our minds when we see these makes us much more likely to share them, meaning they spread like wildfire and bombard us constantly. We might get angry enough to leave an inflammatory comment in approval, or an objection, the latter of which often starts a heated, unproductive argument in ALL CAPS – just to make sure other people know that we're yelling.

Regardless of your outward reaction, you may notice your emotions boiling up. We've been taught by years of toxic dialogue and intentional wedging that we should be angry when the topic comes up. We haven't been taught to engage our brain and explore our emotional response with curiosity.

WHAT TO DO WHEN YOU'RE BEING WEDGED

"He who gains victory over other men is strong;

but he who gains victory over himself is all powerful."

-Lao Tzu

So we're being wedged: it's a consequence of politicians trying to win votes and media trying to win viewers, and destructive to the political process and civil society. Knowing it's happening to us is important.

But fixing it is another story altogether. Many books about politics point out a problem in the political system and call on politicians to make the change themselves. "Someone should do something about this!" is an all-too-common and terribly ineffective response to the problem due to the incentives at work.

We prefer Smokey the Bear's approach: Only you can prevent political forest fires. The American public will need to change in order to overcome the wedge and heal the partisan divide.

Recognizing the problem and understanding why it's happening is an important first step. Then, the real work begins: reprogramming ourselves through deliberate practice to overcome our reflexive, instinctive tribal responses to wedging and instead to challenge what we hear and find common values with our political opposition.

In Part 2: The Wedge Issues, we offer you the opportunity to begin that practice. We have carefully selected and thoroughly researched a few of the top contentious issues of today's political landscape. We illustrate the wedge issue, and then break it down by analyzing the underlying data. The process of deconstructing these wedge issues will help build habits of curiosity, self-awareness, critical thinking, and respect into our consumption of and participation in political discourse.

Throughout the book we have intentionally limited our research to information and data available to anyone with an Internet connection and a library card. Almost all of our citations have web addresses where the information can be accessed from your computer immediately. We hope to show our readers how easy it is to quickly educate oneself on an issue with the right mindset. Explore our citations as you read and consider what other issues you can learn more about with a similar approach to research.

PART II
THE WEDGE ISSUES

"...the smaller the number of individuals composing a majority, and the smaller the compass within which they are placed, the more easily will they concert and execute their plans of oppression."

-Federalist Papers number 10

We chose a few wedge issues to discuss on the basis that they were fairly well-known, tend to have the strongest opinions associated with them, and can be understood quickly.

We're going to walk through each wedge issue with the same structure:

1. **Understand the wedge issue's impact.** We'll explore how it's framed by politicians and the media, what some of the polling looks like, and what emotions are involved. We illustrate some of the 7 wedging tactics used in each issue. This should give you a clear view of the landscape.

2. **Analyze the data around what's really going on.** We'll see how conventional narratives have manipulated data and diverged from reality, and how the narrative about the issue can change when framed with more objectivity and nuance.

3. **Consider the path forward.** Within the framework of our core values, we'll explore where Americans can find agreement and become more effective together. We'll look

into how to potentially take the wedge issue off the table altogether. Finally we'll have some questions you can ask your elected representatives and talking points for your next political discussion.

Our framing will be aimed at highlighting how issues are simplified in political discourse and how complex they are underneath the surface. As you're reading, we encourage you to do the following:

» **Take notice of your feelings when you see data:** what data make you happy, what data are you resistant to believing? What do you accept implicitly, and what do you reject or get angry about?

» **Ask yourself honestly if you want certain things/facts/conclusions to be true,** rather than simply having curiosity for what happens to be true.

» **Take a moment to reflect on your feelings:** "why don't I just have an open mind and desire to seek/know the truth, whatever it may be? Why do I want certain things to be true? How does it relate to my identity? What stakes do I have in the outcome?"

» **Look at the websites of the candidates running in your district/state** (both those you like and those you don't). How do they address these wedge issues? How do they frame the stakes? How do they paint the opposition? Which data do they cite, and which do they ignore? How are they playing on our emotions? Do you think they actually fully believe their own stated positions, or do you distrust what they say?

Discussing these wedge issues with curiosity will be challenging, but revealing. Approached with the right mindset, it can be highly rewarding.

CHAPTER THREE:
GUNS

"If I could have gotten 51 votes in the Senate of the United States for an outright ban, picking up every one of them . . . Mr. and Mrs. America, turn 'em all in, I would have done it."

-*Dianne Feinstein, US Senator (D-CA)*

"From my cold, dead hands."

-*Charlton Heston, then-President of the NRA*

Guns are a classic example of a wedge issue, and a great place for us to start. Artificially divided into two loud and diametrically opposed camps, "gun control" and "gun rights" advocates push guns to the top of the national agenda and drive support to favored candidates every election cycle. They wield huge political power even though only 1% of Americans consider gun control to be one of the country's top priorities.

Like all good wedge issues, instead of being a reasoned, data-driven search for policy solutions, the guns debate devolves into emotional, hyperbolic grandstanding and bumper-sticker politics. Those in the political industry stoke Americans' fears of violence and of government control, taking advantage of sensational, headline-making incidents to fan the flames of antagonism between the two camps and sustain the emotional energy that drives loyal support.

A note here before we get started: every single preventable death is a tragedy. Sometimes people can be concerned that looking at this issue from a high-level data and policy standpoint trivializes the individual tragic incidents that occur. Our aim is to focus on the data only in order to explore which efforts are most effective at reducing preventable, premature, and violent death, and how those differ from the efforts most commonly used for wedging.

THE STATE OF THE DEBATE

Gun Control: Those in favor of stricter gun control often consider private gun ownership to serve only two purposes: violent crime and recreational hunting. They believe that it is a reasonable sacrifice to constrain the latter in order to prevent the tragedy of the former. Current efforts seek to increase the barriers to gun ownership in order to keep guns from being used in violent crime. There is a particular emphasis on banning assault weapons and high-capacity magazines, under the assumption that the deadlier the weapon, the more death it will cause, and therefore that reducing the prevalence of these deadly weapons will lead to fewer deaths per violent incident.

Gun Rights: To those advocating for greater gun freedoms, most gun owners are law-abiding citizens and their 2nd Amendment rights should not be infringed upon due to the unlawful actions of a few. They argue that restrictions to gun ownership are often ineffective at reducing the number of victims of violent crimes. Instead they argue that current laws are not effectively enforced, supporting policies that expand the power of police and the justice system to deter violent acts and remove violent people from society. Some gun rights advocates even contend that gun-control measures are counter-productive, as they will have a disproportionate effect on disarming law-abiding citizens; those who currently come across guns illegally will continue to be able to do so.

A possible wide array of perspectives has been reduced to two blocs that ignore nuance and persist in their sustained virulence against one another, even in the face of both changes in gun control regulation and falling levels of violence.[1]

LAWS COVERING THE SALE OF FIREARMS - AMERICANS' PREFERENCES SINCE 2000

In general, do you feel that the laws covering the sale of firearms should be made:
■ %more strict ■ %less strict or ■ %kept as they are now?

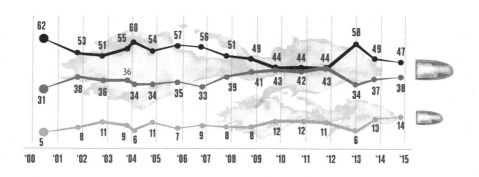

GALLUP | February 8-11, 2015

Above we see a graph that suggests a fairly even split between those that call for stricter gun control, and those that either want laws to be less strict or kept as they are.

What's more, the data available suggest that this is an issue where the emotional response is far out of proportion to the likely harm or risk, whether the rhetoric claims that all of our children are at great risk from school shootings or that gun control risks turning the country into a police state.

UNDERSTANDING THE WEDGE

The image of a gun is a powerful symbol: some see guns as tools of wrongful death while others see them as tools of resisting oppression. Systematic wedging tactics exploit this emotional

---

1   Art Swift, *Gallup*. "Less Than Half of Americans Support Stricter Gun Laws." 10/31/2014. http://www.gallup.com/poll/179045/less-half-americans-support-stricter-gun-laws.aspx, accessed 9/18/2015

potential to stoke the fear that drives viewing, voting, and donating.

Issue Inflation

When polled, only about 1% of Americans rate guns or gun policy as the most important issue facing the country today[2] and it sits in the lower half of issues ranked as a "very important" priority for Americans.[3]

In light of this, keeping attention on guns requires repeatedly framing the issue as critically important, beyond what the facts would justify on their own. Some of the rhetoric is meant to frame the outcome as highly binary: either guns are an unacceptable plague in the country or gun control is a threat to American liberties.

Wedging from the right frames the threat of defeat as the banning of all guns and elimination of Constitutional rights, making citizens vulnerable to crime and government oppression.

"When only cops have guns, it's called a "police state"."

> *– Claire Wolfe, author and columnist, "101 Things To Do Until The Revolution"*

"The war is coming to the streets of America and if you are not keeping and bearing and practicing with your arms then you will be helpless and you will be the victim of evil."

> *-Ted Nugent, American musician, singer, songwriter, hunter, and political activist.*

You may have been reminded that brutal dictatorial regimes like the Nazis, Soviets, and Khmer Rouge banned guns before they massacred their own citizens.

---

2   Rebecca Riffkin, *Gallup*. "Racism Edges Up Again as Most Important US Problem." 7/16/2015. http://www.gallup.com/poll/184193/racism-edges-again-important-problem.aspx?utm_source=Politics&utm_medium=newsfeed&utm_campaign=tiles, accessed 9/19/2015

3   Frank Newport and Joy Wilke, *Gallup*. "Americans Rate Economy as Top Priority for Government." 1/16/2014. http://www.gallup.com/poll/166880/americans-rate-economy-top-priority-government.aspx, accessed 9/19/2015.

"In 1939, Germany established gun control. From 1939 to 1945, six million Jews and seven million others unable to defend themselves were exterminated."

> *-Joe "The Plumber" Wurzelbacher, political commentator*

Wedging from the left frames the status quo as a state of constant fear for Americans and their children, with war-weapons roaming about the country.

"Gun violence is killing America."

> *-Tom Watkins, president of Detroit Wayne Mental Health Authority*

"Our nation's love of guns is killing our children... how many deaths will it take for parents to pay attention?"

> *-Kate Tuttle, Dame Magazine[4]*

Rallying the Tribe against the Enemy

In the guns issue, both camps call the other camp stupid or backwards for the positions they hold.

---

4   Kate Tuttle, *Dame Magazine*. "Our Nation's Love of Guns is Killing Our Children." 2/18/2015. http://www.damemagazine.com/2015/02/18/our-nations-love-guns-killing-our-children, accessed 10/10/2015

From the right, one liners such as, "guns don't kill people, people kill people," are meant to imply that someone is just plain stupid for believing that gun control could reduce murder rates.

"If guns kill people, then pencils misspell words, cars make people drive drunk, and spoons make people fat."

> *- Bill Murray, Actor*

Wedging from the left, on the other hand, frames guns as being part of a backwards culture rooted in violence, machismo, and racism. Gun freedom advocates are called "gun nuts."

"It's not surprising, then, they get bitter, they cling to guns or religion or antipathy to people who aren't like them or anti-immigrant sentiment or anti-trade sentiment as a way to explain their frustrations."

> *-Barack Obama, President of the United States*

"Semi-automatic weapons have only two purposes. One is so that owners can take them to the shooting range once in awhile, yell yeehaw and get all horny at the rapid fire and the burning vapour spurting from the end of the barrel."

> *-Stephen King, author*

Cherry-Picking and Abuse of Data

The gun debate is dominated by cherry-picked data or emotional one-liners that prevent the conversation from becoming a nuanced discussion. Searching online for facts about the effects of guns and gun policy, one finds organizations like the NRA and Mother Jones sniping each other with short-lists of seemingly-decisive facts that prove their point, and retorts calling the others' list a set of myths.

For example, Mother Jones trumpets a positive state-by-state correlation of gun death rate vs. household gun ownership rate,[5] making sure not to point out the total murder or violent death rate (a combined statistic of guns and other weapons), which we show later does not correlate with murder rate.

---

5   Dave Gilson, *Mother Jones*. "10 Pro-Gun Myths, Shot Down." 1/31/2013. http://www.mother-jones.com/politics/2013/01/pro-gun-myths-fact-check, accessed 7/29/2015

Gun ownership vs. gun deaths, by state

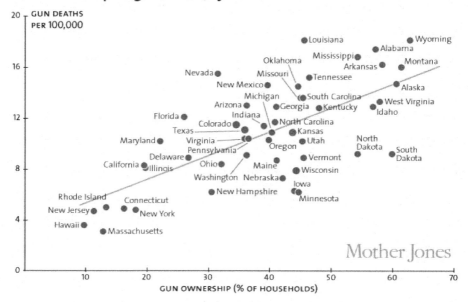

Or a famous Moms Demand Action billboard in Boston has a counter with the number of Americans killed since the Sandy Hook massacre, without elaborating on what killed these Americans.

On the other hand, the Gun Owners Action League chooses a single state (Massachusetts) over an arbitrary time period (1998-2011), claiming that Massachusetts' more restrictive open carry permitting policies led to an outlier increase in gun homicides,[6] saying, "the statistics speak for themselves." You might hear that bomber "Timothy McVeigh didn't use a gun to kill 168 people," used as evidence that guns aren't a problem.

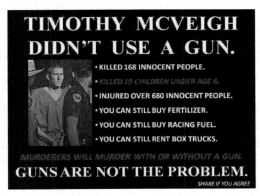

Sensationalized Events

Mass murders are horrible in a way that is very visceral, and are often used to make one's position morally indisputable. These tragedies are unacceptable – and so is the way they are used to score political points.

"Another shooting, another culture war."

   -The News Journal, October 9, 2015

One example is the Umpqua Community College Shooting in Oregon in 2015, in which a student killed 9 other students and then himself.

Left-leaning political news outlets and politicians seized the opportunity to channel the anguish and anger of Americans into rage at groups that oppose their camp's positions on gun control: Republicans, the NRA, and weapons manufacturers.

Former Secretary of State Hillary Clinton reacted to the shootings on the campaign trail, saying, "What is wrong with us, that we cannot stand up to the NRA and the gun lobby, and the

---

6   Gun Owners' Action League. "Massachusetts Gun Laws and Crime Rates as Compared to the Entire Country Since 1998." http://www.goal.org/infographic.html, accessed 8/14/2015

gun manufacturers they represent? ... It's infuriating."[7] Salon's article, "How America's toxic gun culture breeds mass murder," called on Americans to "take the Second Amendment and shove it," and presented gun rights activists as "utterly insane and immoral."[8]

On the other side, right-leaning news outlets and politicians accused the left of strategically co-opting a terrible tragedy in order to push a partisan political agenda.

New Jersey Governor Chris Christie said, "Should he be out there and is he using these families? ... Listen, his statements were obscene. It's that simple... he gives a rant behind the podium in the White House briefing room, a temper-tantrum over things on his liberal agenda that can't get done."[9]

Senator Ted Cruz said, "...they try to use these tragedies as an excuse to come after the constitutional rights of law-abiding citizens. It's unconstitutional, it's cynical, and it's wrong." On the President's speech, he said "...he seeks to tear us apart, he seeks to politicize it and it's worth remembering he is ideological and he is a radical."[10]

The reaction to these events is not limited to rhetoric. Mayor Michael Bloomberg responded to the Sandy Hook massacre by adding $50MM towards gun control advocacy group Moms Demand Action,[11] whose numbers on Facebook swelled after

---

7   Comments made 10/2/2015. Lisa Lerer, *Associated Press*, via US News. "Clinton to Push New Gun Controls After Deadly Oregon Shooting." 10/5/2015. "http://www.usnews.com/news/politics/articles/2015/10/05/clinton-to-push-new-gun-controls-after-oregon-shooting, accessed 10/11/2015

8   Andrew O'Hehir, *Salon*. "How America's toxic culture breeds mass murder." 12/15/2012. http://www.salon.com/2012/12/15/how_americas_toxic_culture_breeds_mass_murder/, accessed 10/11/2015

9   On Fox News, 10/8/2015. Matt Arco, *nj.com*. "Christie blast Obama's 'obscene' reaction to Oregon shooting." 10/9/2015. http://www.nj.com/politics/index.ssf/2015/10/christie_blasts_obamas_reaction_to_oregon_shooting.html, accessed 10/11/2015

10   Comments made on 10/1/2015. Andrew Kaczynski and Mark Arce, BuzzFeed News. "Ted Crus: 'Radical' Obama 'Seeks to Tear Us Apart' With Comments on Oregon Shooting." 10/2/2015. http://www.buzzfeed.com/andrewkaczynski/ted-cruz-radical-obama-seeks-to-tear-us-apart-with-comments#.lmoqGdkeB, accessed 10/11/2015

11   Jeremy W. Peters, *The New York Times*. "Bloomberg Plans a $50 Million Challenge to the NRA." 5/15/2014. http://www.nytimes.com/2014/04/16/us/bloomberg-plans-a-50-million-challenge-to-the-nra.html?_r=0, accessed 9/22/2015

the event. This donation and growth came at the tail of a steady 22-year decline in murder and violent crime in the US.

Gun and ammunition sales spike significantly after highly publicized mass shootings, like Sandy Hook,[12] as well as President Obama's two elections,[13] Searches for "bulk ammo" on Google can illustrate the reaction:

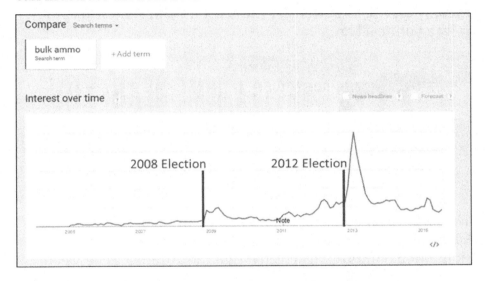

These spikes are driven by the fear pressed into gun owners that after these incidents or the election, severe gun control measures were imminent, and they had better "stock up now."

Manufactured Battlegrounds

In wedge issues, small and often unimportant policy questions are turned into critical symbolic battlegrounds over which to fight the political war. In the issue of guns, the best example is assault weapons.

Highly visible mass shootings like Sandy Hook brought assault weapons back into the spotlight. The movement to ban assault weapons re-emerged after the tragedy in 2012, and in 2013 (after

---

12   Nat Rudarakanchana, *International Business Times*. "Gun Sales Before and After Newtown Shootings: Newtown Anniversary." 12/14/2015. http://www.ibtimes.com/gun-sales-after-newtown-shootings-newtown-anniversary-charts-1509000, accessed 9/28/2015

13   Tony Rizzo, *The Kansas City Star*. Hosted on McClatchyDC, 1/11/2013. http://www.mcclatchydc.com/news/nation-world/national/article24742864.html, accessed 9/28/2015

a bit of the dust settled), about 50%-60% of Americans wanted to ban assault weapons.[14]

In fact, assault weapons are no more lethal than other rifles in the United States, and are used in only 50 murders per year.[15] But assault weapons have been the tool of choice for a number of mass murders and cosmetically resemble machine guns, and thereby serve as a powerful symbolic target around which to rally a political base.

The push to renew the assault weapons ban has yielded fierce backlash from the right. Although wedging rhetoric from the right often points out (correctly) that the differences between assault weapons and other rifles are purely cosmetic,[16] the fight to preserve access to buying new assault weapons is framed as highly critical for gun rights. Because every new gun restriction is framed as a crushing defeat for liberty, the cosmetic features of assault weapons are just as powerful a symbolic target for the right. The partisan establishment of the gun rights camp benefits from the gun control camp's campaign against assault weapons: they use it to energize their own base, too.

---

14   Margie Omero et al, *Center for American Progress.* "What the Public Really Thinks About Guns." 3/27/2013. https://www.americanprogress.org/issues/civil-liberties/report/2013/03/27/58092/what-the-public-really-thinks-about-guns/ and various polls at pollingreport.com, http://www.pollingreport.com/guns.htm, accessed 9/21/2015.

15   Senator Dianne Feinstein, the leader of the push for renewing the Assault Weapons Ban, counts about 48 deaths per year from Assault Weapons since 2004, which is when the ban expired

16   Assault weapons are defined as having two of three characteristics: a folding stock, a pistol grip, and a muzzle flash suppressor. None of these increase the rate of fire, muzzle velocity, or other measurable lethality of the weapon. Assault weapons should not be confused with assault rifles, which are often confused as assault weapons. Assault rifles differ from other weapons in that they are fully automatic, and may have other features like high muzzle velocity.

Analyzing the Data: Undermining the Wedge

Beyond the Binary: Beneath the Rhetoric, Nuance and Common Ground

In reality, the guns issue is highly complex, grey, and full of nuance. The dichotomy of being "pro gun rights" or "pro gun control" is false.

Just as wedging often twists our brains into choosing an extreme, framing focused instead on policy details and problem-solving "de-fangs" the issue and reveals both the nuanced thinking most Americans have about guns as well as the potential for broad agreement.

A Wide Array of Options

If we put ourselves in a curious, policy-making mindset about guns, we can quickly see that there are many positions we can take, all of which follow from different premises, and most of which contain some elements of gun control and some of gun freedom.

Some policies can focus on which weapons should be available to the public, like fully-automatic machine guns, high-caliber tank-buster rifles, clips of certain sizes, assault weapons, handguns, etc. Ultimately, we have to draw a line along the scale somewhere.

Some policies focus on which people should be allowed access to guns. Should convicted violent criminals be able to buy them? What about nonviolent criminals? Should the mentally ill be able to have them? Does "mentally ill" include only the schizophrenic, or does it include narcissists, or the depressed, or the anxious? Should people under 18 be allowed to own a gun, or handle one without supervision? There are a lot of interesting questions here.

Some policies focus on how to regulate gun design and sale to protect personal, family, and community safety. Should one only be allowed to have a gun once one has passed safety training of some sort, like with cars? Should everyone get gun safety training as part of their education? Should it be required to lock a gun in a house with children? Without? Should all guns be required to have trigger locks to prevent accidental discharge? What about biometric locks to prevent unauthorized use? Should people be allowed to openly carry? How about carrying concealed firearms? Should a license of some sort be required, or special permission given in certain circumstances? Should all weapons be open carry only so that people on the street are aware of what's going on around them?

Some policies focus on enforcement. Should background checks be required in order to enforce restrictions on who can have a gun? Should these background checks be required for private sales? What about at gun shows? Should guns be registered to make it easier to catch criminals that have or use guns illegally? Should the authorities be allowed to enter homes of registered gun owners to ensure their weapons are stored in accordance with local laws?

In order to create a reliable voting group, simplicity is critical. It's hard to generate excitement and emotion for oneself as a candidate by discussing complexity. That's why the entrenched "pro gun rights" and "pro gun control" positions have been artificially created through wedging. But the fact is there are dozens of different questions we can consider about gun policy, and thoughtful answers can fall in many different places along a very broad spectrum.

Shared Values and Policy Agreement

Not only can Americans have very diverse and nuanced sets of beliefs about gun control, but there is evidence that we are able to agree on many core values and even many specific policies about guns.

Shared Values: To explore how the battle lines might be artificial and unnecessary we can try looking at the issue from a different perspective. Let's take a moment and start identifying rigorously some of the values that the vast majority of Americans might share and see how they apply to the issue.

1. We don't want to see unnecessary violent and premature death in the US.

2. In particular, we want to protect the most vulnerable and youngest Americans from violent crime.

3. We want a feeling of safety and security in our lives – we don't want to feel like our well-being is at excessive risk at home or in public spaces.

4. We want to accomplish all this without creating a police state or surveillance state, or excessively restricting lawful and peaceful behavior.

5. We want to follow and respect established legislative procedure as we pass the laws we feel are necessary.

6. We want new laws and policies to be effective in accomplishing our core goals.

It's likely most Americans would look at the above and feel they generally agree.

Policy Agreement: When framed vaguely as "more gun control" or "less gun control," we take sides and entrench ourselves, but when we talk about specific policies, we are usually in broad agreement. Very few Americans want to get rid of guns (even handguns), but a large majority wants to make sure we have background checks to keep them out of the hands of likely violent folks; most want to register weapons to make sure we can catch criminals that use them.[17]

---

17 Derek Thompson, *The Atlantic*. "Do Americans Want More or Less Gun Control? Both, Actually." 12/14/2012. http://www.theatlantic.com/national/archive/2012/12/do-americans-want-more-or-less-gun-control-both-actually/266312/

GUN CONTROL SUPPORT

CNN/ORC Poll August 2012

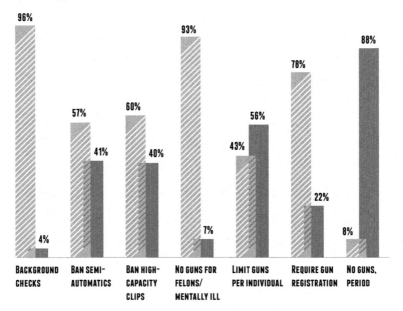

This graph shows us a poll by the Atlantic that asks Americans if they oppose or support certain gun control measures. We see, for example, that about 95% of Americans support background checks before purchasing a weapon; almost as many want to restrict gun ownership for criminals and the mentally ill; almost 80% want guns to be registered. Only 10% wish to see guns banned for the public.

We're going to assume for now that some of the 55% that want to ban semi-automatic weapons really think they mean "fully automatic," as there is a frequent misconception that "semi-automatic" means "automatic,"[18] where a semi-automatic weapon only means that one does not have to reload between each shot. Given that most Americans do not want to ban handguns[19]

---

18   It's hard to find good data on how many people confuse "semi-automatic" (one squeeze, one shot) with "automatic" (one squeeze, many shots) weapons, but anecdotal evidence suggests it happens with some frequency, including to an unfortunate CNN anchor Don Lemon, as featured on Talking Points Memo, "Don Lemon: I Misspoke When I Confused Semi-Automatic and Automatic Guns." By Tom Kludt, 8/21/2014. http://talkingpointsmemo.com/livewire/don-lemon-automatic-guns, accessed 9/18/2015

19   Art Swift, *Gallup.* "Less Than Half of Americans Support Stricter Gun Laws." 10/31/2014. http://www.gallup.com/poll/179045/less-half-americans-support-stricter-gun-laws.aspx,

(which are mostly semi-automatic), it seems unlikely that most Americans would want to ban all one-pull-one-shot weapons. This poll result suggests that there's some confusion around different weapon definitions and their deadliness (we'll cover this in detail when we discuss Assault Weapons); this confusion muddles the debate and takes Americans further out of a technical policy discussion and further into screaming at each other.

Limiting guns per individual is a policy about which there is currently no proposed law or high-visibility political discussion, so we believe that while there's disagreement, it doesn't seem to be as prominent or emotional as other policy issues.

Given all that: looking at the above chart, it seems there's broad support for a few policies, and broad opposition for a few. It really looks like we have potential to have productive and reasonable conversations – and even a large swath of agreement – when we discuss specific policies rather than taking "pro-gun" or "anti-gun" positions.

Almost all Americans who are "pro-gun rights" want some restrictions on gun ownership. And almost all Americans who are "pro-gun control" want to keep guns available for law-abiding citizens. What would happen if we came to the table having all declared that we broadly agree on these two points?

But for as much as we agree, there are still places where we disagree. If the guns issue was ever de-wedged successfully, this disagreement could be both civil and highly productive to the process of creating the best policy to balance our values and use our collective resources as effectively as possible. We would be able to discuss whether specific policies would accomplish what we want, and whether they are worth the trade-offs or costs. Such discussion could lead us to better policies on violent crime, or lead us to focus our efforts onto other issues that we typically rate as more important.

accessed 9/28/2015

Reality Reveals False Wedge Premises

Unfortunately, the strength of the wedge in the guns issue means we're expending effort in fighting one another, without achieving much except making us angrier and chewing up resources that could be better spent. Not only does the issue of guns have a smaller impact (to either side's priorities) than we're led to believe, but the efforts made by either side are not even directed towards outcomes that will deliver what they really want.

Putting the Problem In Perspective

In order to be able to understand whether our current battle-grounds are critical or relevant to what we really want, we must put the debate into perspective.

Often guns get a great deal of focus when discussing violent crime, but they are of course only a part of the discussion. Why is gun violence something that we want to talk about?

Is gun violence a priority simply because we don't want premature (CDC defines "premature" as "before 75") death? Smoking, high blood pressure, elevated blood glucose and being overweight or obese[20] all kill far more people, as do other causes of premature death.[21]

---

20   Bio Med Central, "What's Killing Us? The biggest causes of premature death." 10/22/2014: http://blogs.biomedcentral.com/bmcblog/2014/10/22/whats-killing-us-the-biggest-causes-of-premature-death/, accessed 10/29/2015

21   Statistics for preventable illness, Bio Med Central, "What's Killing Us? The biggest causes of premature death." 10/22/2014: http://blogs.biomedcentral.com/bmcblog/2014/10/22/whats-killing-us-the-biggest-causes-of-premature-death/. For accidental poisoning, unintentional falls, and automobile crashes, the CDC, "FastStats: Accidents or Unintentional Injuries, 9/30/2015: http://www.cdc.gov/nchs/fastats/accidental-injury.htm. For drunk driving, MADD, "About Drunk Driving:" http://www.madd.org/drunk-driving/about/. For power plant emissions, the Huffington Post, "Power Plant Air Pollution Kills 13,000 People Per Year; Coal-Fired Are Most Hazardous: ALA Report," by Joanna Zelman, 5/25/2011: http://www.huffingtonpost.com/2011/03/14/power-plant-air-pollution-coal-kills_n_833385.html. For murder by gun and other methods, gunpolicy.org, "United States – Gun Facts, Figures, and the Law:" http://www.gunpolicy.org/firearms/region/united-states. For suicide by gun and other methods, smartgunlaws.org, "Statistics on Gun Deaths & Injuries," 11/16/2012. http://smartgunlaws.org/gun-deaths-and-injuries-statistics. All accessed 10/29/2015.

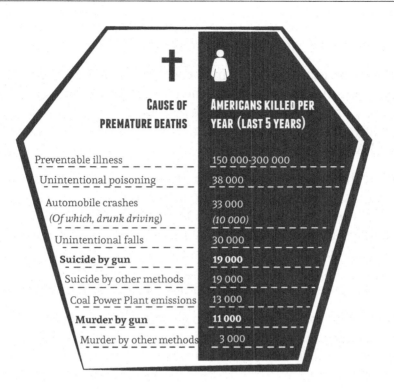

Cause of Premature Deaths	Americans killed per year (last 5 years)
Preventable illness	150 000-300 000
Unintentional poisoning	38 000
Automobile crashes *(Of which, drunk driving)*	33 000 *(10 000)*
Unintentional falls	30 000
Suicide by gun	**19 000**
Suicide by other methods	19 000
Coal Power Plant emissions	13 000
Murder by gun	**11 000**
Murder by other methods	3 000

Unlike many other causes of premature death, gun murders have been on a steady decline for decades. They represented only about 0.5% of premature deaths of Americans in the last five years.[22] In short, if premature death is what we want to prevent, guns are a comparatively small part of the problem.

Certainly, compared to the other causes of premature and wrongful death, the size of the impact of guns does not seem proportional to the emotional response from politicians, media, and wedged American partisans.

And more specifically, the topics within the gun debate that we are most upset about are the topics that have the smallest

---

22   The Population Reference Bureau notes that firearms are responsible for about 1.5% of all premature deaths; because murders are about   of all firearms-related deaths, they account for about 0.5% of all premature deaths. Mark Mather and Paola Scommegna, *Population Reference Bureau*. "Up to Half of US Premature Deaths are Preventable; Lifestyle Choices Key." September 2015. http://www.prb.org/Publications/Articles/2015/us-premature-deaths. aspx, accessed 10/30/2015.

impact: that is, if we want to spend resources reducing gun deaths, then we're focusing on the wrong issues.

Mass Shootings: Mass shootings get huge media attention: the Sandy Hook massacre beat out the presidential election for AP's 2012 story of the year.[23] But these events, although shocking and tragic, have a statistically small impact on the safety and well-being of Americans.

If we use the Congressional Research Service's definition of "public mass shooting" as 4 or more victims dying in a single public incident,[24] then between 1983 and 2013[25] there were 78 public mass shootings with 547 dead and 476 injured victims.[26] By comparison, over 500,000 Americans were murdered in some other fashion over the same time period. You're nearly 1,000 times more likely to be murdered in a non-mass incident.

We know mass shootings aren't becoming more common – media attention is simply getting bigger.[27] Using the FBI's expanded definition in which 4 or more people are injured (still in a public setting without an obvious profit, political, gang, etc motive), we see an average of about 20 incidents per year and about 100 victims (injured and killed) per year. This rate approximately matches the rate independently assessed by

---

23   David Crary, "AP Poll: Mass shootings voted top 2012 news story," 12/20/2012. http://www. ap.org/Content/AP-In-The-News/2012/AP-poll-Mass-shootings-voted-top-2012-news-story, accessed 10/4/2015.

24   You may have seen other stats using other definitions. The BBC uses "4 or more injured in any incident," which makes the mass shooting rate much higher – over one per day. We prefer the FBI's definition as we feel it more accurately reflects what is generally imagined as a "mass shooting," where the BBC definition will include any gang shootout with more than 3 people involved, or other forms of gunfights. BBC: US & Canada. "Oregon shooting: Statistics behind 'routine' US gun violence." 10/2/2015. http://www.bbc.com/news/world-us-canada-34424385, accessed 10/30/2015.

25   That rate has not gone up in 2014 and 2015. We use the dataset through 2013

26   According to the Congressional Research Service, using FBI data: Jerome P. Bjelopera, et al, *Congressional Research Service.* "Public Mass Shootings in the United States: Selected Implications for Federal Public Health and Safety Policy." 3/18/2013. http://www.fas.org/sgp/crs/misc/R43004.pdf, accessed 10/4/2014.

27   From a study by professor Kelly McBride, senior faculty for ethics at the Poynter Institute: Laura Smith-Spark, CNN. "Are mass killings on the increase? Criminologist says no," 4/3/2012. http://www.cnn.com/2012/04/03/us/us-mass-killings/, accessed 10/4/2015.

USA Today,[28] and both have not shown statistically significant increases over the short or long term.

MASS SHOOTINGS IN US, 1976-2011

■ Victims ■ Incidents

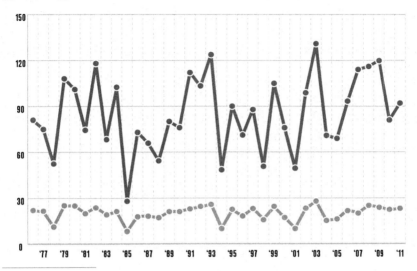

Source: http://www.boston.com/community/blogs/crime_punishment/2012/08/no_increase_in_mass_shootings.html

29

Looking at the above chart of FBI tracking, we see that mass shootings in the US are "spiky." This graph shows total victims—not just those that died, so the total here is going to be higher than the 550 we cited. It appears that the US has somewhere between 10 and 25 mass shootings every year, with usually between 50 and 100 victims per year. One can cherry-pick short-term upward or downward trends, but the key point is that mass shootings have a comparatively small impact, and that impact is not growing over time.

---

28   USA Today. "Behind the Bloodshed: The Untold Story of America's Mass Killings." http://www.gannett-cdn.com/GDContent/mass-killings/index.html#title, accessed 10/30/2015.

29   The keen reader will see that there are way more than 550 victims in this chart. 550 represents the total number of people shot, not deaths. We're using deaths as the metric for comparison between different events because it's the easiest to measure (who "is hurt but doesn't die of" stuff like falling down the stairs or power plant emissions? Very hard to measure – we want to be consistent and focus on the metric with the most available data: deaths). James Alan Fox, *boston.com*. "No increase in mass shootings," 8/6/2012. http://www.boston.com/community/blogs/crime_punishment/2012/08/no_increase_in_mass_shootings.html, accessed 8/24/2015

School shootings are similarly highly unlikely: a child is actually nearly 100 times more likely to be killed by a gun outside a school than in it.[30] Considering that children spend about half of their entire year (6 hours per day, 180 days per year) in schools, they're one of the safest places that a child can be. These school shootings are incredibly tragic and unacceptable, but they're not the bigger danger to children: the data suggests we should focus our efforts on protecting children – even from guns specifically – elsewhere.

Assault Weapons and High-Capacity Clips: As we mentioned earlier, assault weapons absorb a huge amount of emotional energy and inspire hundreds of millions of dollars in political spending from both sides, despite being a very small part of both violent crime and gun rights. Whether trying to save lives or preserve gun rights, there are more productive areas of focus than assault weapons.

30   Dewey G. Cornell, *The Washington Post.* "Gun violence and mass shootings – myths, facts, and solutions." 6/11/2014. http://www.washingtonpost.com/news/the-watch/wp/2014/06/11/gun-violence-and-mass-shootings-myths-facts-and-solutions/, accessed 8/24/2015

HOMICIDE BY WEAPON TYPE, 2011

number of homicides | type of gun used

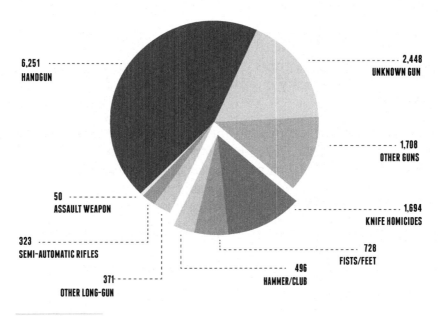

6,251
HANDGUN

2,448
UNKNOWN GUN

1,708
OTHER GUNS

1,694
KNIFE HOMICIDES

50
ASSAULT WEAPON

323
SEMI-AUTOMATIC RIFLES

728
FISTS/FEET

371
OTHER LONG-GUN

496
HAMMER/CLUB

Source: FBI, via http:/www.gunpolicy.org/firearms/region/united-states

In 2011 (which has been fairly representative of the past 10 years), for example, assault weapons were used in 50 murders, where hammers and clubs were used in 10 times as many. We see that handgun deaths account for the largest portion of all murders in the US—over 100 times the number due to assault weapons.

One reason the number is so low is that assault weapons are ultimately no more lethal than most other rifles in the US (it's not that they're scarce – four million assault weapons are floating around the country).[31] Many Americans confuse assault weapons with assault rifles (fully-automatic "machine guns," which are already banned), when assault weapons differ from other semi-automatic rifles in only cosmetics. It's a very unhelpful distinction.[32]

---

31   Paul Whitefield, *The Los Angeles Times*. "4 million assault weapons in America: That should be enough," 3/14/2013. http://articles.latimes.com/2013/mar/14/news/la-ol-feinstein-assault-weapons-ban-good-start-20130314, accessed 8/24/2015

32   Lois Beckett, *The New York Times*. "The Assault Weapon Myth," 9/12/2014. http://www.nytimes.com/2014/09/14/sunday-review/the-assault-weapon-myth.html?_r=0, accessed 9/6/2015.

High-capacity clips (those with over 10 rounds) also get a lot of attention when discussing assault weapons, but the debate usually lacks data. The Department of Justice believes it's simply not clear whether banning high-capacity clips saves lives.[33] It appears that shootings with high-capacity clips kill about 57% more people than shootings without them,[34] but that doesn't imply that high-capacity clips necessarily led to these additional deaths.[35]

But let's assume for a moment that high-capacity clips did drive that entire 57%. Of the 547 killed by mass shootings in the past 30 years,[36] the total additional deaths in shootings with high-capacity clips is 110, or about 3.5 people per year. The highest possible impact of high-capacity clips is very low.

Suicides: The oft-cited 30,000 annual gun deaths in the US include murder, accidental death, and suicide, even though these are all separate issues. Suicide actually makes up 62% of gun deaths in the United States – about 19,000 per year.

Looking closer, we know that guns are used in about 50% of suicides in the United States.[37] For reference, the most common method of suicide varies wildly between countries. Worldwide, the use of pesticides makes up 30% of suicides, the largest chunk. In Hong Kong, jumping from tall buildings comprises the majority.[38]

---

33   Christopher S. Kroper, "An Updated Assessment of the Federal Assault Weapons Ban," National Institute of Justice, US Department of Justice, June 2004. (https://www.ncjrs.gov/pdffiles1/nij/grants/204431.pdf)., accessed 10/29/2015

34   Law Center to Prevent Gun Violence. "Large Capacity Ammunition Magazines Policy Summary," 5/31/2013. http://smartgunlaws.org/large-capacity-ammunition-maga-zines-policy-summary/, accessed 9/5/2015.

35   It could be the case, for example, that shooters with the intent to kill the most people found high-capacity clips in addition to other methods for increasing deadliness, like choosing locations with lots of unarmed people in a concentrated area.

36   Mark Follman, et al, *Mother Jones*. "US Mass Shootings, 1982-2015: Data From Mother Jones' Investigation." 7/16/2015. http://www.motherjones.com/politics/2012/12/mass-shootings-mother-jones-full-data, accessed 9/4/2015.

37   Law Center to Prevent Gun Violence. "Statistics on Gun Deaths & Injuries," 11/16/2012. http://smartgunlaws.org/gun-deaths-and-injuries-statistics/. accessed 9/4/2015.

38   Wikipedia. "Suicide Methods." http://en.wikipedia.org/wiki/Suicide_methods, accessed 9/8/2015.

Some might argue that the presence of many guns in the US leads to a significant increase in suicides, but it's hard to say whether that's true. Of the 19,000 Americans that killed themselves with guns, how many would resort to other methods?

If we compare the US suicide rate to that in peer countries with many fewer available guns, the US fits into the middle of the pack.[39] Japan and South Korea break away from the rest of the OECD, despite being nearly gun-free.

---

39 WHO 2011, via World Health Rankings. "Suicide: Death Rate Per 100,000, Age Standardized." http://www.worldlifeexpectancy.com/cause-of-death/suicide/by-country/, accessed 9/18/2015.

SUICIDE RATE BY COUNTRY
Selected Industrialized Nations (WHO 2011)
Suicide rate (per 100k)

In the years after 2011, South Korea's suicide rate has increased to over 28 per 100,000. The US remains slightly below average in OECD suicide rate.

What this suggests is that there are factors besides gun availability that have a much larger effect on the suicide rate.

Busting Some Common Wedge Myths

The political machine is able to keep our attention focused on these unproductive issues in part by propagating simple one-liner beliefs that are either complete myths or vast oversimplifications of reality to the point of being deceptive. Challenging some of these common myths can create natural skepticism in our minds, allowing us to more easily spot wedging tactics when they're happening.

"Guns in my home make me safer." Those with guns in their homes are 1.9x more likely to be murdered in their home than those without.[40] Most of these homicides are perpetrated by friends or family members.

"More guns means more death." Over the past 25 years, the homicide and violent crime rate in the US has dropped, even as the number of guns per person in the country has grown, and as we've seen earlier in the chapter, there is no correlation between gun ownership and homicide rate across US states or OECD countries.

"Carrying a gun on the street makes me safer." Assault victims carrying guns are about 4.5 times more likely to be shot and 4.2 times more likely to be killed than those without guns.[41] This correlation does not alone clarify the cause, but it should give you pause to consider the conventional belief.

"30,000 Americans die every year from guns." This number is factual, but deceptive. Of those 30,000 deaths, only 11,000 are homicides or negligent manslaughter; the rest are suicides, which are a very different topic than homicide. Uniting the two of them by the tool sometimes used for both obfuscates the complex (and very different) root causes behind violent crime and someone's decision to commit suicide.

Using a whole number, rather than a rate per population, is also just misleading. The whole number of Americans killed by guns is often compared to some other countries, but they have much smaller populations. The only way to make an accurate comparison across geography or time is to use a per-capita rate.

---

40   Linda L. Dahlberg, et al. "Guns in the Home and Risk of a Violent Death in the Home: Findings from a National Study." *American Journal of Epidemiology.* Vol 160, Iss 10: pp 929-936. http://aje.oxfordjournals.org/content/160/10/929.full, accessed 9/7/2015.

41   Charles C. Branas, et al. "Investigating the Link Between Gun Possession and Gun Assault." *American Journal of Public Health*, Nov 2009, vol 99, no 11: pp 2034-2040. http://ajph.apha-publications.org/doi/full/10.2105/AJPH.2008.143099

"Any gun restriction is a violation of the 2nd Amendment."
This is not uncommon to hear, but if this is so, why aren't
gun rights activists fighting for the right to bear machine
guns, grenade launchers, and artillery? What about the 2nd
Amendment specifically allows for the restriction of artillery
(which is functionally a very large rifle) but not other aspects of
weapon ownership?

"Sending my child to a home with a gun is dangerous."
Everytown for Gun Safety and Moms Demand Action[42]
published an emotional whitepaper called "Innocents Lost: A
Year of Unintentional Child Gun Deaths."

The number of children killed by accidental gunfire that year
was 36,[43] or a little less than one for every million children. This
is similar to the 40 kids/year killed by being left in hot vehicles
by their own parents.[44]

For comparison, the same age group saw over 500 accidental
deaths in swimming pools – about 14x more children.[45] Given
that 50 million houses have firearms and only 11 million[46] have
swimming pools, your child is at about 64x greater risk of
death at a house with a swimming pool than a house with guns.
Presumably gun owners who swim should be avoided.

Compared to unintentional death by firearm, children are about
3x more likely to die of burns, 7x more likely to die of accidental
poisoning, and 9x more likely to die of accidental strangling.[47]

---

42   We'll just quickly point out here that these are the same organization so everyone knows
     we've done our homework. They're just two branches with different branding strategies.

43   Citing CDC statistics. John Lott, "What is the risk of a six year old dying from an accidental
     gun shot/" 5/12/2013. http://johnrlott.blogspot.com/2013/05/what-is-risk-of-six-year-old-
     dying-from.html , accessed 10/1/2015.

44   Tom Geoghegan, BBC News, "Hot car deaths: The children left behind,," 21 July 2014. http://
     www.bbc.com/news/magazine-28214266, accessed 8/21/2015 – it's worth noting that
     this article cites all children up to 18 years of age, but we're going to assume for now that
     children over 10 are generally going to be able to get themselves out of the car before dying.

45   Centers for Disease Control and Prevention. "Unintentional Drowning: Get the Facts."
     10/24/2014. http://www.cdc.gov/homeandrecreationalsafety/water-safety/waterinjuries-
     factsheet.html, accessed 8/19/2015.

46   Centers for Disease Control and Prevention. "Healthy Swimming/Recreational Water."
     5/14/2015. http://www.cdc.gov/healthywater/swimming/, accessed 8/19/2015.

47   The National Center for the Review & Prevention of Child Deaths. "United States: Child
     Mortality, 2011." https://www.childdeathreview.org/wp-content/uploads/2011Data/US2011.

We are not saying these are not reasonable concerns for any parent – we say simply that they are best understood in context.

"Current gun laws just need to be enforced." Most guns used in crimes are acquired either via friends or an illegal transfer or sale of some sort. Such friends may have acquired the loaned guns through perfectly legal means.

While it's true that it's already a crime to sell a gun to a convicted criminal and to loan a gun to someone to use in a crime, how can these be enforced? Should the police have the power to search someone's person, car, or home for a gun to check whether it was legally acquired?

The stories we have been told – and repeat to ourselves – maintain the wedge, but don't reflect reality. Understanding that we've been wedged is the first step in overcoming it.

Partisan Efforts are Wasted

Symbolic battles and victories are critical for politicians and advocacy groups to generate the emotion necessary to persist. For both gun control and gun freedom advocates, these symbolic efforts do not change what's truly important to American priorities.

Gun Control

Public advocates for gun control maintain that it is emotionally unacceptable to not support their ideas. But many of the most popular gun control proposals have a poor link between effort and result.

Gun Shows Ban: One proposal on the table to make it harder for criminals to get guns is to shut down gun shows.

That same Fenway billboard.

Shutting down gun shows is a popular gun-control platform because it's a "loophole" through which private owners can sell their guns to other individuals without performing background checks—the idea is that gun shows are a great place for criminals to acquire guns.

But the data doesn't seem to suggest shutting down gun shows would help much.[48] Only 20% of gun-using criminals bought their guns legally—most are acquired from friends (40%) or from an illegal source (39%). Only 0.7% come from gun shows.[49]

European-Style Gun Restrictions: The European Union has a much lower homicide rate than the United States and a much lower gun ownership rate. The correlation makes the EU a tempting place to look for a more successful model to reduce our violent crime rate.

What might happen if the US had as few guns as European countries? There are a number of ways to look at the question.

---

48 Hypotheses exist in the gun control literature that suggest it's possible that gun shows simply make it harder to track guns, and therefore it is easier for these guns to get into the hands of criminals. We haven't yet seen any good evidence in this regard. It's also worth noting that most guns sold at gun shows are sold by licensed dealers that perform criminal background checks; only certain individuals "not in the business" may skip this. David B. Kopel, "The Facts about Gun Shows," 1/10/2000. http://www.cato.org/publications/commentary/facts-about-gun-shows, accessed 10/29/2015.

49 J. Scott Olmsted of American Hunter Magazine, *The Daily Caller.* "Where criminals get their guns." 2/11/2013. http://dailycaller.com/2013/02/11/where-criminals-get-their-guns/, accessed 8/29/2015.

The US *non-gun* violent death rate is already higher than Europe's total, suggesting that the US is a comparatively violent country and (probably) that the biggest factors underlying that violence are something other than gun availability.

While most murders in the United States are perpetrated with guns, many are perpetrated with other weapons (clubs, knives, fists, etc). The murder rate with those weapons in the US is more than 40% higher than the murder rate using all weapons in the EU.

> » 2011 US **non-gun** homicide rate: 1.7[50] / 100k

> » 2011 EU **total** homicide rate: 1.2[51] / 100k

This suggests the following: if all guns were removed from the US, and none of the gun homicides we see would have been perpetrated with other weapons, the US would still have a much higher homicide rate than the EU.

We can explore further whether places with fewer guns have fewer murders.

If we look at the OECD (commonly called our "peer" countries) and remove the United States, we see no evidence to suggest that more guns increases the homicide rate: in fact, there is a slight slope of the line that would suggest the opposite.[52]

---

50   Death Penalty Information Center, "Murder Rates Nationally and By State, 2001-2014." http://www.deathpenaltyinfo.org/murder-rates-nationally-and-state#nat1970, accessed 8/29/2015. Of which 65% from guns.

51   Index mundi. "European Union – Homicide Rate: Intentional homicides (per 100,000 people)." Data from UN Office on Drugs and Crime: International Homicide Statistics database. http://www.indexmundi.com/facts/european-union/homicide-rate, accessed 8/24/2015

52   UNOCD Data, 2013, via John Lott, "So what can the US learn from other developed countries regarding guns and crime," 1/8/2013. http://johnrlott.blogspot.com/2013/01/so-what-can-us-learn-from-other.html, sourcing the UN Global Study on Homicide, 2013. http://www.unodc.org/gsh/en/data.html, accessed 8/24/2015

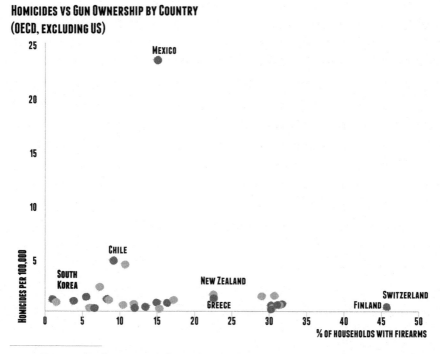

HOMICIDES VS GUN OWNERSHIP BY COUNTRY
(OECD, EXCLUDING US)

Sources: WASHINGTON POST (DECEMBER 17, 2012). "GUN HOMICIDES AND GUN OWNERSHIP BY COUNTRY".
2013 OECD, via https://www.quandl.com/collections/society/oecd-murder-rates

*If more guns generally meant more murders, we should
expect to see the homicide rate be higher in countries where
people owned more firearms—that is, a diagonal line from
bottom-left to top-right. But the trend line seems pretty flat,
and maybe even negative: more guns, less murder.*

*Looking closer: Switzerland might be a special case, as it has
universal conscription. But looking at, for example, New Zealand,
Greece, and Finland we see a 5-10x gun ownership rate of other
countries with identical homicide rates (South Korea, Poland,
the Netherlands). Sweden, Germany, Norway, Iceland, and
Canada have a similar number of guns per capita (about 30 per
100), but have a homicide rate ranging between 0.5 and 3.5 per
100k. The United States has 88 firearms per 100 people and a
homicide rate less than that of Chile (with 9 firearms per 100).*

This suggests that a simple policy of "fewer guns" is unlikely to
reduce the murder rate; in fact, there may be an argument that

the opposite is true. A study with better and more numerous control variables would be required to draw such a conclusion.

We could perform a similar study domestically, as well.

Over the past 20 years or so, we've seen a dramatic drop-off in gun-related deaths in the US despite an increase in the number of guns in the country.[53]

DROPPING HOMICIDE RATE

■ Homicide rate ■ Gun Homicide rate

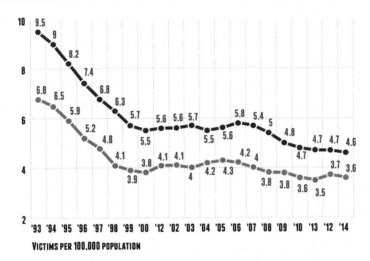

VICTIMS PER 100,000 POPULATION

In this graph we see that both the gun homicide rate and total homicide rate have decreased dramatically since the 1990s, where they peaked. Overall homicides have dropped by more than 50% since 1993, and gun-related homicides have dropped by nearly as much.

But the United States has been undergoing a lot of changes in its demographics, police and justice system, and other major factors that might affect the murder rate.

If we hold time constant and look at a single year (2012), we can compare between the 50 states. We might expect that in states where more people own firearms, we would see more murders.

---

53   Centers for Disease Control and Prevention. "Fatal Injury Reports, National and Regional, 1999 – 2013." http://webappa.cdc.gov/sasweb/ncipc/mortrate10_us.html, accessed 8/24/2015

But comparing states across a scatter plot doesn't show a positive correlation.[54]

HOMICIDES VS GUN OWNERSHIP BY US STATE

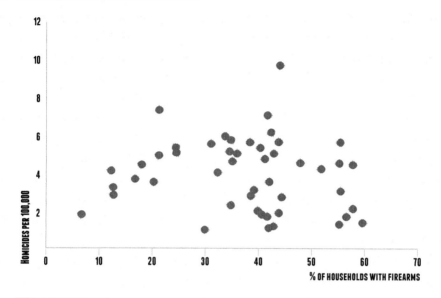

Sources: http://usliberals.about.com/od/Election2012Factors/a/Gun-Owners-As-Percentage-Of-Each-States-Population.htm
"Table 20: Murder by State, Types of Weapons, 2010", Uniform Crime Reports: Crime in the US 2010, FBI.

*Recall the Mother Jones graph early in the chapter, showing a positive correlation between % of households with guns and the **gun** death rate. Restricting the y-axis to the gun death rate is an effective cherry-picking of data. In the graph aboce, we see that the total homicide rate is not correlated with the gun ownership rate. More guns in a state doesn't increase the murder rate, but it does increase the frequency in which guns, rather than other weapons, are used in murders.*

Despite the excitement these proposals elicit from the anti-gun camp, in the end, there doesn't appear to be much data to suggest that simply trying to reduce the number of guns or ban

---

54   FBI statistics via Table 20: Murder by State, Types of Weapons, 2010". *Uniform Crime Reports. Crime in the U.S. 2010.* FBI., and Deborah White, *About News,* "Gun Owners as a Percentage of Each State's Population." 2007. http://usliberals.about.com/od/Election2012Factors/a/Gun-Owners-As-Percentage-Of-Each-States-Population.htm, accessed 8/24/2015

certain types of guns in the United States will reduce violent or premature death in the US.

A Total Gun Ban: Would a total gun ban help reduce violent deaths in the US? The available evidence is mixed. Australia bought back 1 million out of its 3.4 million guns and immediately afterwards experienced a 15% drop in murder rate.[55] However, the murder rate continued to decrease in the 2000s, even though gun ownership has risen again to nearly pre-buyback levels[56] and non-gun homicides dropped just as quickly.[57] Violent crimes do become on average less deadly when perpetrated with knives and crowbars rather than guns,[58] but factors besides the number of guns in the country also contributed to a decrease in homicide rates. The US saw a similar decrease in homicides in both the 1990s and 2000s, even though the number of guns in the country increased steadily.[59]

Much evidence suggests a gun ban might not work. The closest the United States has ever gotten to a gun ban was in the District of Columbia. The DC handgun ban – one of the most stringent in US history – was followed by an increase in violent crime and murders. Murders increased in DC at a similar rate to the rest of the country in the years following the ban,[60] suggesting that the impact of the ban was small at best. One thing we know is that there were still handguns in the city during the period the ban was active.

55   The Australian Bureau of Statistics. "1370.0 – Measures of Australia's Progress, 2010: Crime: Homicide." 09/15/2010. http://www.abs.gov.au/ausstats/abs@.nsf/Lookup/by%20Subject/1370.0~2010~Chapter~Homicide%20(4.4.5.2), accessed 9/22/2015.

56   Nick Ralston, *The Sydney Morning Herald*. "Australia reloads as gun amnesties fail to cut arms." 1/14/2013. http://www.smh.com.au/national/australia-reloads-as-gun-amnesties-fail-to-cut-arms-20130113-2cnnq.html, accessed 9/22/2015

57   John Lott, "Australian gun ownership back up to where it was in 1996, doesn't this gut the claims that Australia's gun buyback [sic]." 1/14/2013. http://johnrlott.blogspot.com/2013/01/australian-gun-ownership-back-up-to.html, accessed 9/22/2015.

58   Adam D. Young, Lubbock Avalanche-Journal. "Experts warn stab wounds common, less deadly but just as punishable." 6/28/2010. http://lubbockonline.com/local-news/2010-06-28/experts-warn-stab-wounds-common-less-deadly-just-punishable#.VWZ6m89Viko, accessed 9/22/2015.

59   "10 Pro-Gun Myths Shot Down." *Mother Jones*, January, 2013. http://www.motherjones.com/politics/2013/01/pro-gun-myths-fact-check, accessed 10/20/2015

60   Adam Liptak, *The New York Times*. "Gun Laws and Crime: A Complex Relationship." 6/29/2008. http://www.nytimes.com/2008/06/W/weekinreview/29liptak.html?pagewanted=all, accessed 9/25/2015.

Gun or handgun bans in Ireland, Jamaica, and Britain were all immediately followed by sharp and sustained increases in homicide rate.[61] It's not entirely clear why this phenomenon happens, but it suggests that banning guns may not in fact reduce the homicide rate.

Let's assume for a moment that the US amended the Constitution to ban privately held firearms in the country. How would we enforce that amendment? Let's explore.

Current estimates suggest somewhere between 270 million and 310 million.[62] Probably tens of millions or more are not registered (which means we don't know where they are).[63] If the US "called in" its guns, how many citizens might not comply, either in principle or because they are violent criminals?

Would we search house-by-house to accomplish the ban? Would we need to pass a Constitutional amendment suspending the 4th Amendment in order to enter people's homes without warrants? How likely would the prohibition of guns drive a gang-run black market, as the prohibition of alcohol and drugs both did?

Eliminating guns from the country entirely seems a truly daunting, potentially unfeasible task, requiring a huge amount of resources that could be utilized in more efficient efforts to reduce premature or violent death.

Expanding Gun Freedom

Gun freedom advocates put great stock in symbolic fights that have very little impact on the lives or freedoms of gun owners, under the specious argument that any gun control law is part of a slippery slope towards the destruction of gun ownership.

---

61   Crime Prevention Research Center. "Murder and Homicide Rates Before and After Gun Bans." 12/1/2013. http://crimepreventionresearchcenter.org/2013/12/murder-and-homicide-rates-before-and-after-gun-bans/, accessed 9/25/2015.

62   Drew Silver, Pew Research FactTank. "A minority of Americans own guns, but just how many is unclear." June 4, 2015. http://www.pewresearch.org/fact-tank/2013/06/04/a-minority-of-americans-own-guns-but-just-how-many-is-unclear/, accessed 9/25/2015.

63   examiner.com. "Gun control, unregistered firearms and the black market." 11/9/2010. http://www.examiner.com/article/gun-control-unregistered-firearms-and-the-black-market, accessed 9/22/2015

Assault Weapons and High Capacity Magazines: Frequently, such an argument takes the form of inflating the importance of more trivial components of guns that are being targeted by gun control advocates.[64] Gun freedom advocates staunchly defend the right to high-capacity magazines, even though their efficacy in law-abiding uses seems limited: it is a tough sell that one needs more than ten rounds for hunting or personal defense. For those worried that they will need to fight the federal government at some point and the extra 4 to 7 rounds per magazine will help: there are already over 40 million high-capacity magazines in the US,[65] and a "ban" would only ban new manufacture and sale (it would not recall these).

Such bans also do not represent a slippery slope. Federal courts repeatedly strike down state bans of magazines fewer than 10 rounds. Such strikes create a growing precedent that restricting magazines to fewer than 10 rounds is excessively prohibitive for gun owners, meaning magazine restrictions can't become a back door to undermining the second amendment.[66]

More clear-cut are assault weapons. Even though assault weapons are merely cosmetically different from other rifles,[67] their potential sales ban is fought bitterly by pro-gun freedom legislators and advocacy groups. During the original Assault Weapons Ban, manufacturers made functionally equivalent weapons that serve the same functions and with the same effectiveness as their assault weapon counterparts.

Open Carry Laws: Advocates often propose expanding gun freedoms beyond the current norm for what appear to be mostly symbolic, not functional, reasons.

---

64 NRA-ILA. "Los Angeles City Council Targets Law-Abiding With Magazine Ban." 7/31/2015. https://www.nraila.org/articles/20150731/los-angeles-city-council-targets-law-abiding-with-magazine-ban, accessed 9/22/2015

65 Patrik Jonsson, *The Christian Science Monitor*. "Gun debate 101: Time to ban high-capacity magazines?" 1/16/2013. http://www.csmonitor.com/USA/Politics/DC-Decoder/2013/0116/Gun-debate-101-Time-to-ban-high-capacity-magazines, accessed 10/30/2013.

66 The most recent example is the decision of the US13th District Court in 2013 against New York State's 7-round restriction. Case 1:13-cv-00291-WMS, filed 12/31/13. Available at http://kingofallwebs.com/Skretny/Skretny-Decision.pdf, accessed 10/30/2013

67 "The Truth About Assault Weapons." http://www.assaultweapon.info/, accessed 9/22/2015.

The expansion of open carry laws (supporting the right to carry a gun visibly rather than concealed) has been an ongoing effort,[68] the NRA calling it important for self-defense.[69] But all 50 states have concealed carry rights, in which citizens can carry guns hidden from view, protecting themselves as they choose. It's not apparent that there is any additional safety benefit of carrying visibly rather than carrying concealed.

Open carry protests and victory celebrations in Texas included organized carrying of rifles into stores and restaurants, in order to exercise their rights. But the demonstration was simply meant to "show off" one's guns and possibly make open carrying more culturally normal.

After hearing complaints from many frightened customers and employees, restaurants began banning open carry in their stores.[70] The insistence on flaunting the symbolic victory drove a backlash against the movement.

Total Gun Freedom: To put a finer point on it: historically, the 2nd amendment has not been interpreted to mean, "having whatever weapon one wants, regardless of its form or lethality," which means that the 2nd Amendment doesn't protect against all possible gun restrictions.

Some people in the gun freedom camp oppose any gun control proposal under the argument that it violates the 2nd amendment. For the sake of argument, let's explore the implications of total gun freedom: a world in which the 2nd Amendment is interpreted to not allow any form of gun control. Total gun freedom might be logistically simpler to enforce than a total gun ban, but it would open up a legal quagmire.

According to the precedent of the past few hundred years of Supreme Court rulings, the rights granted by the 2nd amendment to individuals are somewhat vague. An amendment to the

---

68   Since 1991, 25 states have passed open-carry laws, bringing the total to 42.

69   NRA-ILA. "Right-to-Carry." https://www.nraila.org/issues/right-to-carry/, accessed 10/29/2015.

70   Kolten Parker, mySA. "Whataburger: No 'open carry' in our restaurants despite new Texas las." 7/7/2015. http://www.mysanantonio.com/news/local/article/Whataburger-No-open-carry-in-our-restaurants-6370818.php, accessed 9/22/2015

US Constitution could clarify and expand these rights, but what might it look like?

Would the amendment make all guns free to buy and own, without restrictions? Would this include heavy machine guns? Grenade launchers? Should civilians be able to possess heavy artillery? If not, how can a Constitutional amendment make a clear distinction between the two? Indeed, both rifles and artillery are tubes that use gunpowder to fire a projectile at high speed; one's just bigger.

Would the amendment clarify that anyone could have a gun, including schizophrenics and convicted violent criminals? If anyone at all should forfeit the right to own a gun, how do we enforce this?

The amendment gets unwieldy pretty quickly, and it seems highly unlikely it would ever happen. The one-sentence 27th Amendment to the Constitution took 202 years to ratify.[71] **At the end of the day, gun rights with some restrictions are going to be the law of the land going forward.**

* * *

To understand why these efforts get so much attention, we must remember that politicians and media depend on wedging in order to win elections and keep viewers. Let's assume for a moment that our politicians have teams smart enough to understand that, for example, assault weapons kill only 50 people per year and aren't more lethal than many other rifles. What kind of reaction might their most partisan (and most dependable) political base have if they declared that "assault weapons aren't a serious enough problem to make a priority?" What would happen if a gun freedom advocate said, "we're not going to spend our efforts fighting laws that restrict the sale of merely cosmetic features?" If history is a teacher, their job would be just that – history.

---

71   Which states, "No law, varying the compensation for the services of the Senators and Representatives, shall take effect, until an election of Representatives shall have intervened." Wikipedia. "The Twenty-Seventh Amendment to the United States Constitution." https://en.wikipedia.org/wiki/Twenty-seventh_Amendment_to_the_United_States_Constitution, accessed 9/12/2015

It's this incentive that keeps so much of our attention focused on ineffective or low-priority policy fights.

The obsession over guns *as tools* is a big reason why we can't make greater progress in extracting the wedge. The pro gun control camp vilifies them; the pro-gun freedom camp fetishizes them. This obsession means that the wedge won't remove itself, even as policies change.

EXTRACTING THE WEDGE: CONSIDERING THE PATH FORWARD

Ultimately, extracting the wedge from the guns issue requires doing hard work to grapple with the available data and overcome tribal biases. If we understand both that we're being wedged and that the narratives told to us are oversimplified and often incorrect, what other ways can we look at the issue that could lead us to a more effective national dialogue?

Alternative Paths

Unlike controlling gun usage, reducing premature deaths is a priority for many Americans. Even if we restrict the focus to violent death, the evidence suggests that there are factors besides gun ownership that have a large (and likely larger) impact on the violent death rate in a country. These paths are likely more effective and many of them are less likely to promote wedging.

Social and Economic Factors

You might know that poverty and income inequality are highly linked to violent crime (including gun murders) – much more so than number or density of guns.[72]

Race and gender also show a strong link. Race and gender are two of the most difficult issues for Americans to talk about, but

---

72   Ching-Chi Hsieh and M. D. Pugh. "Poverty, Income Inequality, and Violent Crime: A Meta-Analysis of Recent Aggregate Data Studies." *Criminal Justice Review*, Autumn 1993 vol 18 no 2: pp 182-202. http://cjr.sagepub.com/content/18/2/182.abstract, accessed 9/22/2015.

available data suggest that they are important to consider when exploring how to reduce premature deaths. A few facts:

» Black Americans are 7x as likely as white Americans to be convicted of homicide.[73]

» Twice as many white Americans own guns as black Americans (31% of whites vs 15% of blacks).[74]

So does that mean that a black gun owner is 14x more likely to commit homicide than a white gun owner? Maybe, maybe not. But this 14x (or so) divide is huge and not fully explained by the gap in poverty rate (blacks are 3x more likely to live in poverty than whites).[75]

We also know:

» Men are 9x more likely as women to be convicted of homicide.[76]

» They're also 3x more likely as women to own guns.[77]

By similar logic, this might mean male gun owners are 3x more deadly than female ones. What factors are at play here? Is it testosterone poison? A culture that raises boys to play with guns and be "tough?"

This is a difficult topic to talk about in the United States, but between economics, race, and gender, we have found factors that correlate with murder much more strongly than the prevalence of guns. Understanding and reducing the violent crime

---

73   PR Newswire. "Homicides Fall to Lowest Rate in Four Decades." 11/16/2011. http://www.prnewswire.com/news-releases/homicides-fall-to-lowest-rate-in-four-decades-133967273.html, accessed 9/22/2015.

74   *Pew Research*. "Section 3: Gun Ownership Trends and Demographics." 3/12/2013. http://www.people-press.org/2013/03/12/section-3-gun-ownership-trends-and-demographics/, accessed 9/22/2015.

75   The Kaiser Family Foundation. "Poverty Rate by Race/Ethnicity." 2013. http://kff.org/other/state-indicator/poverty-rate-by-raceethnicity/, accessed 9/28/2015.

76   Alexia Cooper, Erica Smith, *Bureau of Justice Statistics*. "Homicide Trends in the United States, 1980-2008." 11/16/2011. http://www.bjs.gov/index.cfm?ty=pbdetail&iid=2221, accessed 9/28/2015.

77   *Pew Research*. "Section 3: Gun Ownership Trends and Demographics." 3/12/2013. http://www.people-press.org/2013/03/12/section-3-gun-ownership-trends-and-demographics/, accessed 9/22/2015.

and homicide rate in the US requires being able to tackle these factors head-on.

Organized Criminal Activity

Gang violence is responsible for about 50% of violent crime in the US[78] and, according to the Justice Department, their primary funding source is from the drug trade,[79] which is highly profitable.[80]

What would happen if we legalized drugs and undercut gang funding? Legal, industrial production of marijuana should make the more expensive black-market unprofitable[81] and limited legalization has already had a visible impact on the size and violence of both Mexican drug cartels and their US gang buyers.[82]

All of this suggests that, in a world without a wedge driven into the guns issue, approaches to reducing violent and premature death would be very holistic, focusing on a number of factors with strong causal evidence. Resolving the distraction of the guns wedge and working together to reduce violent and premature death could save a lot of lives.

The Effects of Upbringing and Abortion

An argument by Freakonomics authors Levitt and Dubner (originally written in a 2001 academic paper) says that the legalization of abortion in the 1970s decreased the number of unintended

---

78   Matt MacBradaigh, Policy Mic. "Gun Control Debate: Gang Violence Accounts for Half of Violent Crime in America." 3/1/2013. http://mic.com/articles/27281/gun-control-debate-gang-violence-accounts-for-half-of-violent-crime-in-america, accessed 9/22/2015

79   US National Drug Intelligence Center. "Drugs and Gangs Fast Facts." Jan 2005, product # 2005-L0559-001. Archived 7/1/2009. http://www.justice.gov/archive/ndic/pubs11/13157/#relation, accessed 9/28/2015

80   Oriana Zill and Lowell Bergman, *PBS Frontline*. "Do the Math: Why the Illegal Drug Business is Thriving." 2014. http://www.pbs.org/wgbh/pages/frontline/shows/drugs/special/math.html, accessed 9/28/2015.

81   Olga Khazan, *The Washington Post*. "How marijuana legalization will affect Mexico's cartels, in charts." 11/9/2012. http://www.washingtonpost.com/blogs/worldviews/wp/2012/11/09/how-marijuana-legalization-will-affect-mexicos-cartels-in-charts/, accessed 9/28/2015

82   Cathy Reisenwitz, *TownHall*. "US Marijuana Legalization Already Weakening Mexican Cartels, Violence Expected to Decline." 8/11/2014. http://townhall.com/columnists/cathyreisenwitz/2014/08/11/us-marijuana-legalization-already-weakening-mexican-cartels-violence-expected-to-decline-n1876088/page/full, accessed 9/28/2015.

children reaching late adolescence in the early 1990s.[83] Because children of unintended pregnancies tend to have a rougher upbringing, they tend to be more violent, and therefore having fewer of them in the world reduces how violent the country is – and thus reduces the murder rate.

Environmental Factors

Lead is known to be a toxic chemical that negatively impacts brain function. But could it be responsible for violent crime? Maybe. If we plot lead concentration in gasoline with violent crime 23 years later, we see a surprising correlation.[84]

---

83   John J. Donohue III and Steven D. Levitt. "The Impact of Legalized Abortion on Crime." *The Quarterly Journal of Economics*, May 2001, vol 116, iss 2: pp 379-420. http://pricetheory. uchicago.edu/levitt/Papers/DonohueLevittTheImpactOfLegalized2001.pdf, accessed 10/30/2015.

84   Kevin Drum, *Mother Jones*. "America's Real Criminal Element: Lead." Jan/Feb 2013. http:// www.motherjones.com/environment/2013/01/lead-crime-link-gasoline, accessed 9/28/2015.

Sources: Rick Nevin,
USGS, DOJ

Mother Jones

In this graph we see a correlation between the lead concentration in gasoline per population, and the violent crime rate preceisely 23 years later. Such a graph is suggesting that gasoline lead may cause brain damage that causes young adult Americans to be more violent.

In fact, the correlation holds true across different countries, across US states, and between urban and rural areas. Could it be that exposure to lead at a young age leads to violent criminal activity later? Could focusing on these environmental factors be the key to reducing violent crime? It's certainly something to consider.

* * *

We know that gun prevalence has a weak link to homicide, and that factors like poverty, racial and gender demographics, mental health, organized crime, and even the environment have high correlations with violent crime and homicide. Taking a problem-solving approach to homicide and violent crime that explores all the factors behind it will not only lead to greater results and more lives saved, but can also take the wedge out of the national dialogue about guns.

The Way Forward

Even though we all want to protect ourselves and our children from violence while at the same time protecting our liberties, we don't act like we share values because we've been wedged into one side or the other of a war over guns. We even have broad agreement on what gun policies we want to enact, and yet we have been manipulated so thoroughly into ignoring our areas of agreement that we keep looking for ways to fight.

In the meantime, real conversations about how to make the biggest impacts on premature, wrongful, and violent death are left on the sidelines. While we are at metaphorical war over gun policy, professional politicians get campaign dollars, media outlets get viewers, and Americans continue to die.

If you want to start overcoming the guns wedge in your own political conversations, and you only take away one thing from this chapter, just remember that **current gun control and gun freedom platforms are not the best solutions either for those who want to preserve gun freedoms or those who want to reduce premature death.** Gun deaths are a small piece of the pie of premature and wrongful death and there is little evidence to suggest that the most popular gun control policies have a real impact even on that relatively small group of deaths. **Focusing too much on gun control is simply a waste of effort and resources that could be better used elsewhere.**

That doesn't mean some forms of gun regulation aren't smart. And further, it doesn't mean that gun rights are under any real threat. Current gun restrictions focus on cosmetic or trivial aspects of guns. There is little risk of a slippery slope: the Constitutional right to bear arms has been repeatedly upheld, and most Americans agree on many broad forms of gun control. While there will always be sound-bytes of people advocating for "getting rid of guns," it can't happen. In short, **they're not coming to take your guns away.**

As you listen to others discuss guns at dinner, on social media, and elsewhere, keep your eyes and ears sharp for the telltale signs of wedging. Find examples of cherry-picked data, of emotional overload, and of skewed or deceptive framing. Have some empathy for the folks who are stuck on one side of the wedge or the other, and arm yourself to resist being part of the problem. Pose the question to yourself and those around you: if the American gun conversation became one of problem solving and compromise rather than trench-digging and grandstanding, how could our efforts and money be better spent on saving American lives?

Chapter Four:
Abortion

"Militant feminists are pro-choice because it's their ultimate avenue of power over men. And believe me, to them it is a question of power. It is their attempt to impose their will on the rest of society, particularly on men."

> -Rush Limbaugh, political commentator and host of "The Rush Limbaugh Show"

"Denying women access to safe abortion (whether we have been raped or not) is itself a form of figurative, if not literal, violation... Rape denies us bodily integrity; so does restricting abortion. Both are strategies designed to subjugate women."

> -Wendy Simonds, author of <u>Abortion at Work</u>

Abortion is a wedge issue that symbolizes everything wrong with the current state of American politics. It's at the top of the list of issues that Americans get most emotional about.

It's very different from the guns debate in a key way: the debate stems exclusively from strongly held convictions and beliefs that are not based on facts or scientific observation, which means that it has the potential to be stoked by media and milked by politicians without end. Abortion is poised to continue being a major distraction in American politics, unless it can be de-wedged.

THE STATE OF THE DEBATE

Americans stand divided on whether they identify as "pro-life" or "pro-choice," (46% and 47%, respectively).[1] These identities are not particularly well-defined, but pro-choice Americans tend to want to allow abortion in most cases, where pro-life Americans generally believe abortions should have more restrictions.

These positions are rooted in principle, rather than result: even if there was only one abortion per year, this wouldn't change whether people felt it was a personal right or a crime for that abortion to occur. Instead, two core questions lie at the heart of our positions:

1. When does a fetus begin to have the rights of a person?

2. What rights are reserved exclusively to the mother during pregnancy?

Pro-life advocates contend that at some point – often at conception of the zygote or development of the embryo – prenatal humans are alive in a way that grants them rights, meaning that an abortion would kill a human. Those who lean pro-life see a moral ill in aborting a fetus, and therefore advocate either for a ban or limitations on abortion, including term limits or mandatory consultations designed to impart the gravity of the decision upon the expectant mother. Often they believe the morally preferable course of action in the case of unwanted children is to bring the fetus to term and give the child up for adoption. Some people who are pro-life believe that in cases of rape, incest, or danger to the mother, such restrictions should be waived.

Pro-choice advocates are primarily concerned with the rights of women over their bodies and futures. They contend that a fetus, particularly early in term, lacks certain qualities that would

---

1   Lydia Saad, Gallup. "US Still Split on Abortion: 47% Pro-Choice, 46% Pro-Life." 5/22/2014. http://www.gallup.com/poll/170249/split-abortion-pro-choice-pro-life.aspx, accessed 8/12/2015.

make it a full person and thus does not have a right to protection equal to that of a mother. Some also argue that it is not in the best interest of an unwanted child to bring it into the world, and that legal abortions are an important ingredient for a healthy society. Those who lean pro-choice therefore tend to prefer later term limits, if any, and do not want government restrictions on access to abortion.

For some, it's a question of Constitutional law: some people believe the seminal Roe v. Wade court decision was an incorrect interpretation of the Constitution, and others that it was a correct interpretation of the Constitution, regardless of whether they believe abortion is morally acceptable or not.

Many polls suggest that Americans are far apart on this issue, and split down the middle: about 50% are "pro-life" and 50% "pro-choice."[2] The two camps express little interest in discussion with each other. There seems to be no room to agree.

And we certainly act like it. Rather than a policy discussion, the partisans of both sides treat abortion as a very war for the soul of the country. It is an issue that ruins friendships and creates bitter enemies. Abortion is portrayed as high-stakes, uncompromisable, and rooted in the most fundamental of human values – for both sides.

UNDERSTANDING THE WEDGE

Both the professional pundits and partisans on social media declare that what's at stake in the abortion debate are broad concepts like the right to life, women's rights, families, and morality. They suggest that the very fabric of society hangs in the balance. Those that disagree with their position have bad intentions. Our own righteousness, fear, and sense of justice are stoked so strongly that we sometimes feel pressured to support a candidate just because they agree with us on abortion, whatever their other positions may be.

---

2   Ibid.

It's the ultimate in intractable, rage-inducing, bumper-sticker politics. By the one side, abortion is presented as modern-day mass-murder, equivalent to the Holocaust.

By the other, abortion restrictions are framed as an active, deliberate war on women.

The wedge keeps us talking past each other: the two sides of this issue don't actually discuss definitions of life or women's rights: each side claims the moral high ground for themselves and refuses to give an inch. We've been told that we have to fight this war – and win it – because compromise would be unconscionable.

Ripe for Wedging

While no issue in politics is doomed to become a wedge issue, some are more susceptible to wedging than others. Abortion has been milked as the perfect wedge issue for decades due to a few particular characteristics.

It is impervious to data: the "reasons" behind one's stance on abortion rely primarily on an underlying belief in how the rights of fetuses, at various stages of development, compare to the rights of their mothers.

The "size of the problem" doesn't matter so much: in the case of gun control, whether it was 10 people or 10 million people being killed each year would likely change our views on the gravity of the issue and what policies we should enact. On the matter of abortion, any abortion or any denial of an abortion is an unacceptable outcome for those who feel strongly about it.

It's perceived as a matter of fundamental rights, which makes it hard to find room to compromise.

It's extremely visceral: it's got very powerful visual symbolism associated with it, including coat hangers and aborted fetuses. Everyone's stomach churns.

Politicians and media are able to take advantage of this to reliably direct and rally supporters: pro-life and pro-choice tribes will pressure their peers into not "defecting" to a candidate with opposing beliefs on abortion, regardless of other issues on the table.

A Wedge Issue is Born

In this case, we actually have historical evidence of the creation of the wedge. A fascinating moment in the history of abortion is 1995. Here, the significant – and otherwise stable – majority of Americans that identified as "pro-choice" began to slide precipitously, and the "pro-life" identity grew.[3]

---

3   Between 1973 and 1995 Americans identified as pro-choice about twice as often as pro-life. Gallup historical trends on abortion in the United States. http://www.gallup.com/poll/1576/abortion.aspx, accessed 10/23/2015

US ADULTS' POSITION ON ABORTION

With respect to the abortion issue, would you consider yourself to be "pro-life" or "pro-choice"?

■ % pro-life   ▨ % pro-choice

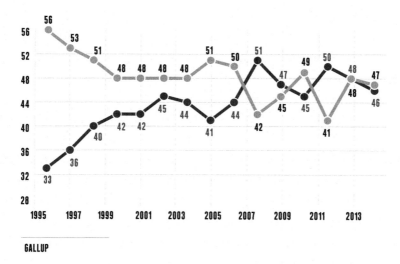

GALLUP

This happened even as there was *no* change on opinions about overturning *Roe v. Wade*, besides a growth in apathy about the question.

US POSITIONS ON OVERTURNING ROE VS WADE

Would you like to see the Supreme Court overturn its 1973 Roe vs Wade decision concerning abortion or not?

■ %No, not overturn ▨ %Yes, oveturn ▨ %No opinion

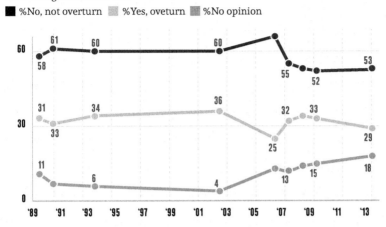

Latest result based on USA Today/Gallup poll conducted December 27-30, 2012.
Wording for pre-2005 trends: The 1973 Roe vs Wade decision established a woman's constitutional right to an abortion, at least in the first three months of pregnancy. Would you like to see the Supreme Court completely overturn its Rroe vs Wade decision, or not? (Split-sample experiment in 2005 indicated wording change had no significant impact on results).

This graph shows us how many people want Roe v. Wade *to be overturned or not since 1989. For the most part, the number of people over the past 25 years that want to overturn or not overturn* Roe v. Wade *has not changed, and those against overturning have always outnumbered those in favor. The most dramatic change is that the percentage of Americans with no opinion at all has grown from a low of 4% in 2002 to 18% in 2013.*

We can also note a brief spike of change in the 2006 mid-terms elections in which opposition to overturning peaked at 66% and support bottomed out at 25%, followed quickly by a reversal. The proximity to the election in which the Democrats took the majority away from the Republicans suggests that a change in wedging tactics and messaging may have occurred in this period.

In fact, the portion of Americans that want to see abortions legal in some form (about 80%)[4] has been essentially unchanged since

---

4   We'll note later that as we ask questions about abortions in a different way, support for abortion grows as high as 92% of Americans. The framing of question is highly important.

Roe v. Wade.[5] Equally consistently, only 1% of Americans have seen abortion as the most important issue in the country.[6]

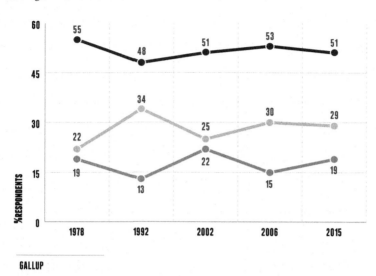

AMERICANS' OPINIONS ON ABORTION LEGALITY

Do you think abortions should be
■ legal under any circumstances ▨ legal only under certain circumstances or
▨ illegal in all circumstances?

GALLUP

7

This phenomenon is our smoking gun. How did Americans' camp identities change so much despite their policy positions remaining steady? How did abortion reach the forefront of the national dialogue and consume effort at dozens of state legislatures even though it's a top priority for a tiny sliver of the nation?

5   Karlyn Bowman and Jennifer Marsico, *The Atlantic*. "Opinions About Abortion Haven't Changed Since *Roe v Wade*." 1/22/2014. http://www.theatlantic.com/politics/archive/2014/01/opinions-about-abortion-havent-changed-since-em-roe-v-wade-em/283226/, accessed 8/13/2015.

6   Karlyn Bowman and Jennifer Marsico, *American Enterprise Institute*. "Americans don't care as much about abortion as the media think." 1/22/2014. http://www.aei.org/publication/americans-dont-care-as-much-about-abortion-as-the-media-think/, accessed 8/15/2015.

7   Gallup historical trends on abortion. http://www.gallup.com/poll/1576/abortion.aspx, accessed 8/24/2015. Note also the framing here: when vague language is used, greater proportions of Americans take the hard-line positions.

The answer is simple: the rage around abortion is manufactured, the camps deliberately carved in order to cultivate the political loyalty possible only from tribal warfighting.

Issue Inflation

Pro-life advocates declare that a fetus, at any stage in development, is alive and human, and that abortion is murder, plain and simple. Abortion is the first step down a moral slippery slope of disrespect for life that will ultimately infect the whole of society.

"There is no cause more important for preserving freedom than affirming the transcendent right to life of all human beings, the right without which no other rights have any meaning."

> *– US President Ronald Reagan, Abortion and the Conscience of the Nation*

"How is the person who considers abortion to be murder any different from the Pole who knew what was going to happen at Auschwitz? If the Pole was morally obligated to attempt to save lives, isn't the person who opposes abortion under the same obligation?"

> *– B.D. Colen, "The Anti-Abortion High Ground"*

Pro-choice activists frame abortion as a matter of fundamental civil rights for women. All restrictions on abortions are restrictions of women's liberty and invasions of personal autonomy. Restrictions on abortion are part of, and lead to, a broader shackling of women by society; a violation, even.

"If we lived in a culture that valued women's autonomy and in which men and women practiced cooperative birth control, the abortion issue would be moot."

> *—Christiane Northrup, MD, author of Women's Bodies, Women's Wisdom*

"Abolition of a woman's right to abortion, when and if she wants it, amounts to compulsory maternity: a form of rape by the State."

> *-Edward Abbey, author and political essayist*

Rallying the Tribe Against the Enemy

Pro-life activists contend that pro-choice Americans are selfish and immoral, lacking compunctions about killing babies or destroying families.

"When life and family are not treasured and preserved in a society, collapse on all fronts is inevitable."

– Fr. Richard Welch, President of Human Life International

"I want to know how these very people who are against war because of loss of life can possibly be the same people who are for abortion? They are the same people who are for animal rights, but they are not for the rights of the unborn."

-Jim Gibbons, Governor of Nevada

Pro-choice activists declare that pro-life Americans want to oppress women and control sexuality:

"...when the Republican Party launched an all-out assault on women's health, pushing bills to limit access to vital services, we had to ask: Why is the GOP trying to send women back... to the back alley?"

Lisa Edelstein, American actress and playwright

"The issue is not abortion. The issue is whether women can make up their own mind instead of some right-wing pastor, some right-wing politician telling them what to do."

—Howard Dean, Governor of Vermont

Partisan citizens get caught up in the rhetoric, flinging attacks on social media that are meant to spread the anger and fear that they feel.

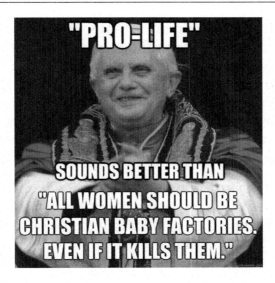

Here an Emperor Palpatine-looking image of Pope Benedict XVI makes him look particularly evil, portraying his pro-life position as completely disregarding the agency and even the lives of women.

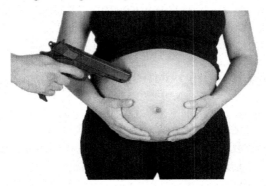

This meme ignores the issue of a mother's agency, using the charged image of a gun threatening a pregnant woman to generate a highly emotional protective response.

Sensationalized Events

The pro-choice and pro-life camps took advantage of a controversy about Planned Parenthood's disposal of fetal tissue as an opportunity to rally support to each side.

The controversy involves Planned Parenthood officials negotiating the price of fetal tissue to be sold to brokers for medical research organizations. Secret videos of the conversations were posted to the Internet, spurring pro-life-affiliated politicians to move to defund Planned Parenthood, painting it as a murder-for-profit factory. But pro-choice-affiliated politicians took the opportunity to rally to the defense of the organization, emphasizing its importance and framing the push to defund as just part of the war on women. Each camp was able to turn the event into an opportunity to plant flags and grandstand, reminding people that they need to be angry.

Why is this simply sensational? Ultimately, what Planned Parenthood does with fetal tissue has nothing to do with how many abortions it performs, including the 1% or so that are performed with federal funds.

Current law allows for "reasonable" fees to cover the costs of donating tissue for research.[8] Whether the laws about fetal tissue donations or cost compensations should be changed could be a totally separate discussion: how the fetal tissue is disposed of is not actually related to the abortions themselves, doesn't change whether they're right or wrong, and doesn't change how many will happen.

Manufactured Battlegrounds

Roe v. Wade

Arguments over the validity of the Roe v. Wade Supreme Court decision are often lumped in with the debate over the morality of abortion. But it wasn't actually a decision about whether abortion was moral or not moral, right or wrong. To summarize it very briefly with an excerpt from Justice Blackmun's majority opinion:

"This right of privacy, whether it be founded in the Fourteenth Amendment's concept of personal liberty and restrictions upon state action, as we feel it is, or, as the District Court determined, in the Ninth Amendment's reservation of rights to the people, is broad

---

8   Will Cabaniss, Joshual Gillin, PolitiFact. "PolitiFact Sheet: 8 things to know about the Planned Parenthood controversy." 8/5/2015. http://www.politifact.com/truth-o-meter/article/2015/aug/05/politifact-sheet-8-things-know-about-plan-national/, accessed 8/30/2015.

*enough to encompass a woman's decision whether or not to termi-
nate her pregnancy."[9]*

The Roe decision is ultimately a very interesting and possibly
complicated piece of constitutional law. We encourage anyone
who cares much about abortion to take a look at the opinions of
the court from *Roe v. Wade* as well as the text of the 14th and 9th
amendments. These are key to understanding *Roe v. Wade*. **The
morality of abortion is not.**

But most people understand little of *Roe v. Wade*. Most younger
Americans don't even know what *Roe v. Wade* is (fewer than
half of Americans under 30 can identify that it's related to
abortion).[10] Instead, Americans tie their support for the decision
to their own beliefs about the morality of abortion, rather than
any understanding of constitutional law. Politicians, of course,
are just fine with this.

ANALYZING THE DATA: UNDERMINING THE WEDGE

Beyond Binary: Beneath the Rhetoric, Nuance and Common Ground

It turns out that beneath the emotion and vitriol of the public
abortion debate, most Americans maintain a very complex
array of beliefs. Statistics show that Americans share many
core values about abortion, agree on a wide variety of moderate
policies, and have internally-conflicted feelings on the matter.
It's an issue that is far from black and white and when we get
away from tribal politics we find that we could agree on and
resolve most abortion policy questions.

A Wide Array of Options

Looking deeper, we find that abortion is not a yes or no question:
there are dozens of nuanced policy questions that can be

---

9   *Justia.* US Supreme Court Case 410 US 113 (1973), *Roe v. Wade.* https://supreme.justia.com/
     cases/federal/us/410/113/case.html, accessed 8/19/2015

10   Barb Listing, LifeNews.com "Just 60% of Americans Know *Roe v. Wade* is About Abortion."
     1/31/2014. http://www.lifenews.com/2014/01/31/just-60-percent-of-americans-know-roe-v-
     wade-is-about-abortion/, accessed 8/9/2015.

asked about the issue, each of which can have a wide variety of answers.

If one believes that abortion should be legal only in the case of danger to the mother, should there be clarity on how much danger is required? Need it be mortal danger, or only danger of injury, and how serious? Every birth has some risk – just how much risk would need to be required?

If one believes that abortion is ever moral, is it always moral regardless of reason? What about if the parents did not prefer the sex or hair color of their child? Would views change if there were a tendency in the US to abort female children in large numbers?

If ever legal, how far into a pregnancy should abortion be legal? All the way up until labor? During labor? What about a day before? If there is an earlier line to be drawn, is it drawn at viability? Heartbeat? Sense of feeling? Moving around? Should the legal line be set at a certain number of weeks or days, or should the line change if a fetus is developing more quickly or slowly than normal?

Is there reason to support legalizing certain cases of abortion even if you believe those cases are immoral?

Should minors require a parent or guardian to be notified of an abortion? If not, what does this mean for other medical procedures – should abortion be an exception, or should minors be able to schedule medical procedures like cosmetic surgery without their parents? If it is an exception, how do we define what makes it different?

Should doctors be required to ensure that a woman is not being pressured by a family member (a husband, boyfriend, parent, etc) to have an abortion before performing the procedure?

Should ultrasounds before the procedure be required to ensure that a woman is making a fully informed decision?

Should abortions be required coverage in all health insurance policies, or should someone be able to choose to pay less for an insurance policy that doesn't cover abortions?

Should someone that murders a pregnant woman be charged with one homicide, or two?

Once we start trying to get to specifics, we find that Americans' opinions vary much more broadly than their simple "pro-choice" or "pro-life" labels might suggest.

Shared Values and Policy Agreement

Seeing protesters, politicians, and social media chatter might suggest that most people have strong, deeply held convictions far on one side or the other of the debate. But given the huge array of questions the issue brings up, it may not be surprising that most Americans have nuanced and often conflicted views about abortion.

In fact, almost half of Americans identify as both pro-life and pro-choice,[11] depending on how the question is framed!

Shared Values: There are many values and feelings most Americans share about abortion. Here are a few:

> » Most people in America believe abortion to be morally complex.

> ◇ 60% of Americans, including 29% of the pro-choice camp, believe that abortion is morally wrong, even though most of these respondents believe it should be legal in some or most cases.

> ◇ Essentially all Americans believe that late-term abortions become morally questionable (and few support them),[12] largely due to the shared belief that at this

---

11   *Public Religion Research Institute.* "Pro-Choice/Pro-Life: Overlapping Identities." 1/25/2015. http://publicreligion.org/research/graphic-of-the-week/pro-choicepro-life-overlapping-identities/#.VcK4dG5Viko, accessed 7/31/2015

12   Karlyn Bowman and Jennifer Marsico. "Opinions About Abortion Haven't Changed Since *Roe v Wade.*" 1/22/2014. http://www.theatlantic.com/politics/archive/2014/01/opinions-about-abortion-havent-changed-since-em-roe-v-wade-em/283226/, accessed 8/22/2015

point fetuses are "viable" or "alive" and should be afforded protection.

» Regardless of how we feel about its morality, at least 80% of Americans believe abortion should be legal, in at least some cases.

» Almost all Americans want fewer unwanted pregnancies and fewer unwanted children.

» A whopping 90% of Americans believe contraception and birth control are morally acceptable[13] (only 7% believe it is unacceptable, which is less than half of the 16% that think drinking alcohol is morally unacceptable).[14]

Policy Agreement: Americans could stand on the cusp of widespread agreement and cooperation on abortion if it were framed as a question of handling an ambiguous and nuanced issue rather than a war.

The brilliantly effective wedging of the American voter has occurred by shifting the debate from finding policy solutions to ensuring that immoral enemies don't get their way. Wedging is most effective where there are the fewest facts and the greatest sense of identity and intractable values. So when we poll Americans about their *identities*, they are split down the middle, and extraordinarily unlikely to move on the matter.

But if we change the framing of the question away from identity and towards policy, the game changes. If we poll people about limitations on abortion (generally, how late in term an abortion should be legal), we still see disagreement on that policy, but we get a broad admission that abortion should be legal, but have some time restriction. This is likely because the question is technical and doesn't do as much to spark the team identification that is used to emotionally manipulate people.

13   Rebecca Riffkin, *Gallup*. "New Record Highs in Moral Acceptability." http://www.gallup.com/poll/170789/new-record-highs-moral-acceptability.aspx, accessed 8/24/2015.

14   Jacob Poushter, Pew Research FactTank. "What's morally acceptable? It depends on where in the world you live." 4/15/2014. http://www.pewresearch.org/fact-tank/2014/04/15/whats-morally-acceptable-it-depends-on-where-in-the-world-you-live/, accessed 8/24/2015.

For example, when Quinnipiac asked a focused question on how late in a pregnancy an abortion should be allowed, 85% of respondents were willing to choose between two options – only 8% insisted that abortion should be either always or never legal.

OPINIONS ON ABORTION AT 20 VS 24 WEEKS

The US Supreme Court has said abortion is legal without restriction in about the first 24 weeks of pregnancy. Some states have passed laws reducing this to 20 weeks.

If it has to be one or the other, would you rather have abortions legal without restriction up to 20 weeks, or up to 24 weeks?

30%
UP TO 24 WEEKS

55%
UP TO 20 WEEKS

■ **7% NEVER LEGAL**   ■ **1% ALWAYS LEGAL**   ■ **7% UNSURE**

QUINNIPIAC UNIVERSITY POLL - July 28-31, 2013. N=1,468 registered voters nationwide

We see that when the question is reframed, 85% of Americans can "live with" abortion being legal and restricted to either 20 or 24 weeks. The difference between those 20 and 24 weeks is very small: the period between 20 and 24 weeks makes up only 1.2% of all abortions.[15] About 2% of abortions occur after 24 weeks, but are almost all cases of danger to the mother (which are often discovered late in the pregnancy). The other 97% all occur before 20 weeks.

What this suggests is that Americans could compromise on some period of abortion restriction. While the 20 or 24 weeks question does not allow Americans to choose other term limits they may prefer even more (18 weeks, 26 weeks, something else),

---

15   Guttmacher Institute. "Fact Sheet: Induced Abortion in the United States." July 2014. http://www.guttmacher.org/pubs/fb_induced_abortion.html, accessed 8/17/2015.

it give us a strong directional hint that potential for a compromise exists.

The reality on the ground is that very few Americans believe abortion should be completely illegal—when given many policy positions to choose from in a poll only 13% choose "illegal under all circumstances."[16] Of those who identify as "pro-life," only 24% believe that abortion should never be permitted.

When respondents are asked about individual cases where abortion might be allowed – including danger to the mother, rape and incest – 88% agree that abortion should be legal some or all of the time.[17] Almost every American wants abortion legal in some way.

At the same time, almost all Americans support some sort of term limit: only 27% of Americans support 2nd trimester abortions and 14% support third-trimester abortions.[18] Of those in the "pro-choice" camp, only 25% believe abortion should be allowed in all cases.[19] When asked whether abortion should be permitted in the case of parents disapproving of the gender of the fetus, 92% of Americans say this should not be allowed.[20]

78% of Americans believe that parents should be notified if a minor has an abortion.[21]

Together, these suggest that almost all Americans fall into a grey area where they want abortion to be legal in some cases, but don't believe it should be legal in all cases. If we were to have

16   Marist Poll, "Abortion in America," January 2015. http://www.kofc.org/un/en/resources/communications/Abortion_in_America_January2015_For_Release_150121.pdf, accessed 8/16/2015.

17   American National Election Studies, "Abortion (2), by Law 1980-2008." 8/5/2010. http://www.electionstudies.org/nesguide/toptable/tab4c_2b.htm, accessed 8/19/2015.

18   *Pew Research.* "The Complicated Politics of Abortion." 8/22/2012. http://www.gallup.com/poll/160058/majority-americans-support-roe-wade-decision.aspx, accessed 8/19/2015.

19   Marist Poll, "Abortion in America," January 2015. http://www.kofc.org/un/en/resources/communications/Abortion_in_America_January2015_For_Release_150121.pdf, accessed 8/16/2015.

20   Ibid

21   Marist Poll, "Abortion in America," January 2015. http://www.kofc.org/un/en/resources/communications/Abortion_in_America_January2015_For_Release_150121.pdf, accessed 8/16/2015.

a discussion based on that realization, it might turn out very differently than the yelling and anger that we're accustomed to.

That grey area is reflected by how many voters actually don't agree with their party's line on this issue. A full 39% of registered Republicans support mostly or fully legal abortion, and almost as many Democrats are against abortion in all or most cases (31%).[22] This isn't reflected by elected politicians in Washington, who almost always toe the "party line" on abortion.[23] A spectrum of opinions, including a wide middle ground, exists in both parties, but it has been suppressed by years of wedging.

What would happen if everyone in the country knew that over 85% of Americans would be willing for abortion to be available with some sort of time restriction? How well would we respond to table-pounding politicians warning about a "War on Women" or a "War on Babies?"

Reality Reveals False Wedge Premises
Putting the Problem in Perspective

Because *Roe v Wade* guarantees that women may have abortions until the fetus is viable, abortions can currently only be made illegal near the 3rd trimester. But as we've seen before, only about 3% of abortions occur after 20 weeks. In addition, because health complications for the mother are usually only apparent very late in the pregnancy, it's likely that many or most of these abortions are cases of danger, which are cases that almost all Americans want to protect. Fighting for changes in abortion restrictions between 20 and 24 weeks will have a very small impact on the total number of abortions performed in the United States.

But most surprisingly, most Americans don't actually consider the issue of abortion to be as important as other issues on the national agenda.

---

22   Lydia Saad, Gallup. "US Still Split on Abortion: 47% Pro-Choice, 46% Pro-Life." 5/22/2014. http://www.people-press.org/2012/08/22/the-complicated-politics-of-abortion/, accessed 8/19/2015.

23   W James Antle III, *The American Spectator*. "The Disappearing Pro-Life Democrat." 3/22/2010. http://spectator.org/articles/39882/disappearing-pro-life-democrat, accessed 10/8/2015

Consistently, when asked to rank their top political priorities, 1% or fewer Americans mention abortion.[24] When voting, only 17% are unwilling to vote for a candidate that disagrees with them on abortion, and 55% don't mention abortion on the list of issues they're even considering at the polls.[25] Wedging tactics are designed ultimately to fire up a fairly small group of hyper-engaged partisans. **Abortion looks like it's a big deal in American politics, but for most people it's not.**

Partisan Efforts Are Wasted

The amount of political energy directed toward abortion simply does not reflect the priorities or values of Americans of either party. Understanding this is key to being able to fight back.

Pro-Choice Efforts

Defending *Roe v Wade*: Every recent United States presidential campaign cycle has included candidates taking their stand on abortion. This often surfaces during conversations about their potential choice for a Supreme Court candidate. And, like clockwork, industry professionals on the left use the presidential election to generate fear in their camp, telling their supporters that upon winning the opposition president will appoint a crazy person as a Supreme Court candidate and doom forever the fate of abortion in America.

In part because the overturning of *Roe v Wade* is so unpopular (even among Republicans), Republican presidential candidates don't tend to name it as a priority in their campaigns. It is more common for Democrats to warn their voters: if a Republican is elected, *Roe v Wade* will be overturned – make sure you turn out to vote for a Democrat in order to defend it.

But *Roe* doesn't need a Democratic president to defend it in perpetuity. While Supreme Court appointments are important in many cases, the next few appointments won't make a difference

---

24   Gallup Historical Trends: Most Important Problem. http://www.gallup.com/poll/1675/most-important-problem.aspx, accessed 10/8/2015

25   Karlyn Bowman, Jennifer K Marsico, *American Enterprise Institute*. "Americans don't care as much about abortion as the media think." 1/22/2014. http://www.aei.org/publication/americans-dont-care-as-much-about-abortion-as-the-media-think/, accessed 10/8/2015

to *Roe*. It's ultimately highly unlikely that the current or near future Supreme Court would overturn *Roe v Wade*, for a few reasons.

First, only two sitting Supreme Court justices have expressed an intent or desire to overturn it: Clarence Thomas and Antonin Scalia. Other conservative judges have clarified that they value precedent in the court: Alito clarified that while he personally advocates the pro-life position, his position as a judge is different and he respects the precedent. Roberts does not believe the Constitution guarantees a right to privacy but made clear that he respects operating within a system of precedent.[26] Kennedy – a common "swing" judge – believes firmly in the right to privacy and has clarified that he "cannot renounce" it and its tie to *Roe*.

Second, at 79 years old, Scalia is one of the oldest judges on the bench. Only Ginsburg is older. Even if Ginsburg retired first and a third opponent of Roe was appointed, Scalia would likely be the next to retire, meaning a fourth could not be appointed.

Third, public support for overturning *Roe* is low and dropping, down to 24%.[27] Supreme Court justices rarely overturn previous Supreme Court precedent, and they're even less likely to do so with very low public support for doing it.

Finally, to challenge *Roe v. Wade*, a plaintiff must have "standing." This means that they must demonstrate clear harm to themselves or other individuals. This is a very hard case to make in the matter of abortion: it would require defining pre-viability fetuses as persons with Constitutional protections, which has been attempted and repeatedly rejected by lower courts. This, ultimately, is why no legal challenge to *Roe v Wade* has ever emerged in upper courts.

Trying to find and appoint a judge (with Senate confirmation) that wants to overturn *Roe v Wade* won't happen. Like in the case

---

26   *Alliance for Justice.* "In Their Words: The Supreme Court Justices on Abortion." 1/8/2014. http://www.afj.org/wp-content/uploads/2014/01/SCOTUS-Abortion-Records.pdf, accessed 10/12/2015.

27   Louise Randofsky and Ashby Jones, *The Washington Post.* "Support Grows for Roe v. Wade." 1/22/2013. http://www.wsj.com/articles/SB10001424127887323301104578255831504582200, accessed 10/12/2015.

of Planned Parenthood, political candidates likely understand that *Roe* is very unlikely to ever be overturned but in election season they make us believe that it's "on the cusp" in order to drive devoted voters to the polls.

Guaranteeing Unlimited Access to Abortion: The Supreme Court has repeatedly upheld restrictions on abortions late in term, often carrying even the votes of more left-leaning judges. There is now consistent precedent that state legislatures can create their own restrictions after 24 weeks and that precedent is unlikely to be overturned.

One could amend the Constitution in order to guarantee unlimited access to abortions, but such an amendment would require 67% Congressional support and ratification by 75% of the states. Given that only 14% of Americans believe 3rd trimester abortions should be legal,[28] achieving a supermajority support for such an amendment seems highly unlikely.

Pro-Life Efforts

Defunding Planned Parenthood: On the right, we've recently seen a lot of discussion about whether Planned Parenthood should receive federal funding. Pro-life advocates insist it should not as it means that federal taxpayer dollars are funding abortions.

But the belief that federal funding is being used to pay for abortions at Planned Parenthood is unfounded. First, federal funding (from Medicaid) for abortions in Planned Parenthood is only permissible in cases of rape, incest, or danger to the mother. These cases are extremely rare – less than 1% of all abortions[29] – and very few Americans believe abortions should not be allowed in these cases.[30] **Besides this very small exception, federal funding for abortions is already banned.** Eliminating funding

---

28   Lydia Saad, Gallup. "Majority of Americans Still Support Roe v. Wade Decision." 1/22/2013. http://www.gallup.com/poll/160058/majority-americans-support-roe-wade-decision.aspx, accessed 10/12/2013.

29   Operation Rescue. "Abortions in America: Incidence of Abortion." http://www.operation-rescue.org/about-abortion/abortions-in-america/, accessed 8/26/2015.

30   Sarah Kliff. *The Washington Post.* "Who rejects abortion in the case of rape?" 8/22/2012. http://www.washingtonpost.com/news/wonkblog/wp/2012/08/22/who-rejects-abortion-in-the-case-of-rape/, accessed 8/26/2015.

completely for Planned Parenthood altogether would simply not accomplish anything for the pro-life camp. Asking whether to defund Planned Parenthood becomes a question of whether to defund STD testing, contraception, and cancer screening, which is what federal dollars are used for.

Perhaps we could argue that one should get rid of abortion funding only for Planned Parenthood. We know that Planned Parenthood uses 3% of its total funds on abortion services.[31] Because only 1% of those are eligible for federal funding, it means 0.03% of Planned Parenthood's $528 million in federal funds are used for abortion. If the federal government passed a ban on funding those few abortions, Planned Parenthood would lose about $158,000 per year out of its combined budget of $1.29 billion.[32] It's unlikely that these abortions would be affected, as other non-federal funds could be used; again, it would likely be other services that suffered.

The funding question for Planned Parenthood is a flashy, symbolic fight, but has very little to do with how many abortions are going to be performed. Planned Parenthood is simply a political symbol; it's clear that efforts to defund it are simply meant to whip up supporters rather than make any substantial change. Like in other symbolic battles, the "defending" side garners just as much political benefit as the "offensive" by rallying its own base to hold the line.

Creating Abortion Restrictions to Reduce Abortion Frequency: Throughout the 2000s, and particularly after 2010, state legislatures have enacted a surge in abortion restrictions.[33]

---

31 Janell Ross, *The Washington Post.* "How Planned Parenthood actually uses its federal funding." 8/4/2015. http://www.washingtonpost.com/news/the-fix/wp/2015/08/04/how-planned-parenthood-actually-uses-its-federal-funding/, accessed 8/26/2015.

32 It's worth repeating that if Planned Parenthood was defunded by the federal government completely, and this money was not replaced with a surge in donations, these other women's health services would take a major hit.

33 *The Guttmacher Institute.* "Laws Affecting Reproductive Health and Rights: State Trends at Midyear, 2015." 7/1/2015. http://www.guttmacher.org/media/inthenews/2015/07/01/, accessed 8/24/2015, accessed 10/12/2015.

STATE-LEVEL ABORTION RESTRICTIONS BY YEAR

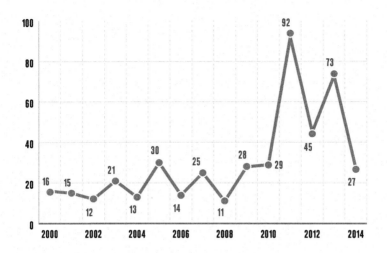

Soure: http://www.guttmacher.org/media/inthenews/2015/07/01/

Most of these require parental involvement for minors or enact waiting periods, which are unlikely to deter many. A few have banned late-term abortions,[34] which we know make up a very small portion of the total.

---

34   Sarah Kliff, *The Washington Post.* "CHARTS: How Roe v Wade changed abortion rights." 1/22/2013. http://www.washingtonpost.com/news/wonkblog/wp/2013/01/22/charts-how-roe-v-wade-changed-abortion-rights/, accessed 10/12/2015.

ABORTION RESTRICTION TYPES 2011-2012

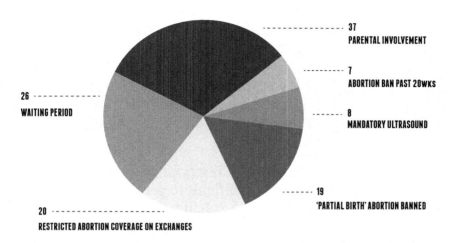

37
PARENTAL INVOLVEMENT

7
ABORTION BAN PAST 20wks

8
MANDATORY ULTRASOUND

19
'PARTIAL BIRTH' ABORTION BANNED

20
RESTRICTED ABORTION COVERAGE ON EXCHANGES

26
WAITING PERIOD

THE GUTTMACHER INSTITUTE

A few states have even pushed for abortion bans after 6 weeks (including North Dakota, Ohio, and Alabama), but the North Dakota ban has been struck down by federal judges as a clear violation of the *Roe v Wade* ruling.[35] It's clear that any other such bans would be similarly struck; they are a waste of effort.

The most effective push to restrict abortion has forced the closing of many abortion clinics across the country by instituting various costly new regulations such as mandates for re-sizing hallways.[36] About 10% have closed since 2010, but the effects are lumpy: Texas has lost half of its clinics, and 4 states – Mississippi, North Dakota, South Dakota, and Wyoming – are down to one each.[37]

It may be tempting to believe that these closings would drive a significant drop-off in the number of abortions, but data suggest

35 NBC News. "Fed Judge Overturns North Dakota's 6-Week Abortion Ban." 4/16/2014. http://www.nbcnews.com/news/us-news/fed-judge-overturns-north-dakotas-6-week-abortion-ban-n82221, accessed 10/12/12015.

36 Carrie Feibel, Kaiser Health News. "Half of Texas Abortion Clinics Close Due to State Law." 7/18/2014. http://khn.org/news/half-of-texas-abortion-clinics-close-due-to-state-law/, accessed 10/12/2015.

37 Esme E. Deprez, Bloomberg. "The Vanishing US Abortion Clinic." 9/14/2015. http://www.bloombergview.com/quicktake/abortion-and-the-decline-of-clinics, accessed 10/12/2015.

that may not be true. Since 2010, abortions have decreased nationwide about 12%. In states with tighter abortion restrictions like Indiana, Missouri, Ohio, and Oklahoma, this drop is a bit more than 15%, but similar drops have been seen in states with unrestricted access like New York, Washington, and Oregon.[38] Of the 6 states with the largest declines in abortion rates, 5 passed no recent abortion restrictions (Hawaii, New Mexico, Nevada, Rhode Island, and Connecticut all had drops over 20%).

It's very likely that these abortion restrictions are making it more financially or logistically difficult to get an abortion in those states, but unlikely that it has had a major impact on the total number of abortions. There is evidence that many people from states where clinics are closing end up driving to a neighboring state.[39]

Don't be too surprised: after Chicago banned the sale of handguns, people still managed to get them elsewhere.[40]

The effort that goes into these restrictions is meant to create strings of symbolic victories that increase re-election prospects, rather than make any substantial changes in the landscape of abortion in the United States.

Eliminating Abortions Entirely: A federal Constitutional amendment banning abortions outright would be similarly necessary to stop abortions from being legally practiced, and it's similarly unlikely.

But even if abortion *were* banned by Constitutional amendment, it wouldn't make abortions go away. Just as prohibition didn't eliminate alcohol and the war on drugs didn't eliminate drugs, we know that pre-Roe state bans on abortions didn't stop them from happening.

---

38   David Crary, Associated Press. "Abortions declining in nearly all states." 6/7/2015. http://bigstory.ap.org/article/0aae4e73500142e5b8745d681c7de270/ap-exclusive-abortions-declining-nearly-all-states, accessed 10/12/2015.

39   Ibid

40   Zack Beauchamp, ThinkProgress. "No, Chicago Isn't Proof that Gun Regulation Doesn't Work." 2/15/2013. http://thinkprogress.org/justice/2013/02/15/1599631/no-chicago-isnt-proof-that-gun-regulation-doesnt-work/, accessed 10/12/2015.

In fact, they may have happened in very large numbers. Harvard professor and historian Paul Boyer estimates that there were maybe 800,000 abortions performed per year in the 1930s[41] even though it was illegal in almost every state. Today's rate of abortions is about 14 per 1000 women (aged 15-44) per year;[42] the 1930s rate was about 26.[43]

What this suggests is that **abortion abolitionists probably would not make meaningful progress towards their goal by banning abortions outright** and would likely create a public health headache for their trouble.

EXTRACTING THE WEDGE: CONSIDERING THE PATH FORWARD

The abortion wedge is probably the single most difficult to resolve due to the amount of anger and toxicity that has been stirred into it over the past few decades. But it is possible.

Since it won't resolve itself through policy, Americans need to find a way to extract the wedge from abortion on their own. We know that Americans can broadly agree when questions of abortion are asked as matters of policy rather than identity. To get to the point of being able to work together and forge these joint policies, Americans need to start working in a different way.

Alternative Paths

The rate of abortion in the United States has been on a steady decline since the peak of 29.3 abortions per 1000 women in 1980

---

41   Boyer, Paul S., ed. (2006). *The Oxford companion to United States history.* Oxford: Oxford Univ. Press. p. 3.

42   Centers for Disease Control and Prevention. "Reproductive Health: Data and Statistics." http://www.cdc.gov/reproductivehealth/data_stats/, accessed 10/8/2015; most recent CDC data is 2014.

43   Calculated using the number of abortions performed per year in the 1930s and an estimate of the number of women between the ages of 15-44.

to about 15.9 per 1000 in 2013,[44] which is the lowest rate since well before *Roe v Wade*.

What's been driving this decline?

Teen pregnancy has been in steady decline during the same time period, accounting for a significant portion of potential abortions averted.[45] Between 1990 and 2010, the teen pregnancy rate dropped by more than half and continues to trend down. Along with it, the teen abortion rate has also dropped by more than half.[46] Unintended pregnancies among older women have also dropped, but by a more modest amount – 5% between 2006 and 2010.[47] This is pretty close to the pace at which the abortion rate dropped, too.

Ultimately it's likely that changes in sexual practices (including use of contraception), which lead to fewer unwanted pregnancies, are the primary drivers behind the dropping abortion rate in the US. Contraceptive technologies have improved and usage of them has increased: the use of long-acting contraceptives (like IUDs or implants) has risen sharply, from about 1% of women to about 8%.[48] These are the most reliable forms of birth control and result in fewer unwanted pregnancies.

Reducing unwanted pregnancies is something most Americans can agree on as a path forward together, regardless of how much we personally prioritize reducing abortions specifically. Working together on how to reduce unwanted pregnancies could be a strong first step for Americans to make progress on the issue

---

44   Abort73.com "US Abortion Statistics: Facts and figures relating to the frequency of abortion in the United States." http://www.abort73.com/abortion_facts/us_abortion_statistics/, accessed 9/25/2015.

45   It's likely that the decline in teen pregnancy has been driven primarily by teens using contraception more often. Some people credit a rise in sexual education.

46   Heather D Boonstra, Guttmacher Institute. "What is Behind the Declines in Teen Pregnancy Rates?" *Guttmacher Policy Review*, Summer 2014, Vol 17, no 3. http://www.guttmacher.org/pubs/gpr/17/3/gpr170315.html, accessed 9/25/2015.

47   Alexandra Sifferlin, *TIME*. "Unintended Pregnancies Decline Across the US." 1/26/2015. http://time.com/3682403/unintended-pregnancy-guttmacher-institute/, accessed 9/25/2015.

48   Janell Ross, *The Washington Post*. "Abortions are way down. Republicans and Democrats should stop congratulating themselves." 6/9/2015. http://www.washingtonpost.com/news/the-fix/wp/2015/06/09/abortions-are-way-down-democrats-and-republicans-should-stop-congratulating-themselves/, accessed 9/25/2015.

of abortion. Certainly trying to ban abortion is likely to be less productive.

Empathy and the Problems of Definition

So much of what we believe about abortion stems from under-lying fundamental premises. While in the future we should healthily continue to disagree and debate fiercely what the best abortion policies should be, first we have to remove the wedge that is maintained through our sense of righteousness and the belief that our opposition are unreasonable or ill-willed.

The key to freeing ourselves from this false impression lies in empathizing with the foundational beliefs of Americans across the spectrum. Our answers to "where does life begin?" vary widely. Being confident that answers other than our own are dead wrong makes it hard not to believe those that disagree with us are foolish or bad: if we entertain the idea that others' beliefs are founded on reasonable premises, however, we can begin to have real conversations.

Having respect for others' definitions of "where life begins" requires realizing that there isn't a watertight answer to the question. Each answer is based on philosophy, theology, intu-ition, and only a little bit of science. By recognizing that our own answer is fuzzy, it becomes easier to understand that reasonable people can disagree with us, even if not everyone that disagrees with us is always reasonable. We become less fundamentalist about a question when we realize that an indisputable answer is elusive.

Of the three most common answers, 52% of Americans believe life begins at conception, 20% believe life begins at viability (the ability to live outside of the womb), and 18% believe that life begins at birth.[49]

First, we should acknowledge that even the framing of the question is questionable. Bacteria, for example, are "alive." By such a definition, it seems easy to agree that a zygote is

---

49   Peter Moore, YouGov. "Three quarters say Longmont attack is murder." 4/7/2015. https://today.yougov.com/news/2015/04/07/three-quarters-say-longmont-attack-is-murder/, accessed 10/12/2015.

alive—just as the egg and sperm were before it. If we frame the question instead as, "when does a fetus obtain the qualities necessary to have rights as a person," the question becomes much more interesting.

Looking at *this* question, we find that each answer is full of complications. These complications make it difficult if not impossible to "prove" to someone else that one answer is absolutely right and another absolutely wrong, highlighting the ambiguity of the question:

> » **At conception:** If personhood begins at conception, we are facing a major health crisis that no one is addressing. 60-70% of all conceived zygotes (that is, eggs and sperm that have already combined,) are naturally terminated in the womb,[50] often while they are only a few cells. If we valued the life of a fetus at this stage the same way that we value the lives of babies out in the world, should we be putting more focus on preventing these terminations to prevent this large mass of deaths?

> » **Viability:** As intensive care and incubator technology improves, we are able to save premature births at earlier and earlier stages—do we need to move our definition of "life" as technology moves? If we developed the technology to grow a fetus to term in a vat after 4 weeks inside the womb, is that fetus alive in a way that an 8-week fetus wasn't alive before the technology was developed?

> » **Birth:** Does a baby just out of the womb have some intrinsic human value, and possess human rights, when a fetus just before birth does not have human value or human rights? What about the process of moving out of the womb actually changes the baby itself, such that we can endow it with the definitions "human" and "alive" in a way we couldn't five minutes earlier? Given that 75% of Americans believe that killing a very pregnant woman is

---

50   Gregg Easterbrook. "Abortion and Brain Waves." *The New Republic*, 1/31/2000. Available at the Wilson Quarterly Archive. http://archive.wilsonquarterly.com/in-essence/when-life-begins, accessed 10/13/2015.

a double-murder, what does this mean for fetus "person-hood" late in term?

The ambiguous and philosophical nature of the question "when does a fetus become human?" means we're ultimately not going to get everyone to agree on the answer. Extracting the wedge can occur if we are able to tolerate and respect someone else's answer as different from our own. Doing so means that we can see that they're not bad people or enemies, but just people with different premises.

The Way Forward

It's frightening to think about "backing down" on the issue of abortion. We've been told so often that our values are under attack by the opposition that it's understandable one might worry that softening one's own stance only allows the opposition to strike. We believe that we have to stay dug-in lest the extreme opposition get their way.

This is a classic problem of brinksmanship: if one side takes a hard line and won't talk, then the other must do so or lose ground. Over time, we might find that the opposition is dug in only because they're as afraid of us as we are of them.

But in this warfighting, we have fallen victim to the lie that Americans are far apart on the issue of abortion and that our differences in policy preferences are driven by deep differences in values. This is simply not true. As we've seen above: with the exception of the fringes of the American political spectrum, **there is broad agreement on the ideal scope of abortion policy in the United States.** A vast majority of Americans believe that abortion should be legal in many cases and illegal in some. A solid majority believe abortion is immoral and many more believe it is morally complicated, but most of those same people believe abortion should be legal under some circumstances anyway. Most Americans feel conflicted about abortion, but this embrace of nuance is simply drowned out by loud, angry minorities on either side of the spectrum. The illusion of a great chasm on abortion is just that.

All this means that despite a 50/50 split in group identity, **the labels of "pro-life" and "pro-choice" are largely meaningless for most Americans when it comes to policy preferences.** For example: let's say someone believed that abortion should be legal, but only until 20 weeks, because they believe the fetus takes on a "human" quality around that time. Is that person pro-life or pro-choice? What if that person believes that an informed choice requires an ultrasound or consultation with a doctor: have they now switched camps? And if that person believes the right time to restrict abortion is after 24 weeks, do they change camps again? These complex, nuanced positions that most Americans believe are not being represented in the political arena: agreeing to let ourselves be labeled by the voices of the political fringes surrenders our political agency and gives power over to political extremes and the politicians they support.

How can we act in a more productive way? The simple answer is to lead by looking for agreement rather than stating a false allegiance to an over-simplified camp identity. This approach opens the door to finding mutual ground within the largely-acknowledged murky grey area of abortion. Whether you seek conflict or agreement, what you seek is what you will most likely find.

We'll end with a brief exercise to prime the pump. Let's imagine that Congress introduced a bill to enforce, clarify, and settle the details of *Roe v. Wade* in a way that would strive to end gridlock on the issue and create compromise: the basics of such a bill are below. Would you or your friends ask your representative to vote for this bill? If not, what would *have to* change, and why? What elements of a compromise would you be absolutely unwilling to accept?

"Congress reinforces the right to access to abortions as outlined in the Constitution and confirmed by the Supreme Court in *Roe v. Wade*. In order to aid implementation, Congress enacts that all states may elect to restrict abortions between 18 and 24 weeks. After 24 weeks, abortions are only allowed in the cases of rape, forcible incest, and danger to the mother. There can be no legislation designed to limit access to abortions before the state's chosen restriction period. States can choose their own legislation over issues around parental consent, ultrasounds, etc."

Even if you don't agree with all of these provisions, would it be worth agreeing to this compromise to take the brinksmanship out of abortion and help Americans move on from the issue?

CHAPTER FIVE:
WEALTH AND TAXES

"In the last recession, 99 percent of us have lost wealth, but did you know that the top 1 percent increased their wealth five times? It tells you they create recessions so they get wealthier."

-Jesse Ventura, former Governor of Minnesota

"Our citizens are tired of big government raising their taxes and cooking up new ways to micromanage their lives, our citizens are tired of big government killing jobs with their do-gooder policies. In short the people are Fed Up!"

-Rick Perry, Governor of Texas

Maintaining a strong US economy is perennially the first or second political priority for Americans. If we consider the country's economic health to include unemployment, poverty, income inequality, and taxes, then it is decisively Americans' primary concern.

Economic issues differ from guns and abortion in this regard: where the latter two issues are hotly contested but ultimately less important to Americans, nothing is more important to us than our economy. It's an issue with a lot of meat that requires a very careful and agile application of policy. It also may be the most complicated issue that the country faces: the US economy is massive, with hundreds of thousands of businesses, hundreds of millions of domestic actors, and billions of foreign actors with whom it interacts. It's poorly understood by laymen and experts alike: experienced economists frequently disagree fiercely on the likely outcome of even simple policy questions related to the economic outlook of Americans.

This complexity makes it difficult for political professionals to engage and inspire their audiences: humans crave clarity over ambiguity. So the political industry oversimplifies issues and finds enemy groups to blame for our economic pains in order to provoke us into political action. Some of the economic issues such as wealth and inequality, income taxes, and inheritance tax, are particularly ripe for wedging tactics: instead of discussing the broadness, complexity, and ambiguity of the economy as a whole, politicians and media focus on these easily-sensationalized issues in order to kindle excitement among voters and viewers.

The pains caused by the 2008 financial crisis made Americans particularly prone to crave a simple, emotionally resonant narrative that laid the blame on a specific group rather than vague "market dynamics." The political industry eagerly complied, each side identifying a convenient enemy: on the one hand, the wealthiest Americans; on the other, the federal government: and so a wedge was born. This wedge both triggered and fed on the rise of the Occupy Wall Street and Tea Party movements, which for many months completely hijacked the national dialogue away from long-term solutions and towards emotional finger-pointing.

ECONOMY, WEALTH, AND TAXES: THE STATE OF THE DEBATE

When discussing the economy, the core concern is generally how to improve the economic outlook for Americans. As a nation, we agree that we want this economic outlook[1] to improve for all Americans over time and to provide opportunity for individuals to improve their economic position through education and effort.

Right-leaning thinkers often believe that too much government stifles the economy and job creation. Many believe that the ability to freely accumulate wealth from work, investment, and entrepreneurship is an important right and incentive and that freedom in this area is critical for driving economic growth. Some also believe that tax rates that are too high are both a threat to national economic health and also a violation of the right to property.

Left-leaning thinkers tend to believe that the government plays an important role in a healthy economy. Some also believe that the tax rate on the wealthy is too low and that the accumulation of wealth by a few is dangerous or unjust: many presume that the economy must be systemically flawed in order to allow significant concentration of wealth and/or that high levels of inequality are bad for national economic health.

Due to the incredible complexity of the system of economic cause and effect, politicians and pundits get the attention they seek by painting pictures that are simple and emotionally attractive. Such simple narratives are available in the issues of taxes and wealth.

Unlike national economic health as a whole, neither the tax rate nor the level of economic inequality in the United States is among the top priorities for Americans to change. Most Americans prioritize other economic issues: the health of the economy as a whole (16% of Americans), unemployment and underemployment (9%), federal deficit and debt (5%), and poverty (4%).[2] The dominance of taxes and inequality over our political dialogue are yet another illustration of how effectively

---

1   We define "outlook" as the likelihood that one's economic outcomes can improve in the future.

2   It is perhaps tempting to link the rate of inequality and the rate of poverty, but we can briefly imagine a country where 100% of people are in poverty (with no inequality), and a country where everyone made between $100,000 and $100,000,000,000 per year, in which there would be high inequality but no poverty.

extreme voices redirect the conversation away from the priorities of the majority.

UNDERSTANDING THE WEDGE

In times of economic plenty, the issue of the economy is fairly resistant to wedging: Americans embrace searching for economic policies that benefit the economy and Americans as a whole. But when economic times are tough, people fear the future and seek the reassurance of a simple story and someone to blame; these feelings are easily exploited. Politicians don't want to tell them, "the causes are complex: it's hard to say exactly what caused the pain and just as hard to know what's going to fix it." A long speech or article exploring the possible factors behind the problem is politically unprofitable. Profit comes instead from identifying an enemy group and claiming that only its destruction will make things better.

The Rise of Tribes: Occupy Wall Street and the Tea Party

Two extreme groups arose in the painful recession following the 2008 financial crisis, claiming to know the cause of our misery: Occupy Wall Street and the Tea Party.

These groups embraced rage and blame as their hallmarks: Occupy blamed greedy corporations and the wealthy for Americans' financial woes; the Tea Party blamed a bloated and power-hungry federal government. Opportunist political hopefuls and media pundits leapt to encourage and inflame these groups, and those who did so best rode these waves of rage to power.

To Occupy Wall Street, the enemy is the top 1% wealthiest Americans. In their view, this 1% manipulates the economy and the government in order to increase their personal wealth and keep the other 99% poor. They need to be beaten or destroyed in order for the economic opportunity of the other 99% to be restored.

An Occupy Wall Street meme with a classic robber-baron that has grown fat feeding upon the flesh and houses of the poor.

To the Tea Party, the enemy is the federal government. In their view, Washington has grown tyrannical; its power and spending having grown too great, it is pushing the country towards socialism and aiming to control ever-larger portions of earned wealth through taxation.

A Tea Party demonstration against spending, taxes, and general socialism, which they inform us is not freedom.

Just as for the Occupy camp, victory for the Tea Party comes not through reform but through the defeat of the enemy—in this case, through a second American Revolution.

A Tea Party meme part of the "Second American Revolution" campaign.

The amount of attention and energy devoted to these movements rivals the most powerful of other wedge issues. Tea Party protesters came to the streets hundreds of times between 2009 and 2012. Occupy protesters camped permanently in their protest sites, often for months.

Political opportunists did not hesitate to take advantage of the powerful wedge that was forming. Politicians like Michelle Bachmann, Ted Cruz, Rand Paul, and a total of 44 Congresspeople were elected in the 2010 and 2012 elections with Tea Party support, often defeating incumbent Republicans in primary elections. The Tea Party Caucus peaked at 48 members in Congress (or about one tenth of the body).

On the opposing side, politicians like Nancy Pelosi and Bernie Sanders, along with much of the Congressional Progressive Caucus (numbering 69 members in Congress) were quick to shift their political rhetoric to endear themselves to the Occupy movement's supporters. Politicians like Elizabeth Warren defeated a number of Republican incumbents in the 2012 elections with Occupy-friendly messaging; even as late as the 2016 presidential race, Bernie Sanders has garnered the support of a double-digit minority of Democrats by singing a similar tune.

Issue Inflation and Oversimplification

Occupy and the left wing camp's perspective on wealth and taxes was simple: economic inequality is fundamentally bad, and the extent of that inequality in the US has reached the level of a crisis.[3] But the camp doesn't dive into asking what is the "right" amount of inequality, either in terms of economic effectiveness or fairness: it has turned the word "inequality" from a term of relative measure into one of morally absolute wrong. By extension, taxes on the rich are too low and need to be raised, because the wealthy need to be brought down.

The Tea Party and the right-wing camp have a similarly simple message: taxes are a bad thing, and they're too high – they neglect to indicate what the right tax rate should be. These high taxes are to blame for economic woes and pose a critical danger to American liberty and economic strength, as they represent a government takeover of the economy. Redistributive efforts to reduce economic inequality would result in a welfare state in which Americans become wholly dependent on the government.

Rallying the Tribe, Calling Out the Enemy

Occupy brilliantly adopted the slogan, "We are the 99%." This identifier implies that almost everybody is already part of Occupy and that the movement represents the interests of an overwhelming majority of Americans. Anyone that opposes Occupy or its aims therefore also opposes the interests of 99% of Americans, favoring instead the interests of only the wealthiest 1%. In the "1%" label they found an equally brilliant tag for their enemy: because there will always be a wealthiest 1%, there will always be an enemy to fight.

The "Main Street" and "Wall Street" labels work the same way: "Main Street" is made up of noble, hardworking, and oppressed Americans. "Wall Street" is populated by corrupt thieves. These groupings shift moral agency: no longer judged by their individual actions, instead some people are evil just because they're wealthy or work in a certain industry.

---

3   Salon's "America's inequality crisis is about so much more than money" and economyin-crisis.org's "Income Inequality is Ravaging America's Middle Class" are just a few.

On the other side, Tea Partiers paint themselves as "patriots," implying that they wish to do what's best for America and that those that disagree with them wish the nation ill. They invoke the symbols of the Boston Tea Party, the original tax revolt, and of the American Revolution and founding fathers. They divide America into "the People" and "the Government," the second stealing from and oppressing the first: as long as the United States exists, the federal government will always be an available enemy.

Each camp claims that the interests of its chosen enemy group are diametrically opposed to the interests of regular Americans: they cannot be worked with; they can only be fought until they are destroyed. Political media outlets like Salon accuse the "1%" of ruining the lives of regular citizens, for example, blaming them for the "ruin" of New Orleans.[4] Others include, "The One Percent are Parasites"[5] and "Let's All Screw the One Percent."[6]

Democrats hoping to win the support of those influenced by Occupy paint wealth, corporations, and profit as morally deplorable. They frame the economy as a zero-sum game, in which those who succeed do so only upon the backs of those who do not, through exploitation and crime.

4   Bill Quigley, AlterNet. "17 shocking stats that show how the 1 percent have ruined New Orleans." Available at salon.com, 7/24/2015. http://www.salon.com/2015/07/24/17_ shocking_stats_that_show_how_the_one_percent_have_ruined_new_orleans_partner/, accessed 8/17/2015

5   Andrew Sayer, Salon. "The 1 percent are parasites: Debunking the lies about free enterprise, trickle-down, capitalism and celebrity entrepreneurs." 4/11/2015. http://www.salon. com/2015/04/11/the_1_percent_are_parasites_debunking_the_lies_about_free_enterprise_ trickle_down_capitalism_and_celebrity_entrepreneurs/. Retrieved 8/17/2015.

6   Paul Rosenberg, Salon. "Let's all screw the 1 percent: The simple move Obama could make to strengthen the rest of us." 12/26/2014. http://www.salon.com/2014/12/26/lets_all_screw_ the_1_percent_the_simple_move_obama_could_make_to_strengthen_the_rest_of_us/. Retrieved 8/17/2015

"Let us wage a moral and political war against the billionaires and corporate leaders, on Wall Street and elsewhere, whose policies and greed are destroying the middle class of America."

> *-Bernie Sanders, Senator from Vermont and 2016 Presidential Candidate*

"The rich have stacked the deck in their favor, and I intend to reshuffle the cards."[7]

> *-Hillary Clinton, former Secretary of State and 2016 Presidential Candidate*

The Tea Party paints the federal government and "establishment" politicians as tyrannical. In addition to other ills, they say the federal government has grown dangerously large and powerful, that its taxation is a threat to the American economy and individual liberty.

According to a 2013 poll by Professor Christopher Parker of the University of Washington, most Tea Party activists believe that President Obama's policies are "socialist" and 71% believe that he might "destroy the country."[8]

Republicans hoping for the support of the Tea Party (whose supporters make up about 10% of all US voters)[9] are pledging to never raise taxes, even in exchange for significant cuts in spending.[10] Their rhetoric simply repeats that the federal government is bad.

---

7   Mara Liasson, *NPR*. "How Would Hillary Clinton 'Reshuffle' Economic Inequality?" 6/12/2015. http://www.npr.org/sections/itsallpolitics/2015/06/12/413964447/how-would-hillary-clinton-reshuffle-economic-inequality, accessed 8/17/2015.

8   Ezra Klein, *The Washington Post*. "'People don't fully appreciate how committed the tea party is to not compromising.'" 10/4/2013. http://www.washingtonpost.com/news/wonkblog/wp/2013/10/04/people-dont-fully-appreciate-how-committed-the-tea-party-is-to-not-compromising/, accessed 8/17/2015

9   Karlyn Bowman; Jennifer Marsico (February 24, 2014). "As The Tea Party Turns Five, It Looks A Lot Like The Conservative Base". Forbes.com. http://www.forbes.com/sites/realspin/2014/02/24/as-the-tea-party-turns-five-it-looks-a-lot-like-the-conservative-base/, accessed 8/17/2015.

10   Paul Waldman, *The Washington Post*. "Nearly all the GOP candidates bow down to Grover Norquist." 8/13/2015. https://www.washingtonpost.com/blogs/plum-line/wp/2015/08/13/nearly-all-the-gop-candidates-bow-down-to-grover-norquist/, accessed 8/17/2015.

"I think it's clear to me that what – when I look at the Tea Party, it's about one-third Democrat, one-third Republican, one-third independents.[11] But 100% of them are sure that the agenda that is taking place in Washington, D.C., is about extremism and is about bankrupting this country and every state within this country."

> -Jeff Sessions, Senator from Alabama

"After the $700 billion bailout, the trillion-dollar stimulus, and the massive budget bill with over 9,000 earmarks, many of you implored Washington to please stop spending money we don't have. But, instead of cutting, we saw an unprecedented explosion of government spending and debt, unlike anything we have seen in the history of our country."

> -Michelle Bachmann, former member of the House of Representatives, (MN-6)

This war of words is simply over who, in the American economy, are the thieves. To the right, those who want to raise taxes and reduce inequality are lazy, rent-seeking, and looking for free handouts off the backs of hard-working Americans. To the left, the rich to be taxed are the thieves, exploiting hard-working Americans to feed their own greed.

ANALYZING THE DATA: UNDERMINING THE WEDGE

Beyond Binary: Beneath the Rhetoric, Nuance & Common Ground

Despite the impressive amount of noise and media attention given to both Occupy and the Tea Party, they only briefly had the support of any significant amount of the American public. Their extreme policy positions never represented the values or preferences of most Americans.

A Wide Array of Views

As in all wedge issues, the dichotomy arranged by Occupy- and Tea Party-friendly partisans is a false one. One need not choose between supporting a tyrannical elite class or a tyrannical

---

11   Author's note: this is not accurate. Tea Party supporters are majority Republican.

government. It's very possible to see both good and ill in how the federal government operates and in how US corporations operate. Most Americans do.

Given the complexity and ambiguity of economics, it is not surprising that the real views of Americans map onto a wide array of policy positions.

One might believe that economic inequality should always be minimized because the most just outcome is the one in which all outcomes are the same. One might believe that efforts intended to reduce inequality should be balanced with those that promote growth, or might simply consider inequality an inevitable outcome of high-growth economies.

Perhaps inequality is only a problem if some are left without things they critically need, and therefore it is most important to focus on unemployment and poverty rates; perhaps inequality is an indicator that the opportunity to succeed is not available to all. On the other hand, perhaps some economic inequality is desirable in order to motivate potential entrepreneurs and drive economic progress. One may see a growing upper class as a positive sign that an economy provides plenty of opportunities to succeed, and that increasing numbers are able to take advantage of it.

There are many different answers regarding how much inequality is the "right" amount, in terms of both fairness and economic growth. Few besides pure communists likely wish to live in the kind of world that is entirely without inequality, in which everyone owns an equivalent amount of property. It's also likely that few want a world of "complete" inequality, in which a few people have all the wealth and the rest live in dire poverty. Most people are going to believe that some inequality is reasonable and valuable for our society: it's a matter of degree.

Regarding taxes, many believe that taxes are a way for everyone to "pitch in" to help society and those in need, but there is disagreement as far as how much is fair, how much not enough, and how much too much for any one person to contribute. Most Americans want to fund the functions of government at different levels, but there is a range of beliefs about which functions are needed, how much they should be funded, and how much of the economy governments at different levels should command. Again, the majority are looking for some balance: none but the fringe believe any working person should pay no taxes or 100% taxes, regardless of their income.

One need not be relegated to being "against" inequality or "against" government participation in creating an effective economic system; one need not be relegated to being for "low taxes" or for "soaking the rich." Such a false dichotomy is a product of the wedge, denying us the opportunity to embrace the ambiguity and nuance of balancing different priorities in creating policy.

Shared Values and Policy Agreement

Despite the reluctance of politicians to engage with it, Americans largely recognize the complexity of these issues, consistently voicing opinions that seek to balance competing priorities within the framework of a uniquely American set of values about the economy.

Shared Values: One thing that sets the United States apart from many of our peer countries (like those in Europe) is our pursuit of an American Dream: above all we want opportunity for everyone to make a living, be comfortable, and be happy if they work hard for it. To a unique extent among citizens of countries in the West – and perhaps the world – Americans celebrate hard work and an entrepreneurial spirit. We want to live in a country where initiative, dedication, and talent can lead to success.[12]

---

12   *Pew Research.* "Emerging and Developing Economies Much More Optimistic than Rich Countries about the Future." 10/9/2014. http://www.pewglobal.org/2014/10/09/emerging-and-developing-economies-much-more-optimistic-than-rich-countries-about-the-future/, accessed 10/16/2015

Americans Stand Out on Individualism

Percent who disagree that success in life is pretty much determined by forces outside our control

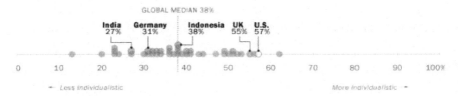

Percent who say it is very important ("10" on a 0-10 scale) to work hard to get ahead in life

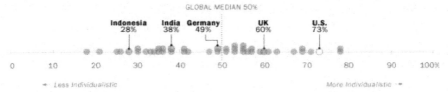

Source: Spring 2014 Global Attitudes survey. Q13b & Q66b.

PEW RESEARCH CENTER

The above graphs show the results of a global study by Pew Research, conducted Spring 2014. The first graph shows the percentage of respondents in a country that disagrees with the idea that "success in life is pretty much determined by forces outside of our control." With 57% disagreeing, the US has the second-highest rate of disagreement in the world: most Americans beleive that success in life is somewhat or largely within the control of each person.

73% of Americans also believe that it is "very important" to work hard to get ahead in life, rating the importance at a 10 out of possible 10. Americans are the third most likely to do this, more than almost all peer countries.

Americans believe, more than any other peer country and almost any country in the world, that hard work and a good education are the top factors to getting ahead economically (much more than connections, a wealthy family, luck, and other factors).[13]

---

13   *Pew Research.* "Emerging and Developing Economies Much More Optimistic than Rich Countries about the Future." 10/9/2014. http://www.pewglobal.org/2014/10/09/emerging-and-developing-economies-much-more-optimistic-than-rich-countries-about-the-future/, accessed 10/16/2015

In fact, a staggering 97% of Americans believe that it's better to provide equal opportunity to get ahead than equal wealth outcomes.[14] This is a truly remarkable data point, and represents perhaps the single most unifying and illustrative value that unites Americans and distinguishes them from the rest of the world.

We support welfare when we see it as an aid to get people back on their feet – rather than something to replace work. This is why the 1993 Welfare Reform Act passed easily: because it was intended to change welfare from more of the latter to more of the former. American unemployment insurance requires that applicants actively look for work and take what comes up in their field. Americans continually seek ways to reform government involvement in the economy to better enable the talented and hard-working to succeed.

All this suggests that **our policy disagreements stem not from real differences in our core values but instead on how we interpret facts about the economy and how the current economic system works.**

Rejecting the Extremes: Even though the hyper-partisan camps of Occupy and the Tea Party have commanded great attention, they don't represent the views of most Americans, who remain steadfastly in a middle ground. Although there was a brief flash of support for both groups, after learning more about them the majority of Americans came to reject both camps.

At its height (around 2010), the Tea Party had the support of about 30% of Americans. Since then, national support has fallen and indifference has grown. In late 2014, Tea Party support had dropped to less than 20%.[15]

---

14   Benjamin I Page and Lawrence R Jacobs. *Class War? What Americans Really Think About Economic Inequality.* University of Chicago Press, 2009.

15   CBS News. "Tea party support hits new lows: Poll." 5/21/2014. http://www.cbsnews.com/news/tea-party-support-hits-new-lows-poll/, accessed 10/16/2015.

TEA PARTY SUPPORT

Do you consider yourself to be

■ % neither   ■ % an opponent of the Tea Party movement or
■ % a supporter of the Tea Party movement

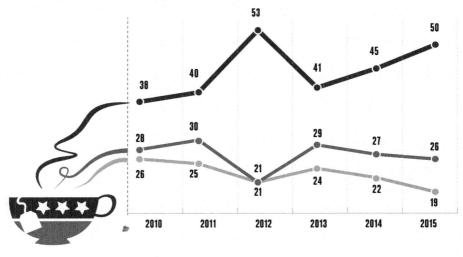

16

At Occupy's height (around October 2011), support for Occupy stood at about 43%,[17] with about 20% opposing its aims. But the excitement faded quickly. By May 2012, support had dropped to just 16%.[18] After that, interest diminished enough that major polling groups stopped asking about Occupy. Three years later, most Americans said that the Occupy protests had little or no impact.[19]

16   Gallup In Depth: Tea Party Movement. http://www.gallup.com/poll/147635/tea-party-movement.aspx, accessed 8/17/2015

17   Brian Montopoli. "Poll: 43 percent agree with views of "Occupy Wall Street." 10/26/2011. http://www.cbsnews.com/news/poll-43-percent-agree-with-views-of-occupy-wall-street/, accessed 8/17/2015

18   Harry J Enten, *The Guardian*. "Occupy Wall Street's people power loses popularity." 5/14/2012. http://www.theguardian.com/commentisfree/cifamerica/2012/may/14/occupy-wall-street-people-power-popularity, accessed 8/17/2015

19   Peter Moore, YouGov. "The limited impact of Occupy Wall Street." 9/18/2014. https://today.yougov.com/news/2014/09/18/occupy-wall-street/, accessed 8/17/2015

Opportunity Lost

This wedge issue also stands out from others in part because the Tea Party and Occupy Wall Street movement shared the belief that the core problems they saw were caused in part by the excessive power wielded by the marriage of corporations and government. For example: both the Tea Party and the Occupy movement scorned the TARP bailouts as handouts to cronies and looked to the Federal Reserve with distrust. Both felt that much of the government response to the recession served special interests at the expense of regular Americans. Both believed that corporations and government were in bed together and needed to be separated. Most importantly, neither supported the Republican or Democratic parties, believing each to be too entrenched with the interests of the establishment.

Odd as it may seem in retrospect, these concurrent movements had a lot of potential to team up to accomplish their biggest goals: breaking what they saw as crony capitalism, where big corporations and big government got in bed together, and reducing government debts that future generations will need to pay. In a political system capable of forming temporary coalitions on areas of agreement, they may have become a powerful force.

But that wasn't how it turned out. As the dust settled, the momentum of these movements started to fizzle. And throughout their dizzying highs, the only people they hated more than the business-as-usual political and corporate "cronies" was each other. Another opportunity for people to find common ground and drive reform was lost due to the manipulation of these groups by wedging tactics.

OCCUPY WALL STREET SUPPORT
% supporter of Occupy Wall Street

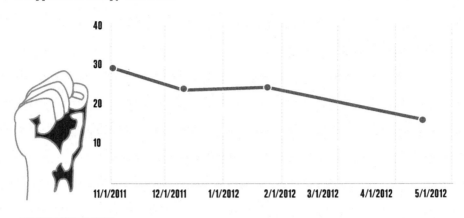

POLLS BY THE GUARDIAN
http://www.theguardian.com/commentisfree/cifamerica/2012/may/14/occupy-wall-street-people-power-popularity

Economic inequality, taxation, and spending remain powerful wedge issues, but the political extremism, emotional excess, and lack of focus on practical problem-solving led Americans to become disillusioned and seek other avenues to address their concerns.

Policy Agreement: Americans broadly believe the path forward for the economy is to focus on economic growth and job creation. They favor government policies focused on enabling the market to create these jobs and foster an overall healthy economy that benefits all Americans.

On Income Inequality

A large majority of Americans are concerned about the level of income inequality specifically because we believe it drives unequal economic opportunity, that core shared American value.[20] We believe it's harder for less wealthy people to move up the ladder, and we want the economic outlook for these Americans to be a bright one.

---

20   David Madland, Center for American Progress. "Public Opinion Shows Dissatisfaction with Our Economic System." 3/5/2012. https://www.americanprogress.org/issues/economy/news/2012/03/05/11193/americans-care-about-economic-inequality/, accessed 8/17/2015.

MOST AMERICANS BELIEVE THE ECONOMIC SYSTEM IS UNFAIR

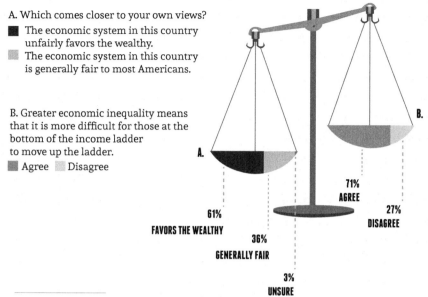

A. Which comes closer to your own views?
- ■ The economic system in this country unfairly favors the wealthy.
- The economic system in this country is generally fair to most Americans.

B. Greater economic inequality means that it is more difficult for those at the bottom of the income ladder to move up the ladder.
- ■ Agree ■ Disagree

B.

71%
AGREE

27%
DISAGREE

61%
FAVORS THE WEALTHY

A.

36%
GENERALLY FAIR

3%
UNSURE

A. Source: Dec 7-11, 2011
PEW RESEARCH CENTER POLL. N=1,521. Margin of error ±3.5.
B. Source: Jan 27-Feb 8,2009
PEW/GREENBERG QUINLAN ROSNER POLL. N=1,000.

The differences in our opinions on economic policy do not stem from whether we want to see improved economic opportunity for lower- and middle-income Americans, but seem to be rooted in *how we believe the economy works*. Most Americans don't want to respond to this perceived unfairness by simply redistributing money—instead, Americans want the government to focus on efforts to drive economic growth, which they believe will create opportunity for all Americans and improve outcomes for all.[21]

---

21   Emily Ekins, reason.com "Poll: 74 Percent Say Congress Should Prioritize Economic Growth Over Reducing Income Inequality." 10/2/2014. http://reason.com/poll/2014/10/02/poll-74-percent-say-congress-should-prio, accessed 10/16/2015 There is some evidence that certain levels of income inequality have different impacts on economic growth, so these may be intrinsically linked. The use of this poll is meant to give a general sense of the tenor of Americans.

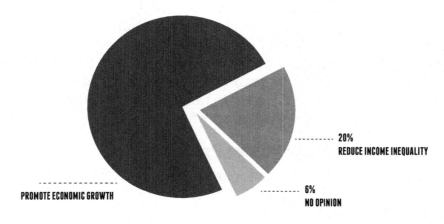

AMERICANS WANT CONGRESS TO PRIORITIZE ECONOMIC GROWTH OVER REDUCING INCOME GAP

When it comes to priorities, would you rather see Congress prioritize policies aimed at reducing income inequality or policies aimed at promoting economic growth?

20%
REDUCE INCOME INEQUALITY

6%
NO OPINION

PROMOTE ECONOMIC GROWTH

REASON-RUPE POLL – Aug 6-10, 2014

On Taxes

The conventional wisdom on taxes suggests there's very little overlap between left- and right-leaning Americans: one wants to raise taxes to fuel spending, the other wants to cut taxes and cut spending. As we often find, thoughtfully exploring more specific policy questions helps us break away from binary roles we've been told to play and find opportunities for agreement.

In taxes, the area of agreement is in reducing tax "loopholes," or deductions that favor some more than others. The current tax code allows some Americans in each tax bracket to use deductions to pay lower rates than some in that tax bracket, or even some in lower brackets. One example of the effects of such loopholes would be Warren Buffett paying about 11% in effective income taxes, compared to a marginal rate (on almost all of his $63 million in income) of 35%.[22] Another example is in corporate taxes, in which some corporations pay close to the nominal rate

---

22   Richard Wolf, USA Today. "Comparing tax rates for Obama, Romney, and you." 8/20/2012. http://usatoday30.usatoday.com/news/politics/story/2012-08-17/obama-romney-tax-income-comparison/57161254/1, accessed 10/15/2015.

of 40%, but others like General Electric or Prudential end up paying 0% over years.[23]

Americans struggle to agree on broad concepts like "raising" or "lowering" taxes, but 82% believe in placing a limit on tax deductions, which would mean both a higher effective tax rate on higher-income Americans and also a more uniform tax burden on people within each bracket. 79% of Americans also favor adjusting the corporate tax code so that American corporations pay as much on foreign profits as profits generated in the US.[24]

Reality Reveals False Wedge Premises

Occupy and the Tea Party both manage to touch on issues important to Americans, and identify problems that many Americans believe need to be prioritized. But in their zeal, both movements distract themselves and the voters they're looking to attract by focusing instead on problems that are flashy and emotional but don't fit into the priorities most Americans hold.

Putting the Problem in Perspective

Between the Tea Party and Occupy, we might believe that the average American is being squeezed into oblivion: on one side by the greed of the 1% and on the other side by an out-of-control government.

While the US and many of its families do face economic challenges of various forms, the story of a hand-built crisis is a myth: it gets people excited, but doesn't reflect reality. This warping draws legislative focus away from where it could be most effectively applied and pits each camp's efforts toward reinforcing their narrative and undermining that of their rival.

---

23 Eric Pianin, *The Fiscal Times*. "15 Fortune 500 Companies Paid No Federal Income Taxes in 2014." 4/9/2015. http://www.thefiscaltimes.com/2015/04/09/15-Fortune-500-Companies-Paid-No-Federal-Income-Taxes-2014, accessed 10/15/2015

24 Harry Gural, Americans for Tax Fairness. "New Poll Shows Americans Strongly Want to Close Tax Loopholes Benefiting the Rich and Corporations in Next Budget Deal." 11/13/2013. http://www.americansfortaxfairness.org/new-poll-shows-americans-strongly-want-to-close-tax-loopholes-benefiting-the-rich-and-corporations-in-next-budget-deal/, accessed 10/15/2015

Busting Some Common Wedge Myths

"The Shrinking Middle Class": A common refrain of concern about economic inequality is that the "middle class is shrinking." Hearing this cry, we might infer that the problem is that as the rich get richer, Americans in the middle of the pack get poorer.

But as we examine this idea, a number of questions arise. First, it's hard to say what the "middle class" even means. If the middle class is a relative definition (that is, "the middle 1/3 of the country" or similar), then it is by definition impossible for the middle class to shrink. The "absolute" definition of a middle class, one that could change relative size, requires defining some ultimately arbitrary income bracket—between $X and $Y.

Does "a shrinking middle class" suggest that the middle 50% (or so) of American households make less money than they used to? Or does it mean that fewer American families are within this "middle" (between $X and $Y) range of income?

Looking to the first question: when you control for inflation and cost of living, the median family's real[25] income has grown to about 9% higher than it was in the early 1990s (after it bottomed-out from that decade's recession).[26] For the middle 20% and middle 60% of families, the story is similar:[27] income has moderately grown, not shrunk.

If we look at the second question, we do indeed see fewer families with a "middle" income—in this case, defining it as between $25,000 and $75,000 (a cut-off chosen by the IRS). **But those families aren't moving into lower tax brackets; they're moving into higher ones.** Controlling for inflation, the proportion of families in this "middle" group has been on a steady

---

25   This defined as income adjusted for monetary inflation and cost of living, or CPI.

26   *The State of Working America.* "Income Growth for families at the 20th, 50th, and 95th percentiles, 1947-2013." 9/24/2014. http://stateofworkingamerica.org/charts/real-income-growth-for-different-income-percentiles-diverged-in-the-1970s-with-real-incomes-flattening-in-the-20th-percentile-and-the-median-and-increasing-in-the-95th-percentile/, accessed 8/25/2015

27   "The Bigger, the Less Fair." *The Economist*, 3/14/2015. http://www.economist.com/news/finance-and-economics/21646266-growing-size-firms-may-help-explain-rising-inequality-bigger?fsrc=scn/tw/te/bl/ed/inequality, accessed 8/25/2015

decline since the 1970s, accompanied by a growth in the proportion of families making $75,000 or more.[28]

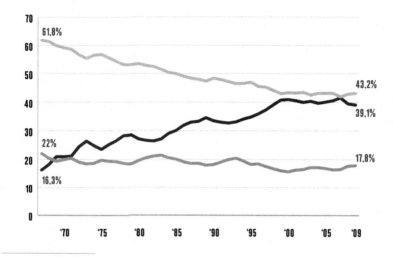

PERCENT DISTRIBUTION OF US FAMILIES BY INCOME LEVEL IN CONSTANT US DOLLARS, 1967-2009

■ upper-income ($75,000 and over)   ■ middle-income ($25,000 to $75,000)
■ lower-income ($25,000 and under)

Source: **2012 US CENSUS:** *Income, Expenditures, Poverty, and Wealth.* Table 696.

We can see also that the portion of families making less than
$25,000 hasn't grown. This meshes well with census data that
also shows that the poverty rate has wavered consistently
between 11% and 15% over the same time period.[29]

Some of the growth in high-income families is driven by an
increase in the number of women in the workforce (meaning
more families with two earners), but not all of it – the rate of
growth of families making over $75,000 was higher than the rate
of women entering the workforce. In the early 1990s the workforce stabilized,[30] suggesting that all the growth we see after
about 1992 is due to increases in per-earner incomes.

---

28   2009 US census, http://www.census.gov/compendia/statab/cats/income_expenditures_
     poverty_wealth.html, table 696, accessed 8/25/2015

29   2012 US Census, via http://www.theatlantic.com/business/archive/2011/09/the-5-most-
     astounding-facts-from-the-census-poverty-report/245023/, accessed 8/25/2015

30   Bureau of Labor Statistics, via http://angrybearblog.com/2013/09/did-the-baby-boom-labor-
     force-surge-cause-the-great-inflation.html, accessed 8/25/2015

By this definition, the middle class is shrinking, but the evidence suggests that this is **because middle-class families are being drawn into the upper class,** rather than pushed out into the lower class.

Further, since the financial crisis, the top 10% appear to have taken bigger hits to income (including capital gains) than the lower 90%.[31] After including tax breaks and transfers from the government, the bottom 90% actually lost *no income at all over this time period.* **Income inequality may in fact be shrinking, even as the economy recovers.** It will be worth watching this trend further to understand what inequality in the post-recovery economy will look like.

---

31 According to a study by Emmanuel Saez and the Congressional Budget Office. Featured in The New York Times. David Leonhardt, "Inequality Has Actually Not Risen Since the Financial Crisis." 2/17/2015. http://www.nytimes.com/2015/02/17/upshot/inequality-has-actually-not-risen-since-the-financial-crisis.html?_r=0, accessed 10/29/2015.

The Rich Have Gotten Poorer Since 2007

Since the financial crisis and recession began, the incomes of the highest-earning households have fallen even more than the income of others.

Change in average pretax income of different percentiles, since 2007

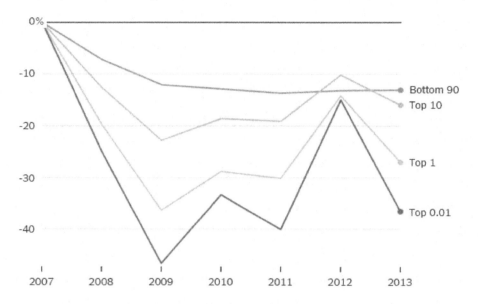

Income includes capital gains and is adjusted for inflation.

Source: Analysis of Emmanuel Saez data

"Taxed Enough Already!": The Tea Party's fierce messaging that tax rates are oppressive implies that tax rates for most Americans have been growing significantly, and are now comparatively high.

Exactly how much one pays in taxes goes beyond the federal income tax rate. In addition to payroll taxes like Social Security and Medicare taxes, Americans pay federal taxes on capital gains and interest, business profits, and a bunch of other stuff like road tolls, registration fees, excise taxes, tariffs, etc. What we actually pay is a total of all these, minus the deductions and exemptions we take.

The graph below by Bill Marsh shows what the average person in different tax brackets actually pays (their "effective tax rate").

Since the 1990s, the tax burdens on every income group have dropped, particularly for the highest 20% or so.

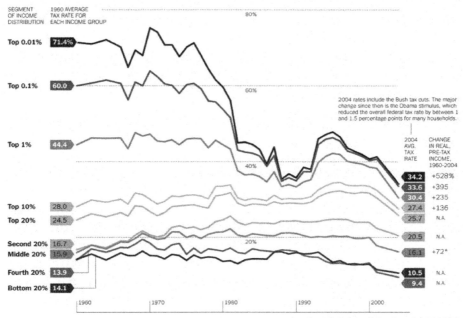

32

We can also evaluate the total tax burden by measuring how much of the GDP that the federal government receives through taxes. Since 1945, the portion of the GDP the federal government has collected in revenues has wavered between 15% and 20%, never leaving that range.[33]

Ultimately, Americans aren't paying more in taxes than they used to. Every income bracket has seen a decline in effective tax rates since the 1990s and into the 2000s and the amount of the GDP that the federal government controls has been strikingly constant over the past 70 years: government revenues have grown at the same rate as the economy as a whole.

32   The New York Times, via the Atlantic: Derek Thompson. "How We Pay Taxes: 11 Charts." 4/16/2012. http://www.theatlantic.com/business/archive/2012/04/how-we-pay-taxes-11-charts/255954/, accessed 8/25/2015. As the article explains, the tax rate has dropped a bit since 2004, but is essentially the same.

33   The St. Louis Federal Reserve. "Federal Receipts as Percentage of Gross Domestic Product." 2014. https://research.stlouisfed.org/fred2/series/FYFRGDA188S, accessed 8/26/2015

"Raising/Lowering Taxes Will Mean $X In Added/Lost Revenues": Politicians often claim that they know what changes in government revenues will be for a tax raise or tax cut. Often, the projections for tax hikes follow a simple straight line: 10% higher taxes means 10% more government revenue. Yet just as often, proposed tax *cuts* are claimed to have almost the same outcome, with politicians suggesting that a tax cut will increase government revenues by stimulating the economy.

In a given situation, both can't be true. In fact, tax revenues relate to tax rates in a somewhat complex way.

Imagine we start at an incredibly high tax rate, like 99%: in this case lowering taxes might actually increase government revenue. This might be because at 99% taxes, there is little incentive to work or those being taxed at the highest levels might move to another country instead. When France raised its top tax rate to 75%, it ended up vastly over-estimating how much money it would make, largely because it simply projected linearly, not taking into account the effect on the economy and incentives for the super-wealthy.[34]

Thinking along these lines, it seems likely that both a 0% and 100% tax rate would result in $0 in government revenue, presuming that at a 100% tax rate no one would be motivated to work to earn any money in this country, since they wouldn't get to keep any of it. It seems that the relationship between tax rate and government revenue could be represented by some sort of curve, dropping down as it approaches 0% and 100% on either side, with the tax % that would lead to the maximum amount of government revenue falling somewhere in between.

The ontological model for this (that is, the tool that's useful for thinking about it) is called the Laffer Curve. It was first drawn on a napkin in the 1970s by economist Arthur Laffer.

---

34   Andrew Lundeen, *Tax Foundation.* "France's 75 Percent Tax Rate Offers a Lesson in Revenue Estimating." 5/28/2014. http://taxfoundation.org/blog/france-s-75-percent-tax-rate-offers-lesson-revenue-estimating, accessed 10/15/2015

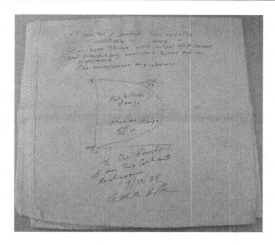

The curve is a pedagogical tool meant to show us both that tax rates don't have a linear impact on revenue, and that at some point revenues are going to drop as taxes are raised further. Unfortunately, we currently have no way of knowing where the "peak" of the curve would be: that is, at what tax rate the government generates the most revenue. Economists' estimates for this peak vary wildly, but most of the time the answer is above 50%.[35]

It's also very possible that there is not a single absolute peak, but that in different countries, in different situations, the peak will move. It could be that setting a certain tax rate causes the curve itself to shift for that country, as its economy reacts to the new tax rate. The phenomenon is extremely complicated.

Of course, maximizing government revenue may or may not be one's goal. But seeing how the complexity of economic factors plays out in this scenario should help remind us to be skeptical when someone claims they have good foresight into what will happen when taxes are increased or decreased. Are your elected representatives analyzing and discussing how changes in taxation impact total revenues when they propose a change? Or are they giving the easy answer?

35   Fullerton, Don (2008). "Laffer curve". In Durlauf, Steven N.; Blume, Lawrence E. *The New Palgrave Dictionary of Economics* (2nd ed.). p. 839

Partisan Efforts Are Wasted

Cutting CEO Pay

Occupy supporters frequently point to the CEO-worker pay ratio as evidence of a major problem in the US economy.[36] This ratio compares the average pay of CEOs in publicly traded firms to the average pay of non-supervisory workers in those firms. In 1982, the ratio was 42:1 (CEOs made 42x what workers made). By 2013, that ratio had climbed to 331:1.[37]

The rapid and dramatic increase of this ratio has caused it to come under the limelight, with many Occupy supporters calling for limitations on CEO pay. This fixation seems to imply that if CEOs were paid less, other Americans might be better off.

Let's consider for a moment that US corporate profits hit a record $1.7 trillion in 2014.[38] Clearly, US corporations have enough money to pay other workers more, even with high CEO salaries. But if existing profits are already going to shareholders, rather than workers, what evidence do we have to suggest that the revenue freed up by limiting CEO wages would go to worker wages, rather than profits? Approaching the issue of wages from other angles is likely to yield greater impact.

The disconnect between Occupy supporters and most other Americans is not that Americans don't believe that employment and worker income are not priorities. But in focusing on unproductive side issues like CEO salaries in a bid to maintain focus on an enemy group, Occupy distracts itself from focusing on solutions to increase employment rates and wages for Americans.

---

36   William Lazonick, Occupy.net "How High CEO Pay Hurts the 99 Percent." 2013. http://occu-pywallstreet.net/story/how-high-ceo-pay-hurts-99-percent, accessed 8/25/2015

37   AFL-CIO. "Executive Paywatch: High-Paid CEOs and the Low-Wage Economy." http://www.aflcio.org/Corporate-Watch/Paywatch-2014, accessed 8/25/2015

38   Tim Fernholz, *Quartz*. "What another record year of corporate profits means for the US economy." 3/27/2014. http://qz.com/192725/what-another-record-year-of-corporate-profits-means-for-the-us-economy, accessed 8/25/2015

Cutting Congressional Pay

One plank of the Tea Party's platform to significantly cut back government spending is a call for Congress to take a pay cut.[39] Citing "a time of fiscal challenge," some Tea Party-friendly Congresspeople are choosing to forego some of their benefits (like pensions),[40] demanding that others do the same. Congressional pay gets special attention as a form of government waste that needs to be brought under control.

This focus might suggest that reducing Congressional compensation could have a measurable impact on the federal deficit or taxpayer burden. But in reality, it's a drop in the ocean.

The base salary for a Congressperson in the House of Representatives is $174,000, with leadership positions paying up to $210,000.[41] Between the 541 members of Congress, total salaries are $96 million. There are benefits besides this, including travel budgets (primarily to DC from their home districts and back), the Congressional health care plan, and retirement plans, which differ a bit based on age, position, and time served, but the total per Congressperson comes out to about $286,000 each,[42] or about $155 million total.

How does Congressional compensation stack up as a part of federal government spending? The 2015 fiscal year federal budget is about $3.8 trillion.[43] Out of every dollar spent by the federal government, 0.004 cents goes to Congressional benefits. If all Congressional pay were refunded directly to taxpayers, each worker would receive about a dollar per year.

39 Teaparty.org. "Are Members of Congress Overpaid? You Decide." 8/29/2014. http://www.teaparty.org/members-congress-overpaid-decide-53185/, accessed 8/25/2015

40 Shane Goldmacher, *The National Journal*. "Nearly One in Five Members of Congress Gets Paid Twice." Available at Taxpayers for Common Sense, June 28, 2013. http://www.taxpayer.net/media-center/article/nearly-one-in-five-members-of-congress-gets-paid-twice, accessed 8/25/2015

41 Ida A. Brudnick, Congressional Research Service. "Congressional Salaries and Allowances: In Brief." 12/30/2014. http://library.clerk.house.gov/reference-files/114_20150106_Salary.pdf, accessed 8/25/2015

42 David Williams and Michi Ijazi, Taxpayers Protection Alliance. "TPA Releases Report on Congressional Pay and Benefits." 8/29/2014. https://www.protectingtaxpayers.org/index.php?blog&category_id=42, accessed 8/25/2015

43 National Priorities Project. "Federal Spending: Where Does the Money Go." 2015. https://www.nationalpriorities.org/budget-basics/federal-budget-101/spending/, accessed 8/25/2015

In fact, perhaps we might happily pay $3 for Congressional benefits and salary rather than $1 if we believed it would get us better candidates.

Just as with CEOs, focusing on Congressional pay redirects blame to a convenient enemy group, but misses the mark on actually helping address the priorities of Americans. In regards to reducing the federal deficit, more progress could be made focusing just about anywhere else.

EXTRACTING THE WEDGE: CONSIDERING THE PATH FORWARD

The simple explanations offered in response to the economic concerns of Americans neither tell the whole story nor arm us with the ability to make informed decisions about potential policy changes. As long as we let those simple explanations – and the anger associated with them – dominate the national dialogue, we'll never form a coalition to pass the policies that will create the economic opportunity and security that the country needs.

Embracing Ambiguity

Economics is a science that is often poorly understood. The complexity of the constantly-changing global economy defies full comprehension and those who dedicate their lives to studying it don't agree on how many of its elements work. Each time we observe an economic phenomenon like the recession, or each time a policy change like increasing minimum wage is introduced, economists will present an array of disagreeing theories to explain what happened or predict what will happen.

We can contrast this to sciences like physics, in which experts are able to achieve broad agreement when trying to explain most elements of how the world works. Scientists agree on how momentum, thermodynamics, and gravity work. When new data contradicts an old model or theory, physicists have an agreed-upon method by which they perform experiments on new hypotheses and achieve consensus on an updated model.

Modern humans are able to accurately and consistently launch huge payloads to distant planets, and when we fail we are able to understand why and how.

It's not yet so with economics. There are some broadly agreed-to principles about how economies work, and we can largely explain why certain countries generally thrive and others generally struggle: a great example is the difference between North Korea and South Korea. Certain economic policies like price-fixing, over-printing of currency, and central planning are consistently dangerous to an economy. Certain phenomena like "negative externalities" (pollution being a classic example) and the "tragedy of the commons" are commonly agreed to be places where the market can fail.

But there are large areas of ambiguity and disagreement. With access to the same information, different economists will often create mutually contradictory models, none of which can be fully verified. The different theories about economic boom-and-bust cycles and the impacts of regulation and income inequality on innovation and growth that underlie different economic policy proposals haven't yet been reconciled.

With respect to the minimum wage, for example, different economists have published papers saying that increasing it would increase,[44] decrease,[45] or not seriously affect[46] unemployment. The CBO estimates that a slightly higher minimum wage would slightly reduce unemployment, but that significantly higher minimum wages would increase it.[47] But there isn't agreement.

Regarding the financial crisis and recession of 2008, some economists blame low regulation on the financial industry and

---

44   The Mises Institute: https://mises.org/library/yes-minimum-wages-still-increase-unemployment, accessed 10/15/2015

45   The Center for Economic Policy Research: http://www.cepr.net/blogs/cepr-blog/2014-job-creation-in-states-that-raised-the-minimum-wage, accessed 10/15/2015

46   Studies by Katz and Kreuger (1992), Card and Kreuger (2000), Dube, Lester, and Reich (2010 and 2011), Allegrett, Dube, and Reich (2011): https://www.americanprogressaction.org/issues/labor/news/2014/02/18/84257/evidence-shows-increasing-the-minimum-wage-is-no-threat-to-employment/, accessed 10/15/2015

47   Congressional Budget Office. "The effects of a minimum-wage increase on employment and family income," February 2014. http://www.cbo.gov/sites/default/files/cbofiles/attachments/44995-MinimumWage.pdf, accessed 10/15/2015

excessive speculation,[48] while others blame misguided government-sponsored subsidies and low interest rates in the housing market that drove a dangerous bubble in the market.[49] [50] The US official Financial Crisis Inquiry Commission blames both.[51]

This ambiguity in our understanding of our massively complex economy means that simple answers are invariably going to fail to represent reality accurately. The insistence on having a simple, clear answer is important for the political industry, but it leads to destructive wedging: each camp is told to believe its answer is obviously correct and that the opposition's answer is based on foolishness or malice.

Resolving the wedge requires embracing complexity and ambiguity. We must have the courage to accept that there is much about economics that we don't understand as a society. This acceptance gives us the power to be skeptical when politicians or media present us with what looks like a clean, simple, open-and-shut answer, particularly if it conveniently finds some enemy group to blame for the economic pains we may feel. It also gives us the empathy to understand that someone that shares our values may have a different belief about the best path forward for the economy: this empathy and respect is needed to have effective conversations where we can learn more about what might be the best policy.

Alternative Paths

While the path forward is a murky one, we have some common ground to start with: the vast majority of Americans want to

---

48   *The Economist* and *Forbes* both outline the arguments clearly: http://www.economist.com/news/schoolsbrief/21584534-effects-financial-crisis-are-still-being-felt-five-years-article and http://www.forbes.com/sites/stevedenning/2011/11/22/5086/, accessed 10/15/2015

49   Norbert J Michel, The Heritage Foundation, "Government policies caused the financial crisis and made the recession worse." http://www.heritage.org/research/commentary/2015/1/government-policies-caused-the-financial-crisis-and-made-the-recession-worse, accessed 10/15/2015

50   One of the members of the Financial Crisis Inquiry Commission argues that without the government's intervention, there would be no housing crisis. Peter Wallison, *The Atlantic.* "Hey, Barney Frank: The Government Did Cause the Housing Crisis." http://www.theatlantic.com/business/archive/2011/12/hey-barney-frank-the-government-did-cause-the-housing-crisis/249903/, accessed 10/15/2015

51   The Financial Crisis Inquiry Commission. "The Financial Crisis Inquiry Report," February 25, 2011. http://www.gpo.gov/fdsys/pkg/GPO-FCIC/pdf/GPO-FCIC.pdf, accessed 10/15/2015

grow the economy in a way that will increase economic opportunities and outcomes for everyone, as well as set a tax and spending rate that will balance the national budget. Some of the more broadly-accepted parts of economic theory give us a handful of policies that are promising and merit exploration.

It's likely that the kinds of policies that drive growth focus neither on going after the rich nor slashing taxes. For example, countries that have targeted the wealthy have seen backlashes: in France, a 75% tax rate on the wealthy led to a mass exodus of the top tax bracket and a decline in both domestic investment and tax revenues. It was later canceled.[52] South American nations like Venezuela[53] and Bolivia[54] that have broken up or nationalized industries like oil or finance have seen businesses flee the country and nationalized industries stagnate and wither, leading to national defaults, food shortages, and persistently high unemployment. Southern European countries like Spain, Portugal, Greece, and Cyprus have unemployment rates in the 20%'s or greater due in part to policies that have hampered businesses and taxed the economy heavily.[55]

But there is also no evidence that cutting taxes further will lead to greater economic or job growth. Within the latter half of the 20th century, there is not a clear correlation in the US between marginal tax rates and GDP growth.[56] Often, much higher tax rates have been part of much higher growth. Within this scope, there are many policies and tax structures we could explore that could improve the American economic outlook, many of which

52   Anne Penketh, *The Guardian*. "France forced to drop 75% supertax after meagre returns." 12/31/2014. http://www.theguardian.com/world/2014/dec/31/france-drops-75percent-supertax, accessed 10/15/2015

53   Stephen Keppel, ABC News. "5 Ways Hugo Chavez Has Destroyed the Venezuelan Economy." 1/17/2013. http://abcnews.go.com/ABC_Univision/News/ways-chavez-destroyed-venezuelan-economy/story?id=18239956, accessed 10/15/2015

54   Associated Press. "The troubling trend of nationalization." 2012. Via NBC News. http://www.nbcnews.com/id/12600039/ns/business-oil_and_energy/t/troubling-trend-nationalization/#.Vh9ESPmrSM8, accessed 10/15/2015

55   Derek Thompson. "Why is Unemployment in Spain So Unbelievably High?" *The Atlantic*, 12/1/2011. http://www.theatlantic.com/business/archive/2011/12/why-is-unemployment-in-spain-so-unbelievably-high/249300/, accessed 11/3/2015.

56   William G Gale and Andrew A Samwick. The Brookings Institute. 9/9/2014. http://www.brookings.edu/research/papers/2014/09/09-effects-income-tax-changes-economic-growth-gale-samwick, accessed 10/15/2015

could be embraced by most Americans. We explore below a few that show promise, but have been pushed to the back of the debate by wedging tactics.

Reforming Education

In the United States, there is a consistently strong correlation between states with high levels of advanced education, and high levels of employment, income, and productivity – there is strong evidence for a causal relationship.[57] In short, when Americans are better-educated, they contribute more to the economy and earn more, as well.

What this means is that those who are persistently unemployed or in poverty tend to be those with less education, and that lack of education holds them back from making economic advances. The US economy has consistently created jobs that employ those with technical educations and it's likely that improving the education outcomes of lower-income Americans would drive the economy to create more.

In fact, there are already 3-4 million skilled technical or trades jobs that are going unfilled because Americans don't have the training to perform them.[58] Finding ways to train and educate Americans to fill these roles would both decrease unemployment and drive economic growth.

Focusing on education and enabling Americans to acquire skills to succeed in the job market could be a path that is both highly effective and acceptable to most Americans. This is by no means simple, but a conversation about improving the technical education of Americans is likely to bear more fruit than shouting about taking down the 1% or defunding the government.

---

57 Noah Berger and Peter Fisher, The Economic Policy Institute. "A Well-Educated Workforce is Key to State Prosperity." 8/22/2013. http://www.epi.org/publication/states-education-productivity-growth-foundations/, accessed 10/15/2015

58 Lorraine Woellert, Bloomberg Business. "Companies Say 3 Million Unfilled Positions in Skill Crisis: Jobs." 7/25/2012. http://www.bloomberg.com/news/articles/2012-07-25/companies-say-3-million-unfilled-positions-in-skill-crisis-jobs, accessed 10/15/2015

Increasing Skilled Immigration

This may seem counter-intuitive, but there is growing consensus that higher skilled immigration means more jobs for the Americans already here. This bucks the common wisdom that immigrants "take jobs from" or "compete with" native-born Americans. There is conflicting evidence about the effect of low-skilled migrants,[59] but there is fairly strong evidence that immigrants with advanced degrees – especially in scientific and technical fields – tend to create far more new jobs for natives than they occupy.[60]

ADVANCED DEGREES
2000-2007

ADVANCED
DEGREE
AND IN STEM
OCCUPATION

100 FOREIGN BORN WORKERS
= 262 ADDITIONAL JOBS

Every additional 100 foreign-born workers who earned
an advanced degree in the US and then worked in
STEM fields created an additional 262 jobs for US natives.

ADVANCED
DEGREE

100 FOREIGN BORN WORKERS
= 44 ADDITIONAL JOBS

Every additional 100 foreign-born workers with an advanced
degree created an additional 44 jobs for US natives.

For clarity: the study shows that 100 foreign-born workers with advanced degrees actually create 144 jobs; the 44 "additional" is the excess: 144 new jobs, minus an original 100 occupied by immigrants.

---

59   This is a good example where different models yield fairly different results. James Pethokoukis, *American Enterprise Institute.* "How does immigration affect US wages and jobs?" 1/29/2013. http://www.aei-ideas.org/2013/01/how-does-immigration-affect-us-wages-and-jobs/, accessed 10/15/2015

60   Ibid.

These skilled immigrants drive new jobs in a few ways. Some start their own businesses. Others work in innovative positions for domestic businesses, helping create new processes or products that lead to new hiring. Others simply contribute much-needed skilled labor that helps enable businesses to grow. All make and then spend money domestically, thereby creating new demand for service jobs in their communities.

The federal government only allows 65,000 "H1-B" visas for skilled worker immigrants per year.[61] In 2015, applications for all of these visas were submitted in 7 days after opening, and demand far exceeds the supply: in the past year, 233,000 applications were submitted.[62]

Given that these skilled migrants create new jobs in the US economy, increasing the number of skilled worker visas may prove an effective way that most Americans could support to increase employment, growth, and income in the United States. What's not clear is whether this trend would change if the numbers of immigrants became very large (say 10x or 100x the current level of skilled immigration).

The US is becoming an increasingly skilled economy; the largest computational, Internet, biotech, space, and robotics companies exist in the US, and these fields are expected to keep growing. There's strong evidence to suggest that skilled immigration will be part of the fuel that drives this engine and improves the economic outlook of the country.

The Way Forward

Amidst the mayhem of the rise of the Tea Party and Occupy movements, it appeared that Americans were farther apart than ever on how to resolve improving the economic outlook of the American people. The wedged argument started immediately with – and never graduated from – angry expressions of blame

---

61   Miriam Jordan, *The Wall Street Journal*. "Demand for Skilled-Worker Visas Exceeds Annual Supply." 4/7/2015. http://www.wsj.com/articles/u-s-demand-for-skilled-worker-visas-exceeds-annual-supply-1428431798, accessed 10/15/2015

62   Miriam Jordan, *The Wall Street Journal*. "Skilled-Worker Visa Applications by US Companies Reach High." 4/14/2015. http://www.wsj.com/articles/skilled-worker-visa-applications-by-u-s-companies-reach-high-1429056123, accessed 10/15/2015

and hatred. These groups looked for people to blame, rather than for solutions. They viewed each other as enemies on this issue: not to be worked with, but to be crushed.

The vast majority of Americans believe that all people should have great economic opportunity and believe in a safety net for when Americans fall on hard times, but don't believe in trying to make everyone equal. They believe that economic growth and employment are the best methods for improving the economic outlook of the country. **The focus on creating enemy groups out of the rich, corporations, or the government is purely a distraction from the core priorities of Americans.** Americans' priorities require making policy changes, but trying to destroy or stifle enemy groups won't accomplish their goals.

If we really want to improve the economy, our role as citizens must include **demanding evidence.** When our elected representatives or media outlets make claims about economic and tax policy, we must challenge them to describe in detail what the effects will be for Americans across the economy, and to show that the evidence in the field supports it. Such a demand for evidence will deny the political industry the opportunity to dodge reality and profit from emotionally-charged stories, and will re-direct the national dialogue towards problem-solving.

CHAPTER SIX:
DRIVING THE WEDGE
INTO BIGGER ISSUES

As we observed in the chapter on Inequality and Taxes, wedge issues often exist within the umbrella of a bigger issue: inequality and taxes are just small parts of the bigger question of how we achieve a healthy economy in the United States and how we make sure its benefits go to improving the lives of American citizens.

Such wedge sub-issues serve an important purpose in electoral politics and in news media. Many of the nation's challenges are difficult to fully comprehend and their root causes even more difficult to identify. Communicating to the public the nuance and risks behind laws made up of hundreds or thousands of pages is daunting for politicians and pundits, even when they themselves have a firm grasp of the content. And it's not likely to be well received: dry, nuanced, detail-driven discussions quickly lose the interest of our modern TV-age electorate. Wedged partisans crave simple, emotionally resonant battleground issues and most of the middle ground is no longer even tuning in.

The political industry cannot simply ignore these hugely complex issues in their communication with the public. So they choose isolated sub-components to make into wedge issues, creating the emotionally engaging, black-and-white story that will drive us to tune in and share, to vote, and to spend our money.

Below we briefly explore three instances in which the American political dialogue has been taken over by these wedge sub-issues and the greater issue at hand has been obfuscated. By understanding how some of these examples work, you'll be able to take a step back next time you see such distracting wedging in action and focus your problem-solving energies on the larger, truly important issue at hand.

ILLEGAL IMMIGRATION FROM LATIN AMERICA

"Illegal immigration is crisis [sic] for our country. It is an open door for drugs, criminals, and potential terrorists to enter our country. It is straining our economy, adding costs to our judicial, healthcare, and education systems."

> -Timothy Murphy, member of the House of Representatives (PA-18)

"[Opposing the President's executive action on immigration] is mean and xenophobic."

> -Luis Guitierrez, member of the House of Representatives (IL-4)

Immigration into the United States is the top priority issue for about 6% of the country (sometimes as high as 15%),[1] putting it on par with issues like education and the federal debt. Its impact on the US economy, as well as on government services, entitlement programs, and infrastructure, is complex and uneven.

Immigrants to the United States include skilled and unskilled labor, entrepreneurs, the very old and young. Immigration from different cultures comes in fits and starts, often settling in high concentrations in a few places.

---

1   Various polls on Pollingreport.com. "Problems and Priorities." http://www.pollingreport.com/prioriti.htm, accessed 10/3/2015

Immigration has historically been a critical part of the engine of the US economy, but the boons and burdens are often distributed unevenly, and the benefits often come with challenges. Different kinds of immigration policy help certain American groups more than others.

The issue of immigration has an interesting twist that sets it apart: opinions about immigration policy are less likely to settle along party lines than other issues we've addressed, as different interest groups within each party have different priorities. Some Democrats want to make sure immigration policy allows families to reunite, and to expand the scope of US multiculturalism. Others worry that labor migration will depress wages for American workers, especially unskilled laborers. Within the Republican Party, some welcome immigration as a way to power the economy, where others worry about a burden on government services and welfare programs. Some struggle to stomach any "legitimization" of breaking the law by accepting immigrants that don't have visas. Some of these opinions cross party lines, making it challenging for either party to form a voter-inspiring, unified platform. What results is an often confusing set of intellectual gymnastics, in which politicians or pundits espouse contradictory positions in an effort to rally different political interest groups within the party.

Immigration also carries complex political incentives for each party. Consultants and leaders of each party predict that certain kinds of immigrants into certain areas of the country are going to grow their voter base; other groups landing in other regions will grow that of their opponent. Hispanics have historically tended to vote more often for Democrats, meaning both parties predict that increased immigration from Latin America will increase the number of Democratic voters in the country. The parties believe that changes in immigration policy are likely to have an impact on the strength of the party in the future, leaving politicians awkwardly trying to balance the interests of current political constituents with the potential for growth of future political constituent groups.

From the perspective of a politician, immigration policy decisions quickly become dauntingly complex, without a clear winning policy move for either party. What level of immigration of migrants with different skillsets is the right mix for the US economy? What should we do to limit the encouragement of new illegal immigration with the need to ensure the safety and economic well-being of the 11 million illegal immigrants[2] already in the United States?

The Oversimplification and Battle Lines

For the cases of both legal and illegal immigration, there are no policy solutions apparent that are wins for all and losses for none. So politicians instead narrow their focus to a sub-issue small enough to draw tribal battle lines around: illegal immigration from Latin America.

Constrained to law-breaking activities from a particular region and ethnic group, "for" and "against" camps become easier to identify and political professionals can go ahead and break down the issue into engaging, one-line statements that are designed to trigger group loyalties, be impossible to disagree with, and discourage a nuanced discussion of the highly complex problem.

The right-wing camp emphasizes that these immigrants violated American law in order to get here. They appeal to our desire for order and safety, citing the dangers of setting the precedent that people can break our laws without consequences. Congressman Paul Broun (R-GA) says, "Illegal aliens are criminals and we need to treat them as such." Congressman Vern Buchanan (R-FL) says, "Congress should reject amnesty and heed the American people's call for border security and keeping terrorists, drug lords, and illegal gang members out of the United States." Governor Jan Brewer (R-AZ) says, "We cannot afford all this illegal immigration and everything that comes with it, everything from the crime and the drugs to the kidnappings and the extortion and

---

2   Jens Manuel Krogstad and Jeffrey S Passel Pew Research FactTank. "5 facts about illegal immigration in the US." 7/24/2015. http://www.pewresearch.org/fact-tank/2015/07/24/5-facts-about-illegal-immigration-in-the-u-s/, accessed 10/3/2015

the beheadings and the fact that people can't feel safe in their community. It's wrong!"

The left-wing camp instead calls these 11 million people simply "undocumented people/workers," emphasizing the vulnerability of people living here without the legal protections afforded to citizens or documented migrants. This camp declares itself "pro-immigrant rights." Congressman Bob Menendez (D-NJ) calls amnesty "the civil rights issue of our time."

Joshua Hoyt, of the advocacy group One People's Project, says of illegal immigration, "We don't have a leader like Martin Luther King or Cesar Chavez, but this is now a national immigrant rights movement."

Though positioned as opposition on the issue, both parties benefit politically from the framing of the issue as a false choice: political leaders are able to rally their bases while escaping the difficult task of finding and implementing a solution.

Rallying the Tribe, Calling Out the Enemy

The pro-immigrant rights camp accuses the Republican party of being motivated primarily by racism. The official Democratic National Committee twitter account claimed that "ethnic cleansing" was a priority for Republicans with regard to immigration reform.[3]

The left calls out the right for threatening the family cohesion of migrants living and working in this country. Advocacy groups like Families for Freedom[4] and the Human Rights Watch[5] talk of "tearing families apart." If you're a "pro-family" party, how can you seek to "tear families apart?" How can one oppose the "dreams" of young people in the country?

3   Official DNC Twitter account. https://twitter.com/TheDemocrats/
     status/535572411278954496/photo/1, accessed 10/3/2015

4   Minerva Carcano, Groundswell. "Suspend Deportations & Stop Tearing Families Apart."
     2015. http://action.groundswell-mvmt.org/petitions/suspend-deportations-stop-tearing-
     families-apart-while-congress-seeks-immigration-reform, accessed 10/15/2015

5   Human Rights Watch. "US: Drug Deportations Tearing Families Apart." 6/16/2015. https://
     www.hrw.org/news/2015/06/16/us-drug-deportations-tearing-families-apart, accessed
     10/15/2015

"When Scott Brown voted against [The DREAM Act], he denied the dreams of young people who did nothing wrong..."

  -Elizabeth Warren, Senator from Massachusetts

On the other side, those in the anti-illegal immigration camp accuse Democrats advocating for amnesty of "rewarding criminal behavior" and irresponsibly encouraging further illegal immigration in the future. Such rewarding is unfair to those who seek legal route into the country. Such sentiments are repeated by the US Daily Review,[6] who says, "The senate is primed to pass an immigration bill that promises only more chaos, confusion, and lawlessness." The Center for Immigration Studies,[7] The Heritage Foundation's blog,[8] and many Republican Congresspeople make the same argument.[9]

According to the right wing, their opposition is simply unwilling to make hard decisions, and instead forces communities in the southwest to bear the threat of criminal activity and the burden of an influx of new users into their education, hospital, and welfare systems.

"The Democrats are getting more and more open that they are the party of illegal immigration... in support of allowing violent illegal aliens to go free."

  -Ted Cruz, Senator from Texas and 2016 US Presidential Candidate

6   US Daily Review. "Senate Amnesty 'Rewards Criminal Behavior.'" July 6, 2013. http://usdai-lyreview.com/senate-amnesty-rewards-criminal-behavior/, accessed 10/15/2015

7   Ronald Mortensen. "DREAM Act: Rewarding Illegal Behavior to Build the New American Utopia." October 9, 2012. http://cis.org/mortensen/dream-act-rewarding-illegal-behavior-build-new-american-utopia, accessed 10/15/2015

8   Nathaniel Ward. "The Flawed 'Gang of Eight' Immigration Plan, April 18, 2013. MyHeritage. https://www.myheritage.org/news/the-flawed-gang-of-eight-immigration-plan/, accessed 10/15/2015

9   Devin Dwyer. "Senate Republicans Block DREAM Act for Illegal Immigrant," Dec 18, 2010, ABC News. http://abcnews.go.com/Politics/dream-act-senate-republicans-block-act-for-illegal-immigrant-students/story?id=12429589, accessed 10/15/2015

"...Healthcare for illegal aliens is costing state taxpayers well over $1 billion a year. Eighty-four hospitals across California have already been forced to close because of unpaid bills by illegal aliens."

-Ann Coulter, author and political commentator

"Could legalizing an estimated 11 million illegal aliens tip our precarious national finances into insolvency? Could be."

-Jim Robb, columnist at Townhall[10]

Both camps accuse the other of being politically motivated in their policy positions. Republicans accuse the Democrats of wanting to buy 11 million Democratic votes by providing welfare services from taxpayer dollars and granting voting rights to the illegal immigrants in the country.

"President Obama famously said his goal was to fundamentally transform the United States of America. And one of the critical tools he is using to try to do that is to allow millions of people to come here illegally."

-Ted Cruz, Senator from Texas and 2016 US Presidential Candidate

Democrats similarly accuse Republicans of favoring deportation in order to drive away voters that would challenge Republican supremacy in southwestern states. Huffington Post says that Republicans oppose amnesty because of electoral calculations: a fear of 11 million new left-leaning, Hispanic voters.[11] An article from Alabama's AL.com asks, "Why do Republicans resist immigration reform? Here's why:" going on to answer that, "if large numbers of Hispanics get added to the voter rolls, the Democrats will gain an edge – an edge that could tip the balance in states and districts that are closely divided."[12]

---

10   Jim Robb. "Is Amnesty Worth a National Bankruptcy?" Townhall, Feb 12, 2013 http://townhall.com/columnists/jimrobb/2013/02/12/is-amnesty-worth-a-national-bankruptcy-n1510144, accessed 10/15/2015

11   Giancarlo Sopo. "Republicans' Electoral (Mis)Calculations on Immigration Reform." Huffington Post, January 17, 2014. http://www.huffingtonpost.com/giancarlo-sopo/republicans-electoral-immigration-reform_b_4611582.html, accessed 10/15/2015

12   Brendan Kirby, "Why do Republicans resist immigration reform? Here's why." AL.com, November 20, 2014. http://www.al.com/opinion/index.ssf/2014/11/

Both camps shore up loyalty from their own partisan die-hards by painting the other as full of malicious intent towards the country or towards the families of a vulnerable population, in order to gain political advantage. The focus on war-fighting prevents progress towards resolving the issue of illegal immigration in a way that balances the needs and priorities of different people affected by it.

Beneath the Rhetoric, Nuance and Agreement

With a more nuanced, policy-centric look at illegal immigration, we see a series of priorities that must be balanced when considering immigration policy. Some of these include:

» Keeping unemployment down

» Continuing to service "low-end" jobs currently performed by migrants, like in the agricultural industry

» Ensuring that illegal immigrants are not exploited due to their status

» Limiting burdens on the welfare state and taxpayer

» Keeping schools properly staffed

» Not tearing apart families by deporting parents of children born on US soil as citizens

» Controlling property and violent crime

» Minimizing drug and weapons importations along the border

» Helping bring in new Americans that want to live and work here

» Preventing a stifling of the US economy if labor migration is too low

Perspectives on immigration are often driven strongly by emotions and group identity, as with many wedge issues about which we're struggling to hold a dialogue. But when we focus on specific policies, we see a level of agreement that might be surprising.

For each of the following elements that might be part of a new law, please tell me if you favor or oppose it as part of an immigration bill. **(Rotate list.)**

	Favor	Oppose	Not Sure
Allowing immigrants living in the country illegally to become citizens, provided they don't have criminal records, they pay fines and back taxes, and they wait more than 10 years	74	21	5
Strengthening border security and creating a system to track foreigners entering and leaving the country	85	12	3
Requiring employers to check potential employees' immigration status or face penalties	85	13	2
Deporting those living in the United States illegally and increasing border security so no immigrants can enter the country without permission	65	29	6

13

What might be most fascinating about this poll is that Americans seem to have significant agreement over two mutually-contradictory policies. The first policy allows illegal immigrants to become citizens over time; the second would deport them. At least 40% of those polled answered "favor" to both of these policy proposals: it suggests many Americans are conflicted or confused about what to do with regards to illegal immigration, rather than united in one camp or the other. This might indicate that there could be a solution between these polar policies that would be politically palatable if the voices of this group were heard in the US political system.

Analyzing the Data: The Wedge Obfuscates Real Complexity

Like with other wedge issues, most of the oversimplifications around illegal immigration simply provide false comfort for a given camp's followers.

The narrative that illegal immigrants are a significant burden on the welfare state is largely untrue. On social services or welfare, there are a few that illegal immigrants can receive – but most, they just simply cannot.[14]

---

13   Bloomberg News National Poll, May 31 – June 3, 2013. http://media.bloomberg.com/bb/avfile/rSyhOIf9XBrY, accessed 8/6/2015

14   The Southern Poverty Law Center. "10 Myths About Immigration." Teaching Tolerance, No 39: Spring 2011. http://www.tolerance.org/immigration-myths, accessed 10/3/2015

NOT Eligible for:	**Eligible for:**
Social Security	Medicare[15]
Welfare	Emergency medical treatment
Food Stamps / EBT	Schooling
Subsidized Housing	

Would Americans want the children of illegal immigrants to live in the country without schooling or emergency medical treatment? What might this mean in the long term for a portion of the population that might live here most of their lives? Without such services, a permanent underclass of sick, poor, and uneducated residents may emerge and persist.

Similarly, the "deport" strategy has large complications. How might federal or state agents find illegal immigrants? Unless the latter break a domestic law that creates plausible reason to check documentation, agents lack the constitutional authority to move home-to-home and search for illegal immigrants: it is a violation of the fourth amendment.

Even calling illegal immigrants "criminals" oversimplifies the issue. These migrants have broken the law, but most Americans break the law: some smoke marijuana, some exceed the speed limit, and almost everyone violates copyright.[16] What type or level of criminal behavior should provoke federal or state agents hunting down those who broke the law?

But simply allowing amnesty for those who migrated illegally to the United States is unlikely to come without problems. After the 1986 Immigration Reform & Control Act, the US saw a significant increase of illegal immigrants that were mostly the family

---

15   The federal government is planning to halt this, but it's only $70MM/yr: Tom Howell Jr, The Washington Times. "Illegals still get Medicare benefits, but feds vow crackdown, $70M savings." http://www.washingtontimes.com/news/2014/jan/7/illegal-aliens-may-lose-of-some-medicare-benefits/?page=all, accessed 10/3/2015

16   Centre for Research on Globalization. "Federal Copyright Laws: Americans Break Them Every Day Without Even Knowing It." 5/8/2014. http://www.globalresearch.ca/federal-copy-right-laws-americans-break-them-every-day-without-even-knowing-it/5381302, accessed 10/5/2015

members of those that had received amnesty.[17] It is likely that the amnesty was a major driver for the surge of illegal immigration through the 1990s and 2000s, in the hopes that amnesty might come again.[18]

U.S. Unauthorized Immigrant Population Levels Off

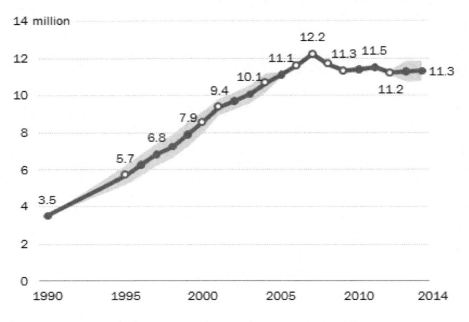

Note: Shading surrounding line indicates low and high points of the estimated 90% confidence interval. White data markers indicate the change from the previous year is statistically significant (for 1995, change is significant from 1990). Data labels are for 1990, odd years from 1995-2011, 2012, 2014.

Source: Pew Research Center estimates based on residual methodology applied to March supplements to the Current Population Survey (1995–2004, 2013-2014) and American Community Survey (2005–2012). Estimates for 1990 from Warren and Warren (2013).

PEW RESEARCH CENTER

This graph from Pew shows estimates of how many unauthorized immigrants are in the United States. We can see that between 1990 and 2007, there was uninterrupted linear growth. The unauthorized

---

17   Steven A Camarota, Center for Immigration Studies. "New INS Report: 1986 Amnesty Increased Illegal Immigration." 10/12/2000. http://www.cis.org/articles/2000/ins1986am-nesty.html, accessed 10/3/2015

18   Jeffrey S Passel and D'Vera Cohn, Pew Research FactTank. "Unauthorized immigration population stable for half a decade." 7/22/2015. http://www.pewresearch.org/fact-tank/2015/07/22/unauthorized-immigrant-population-stable-for-half-a-decade/, accessed 10/4/2015

immigrant population peaked in 2008 at about 12.2 million and then dropped, probably due in part to the recession. The Obama administration also increased border security and deportations. Since that drop, the population has stayed remarkably steady.

The United States has an immigration process and presumably wants to use it by its precepts. If the United States allowed all undocumented migrants to stay, it could receive an unlimited amount of immigrants. What would need to change in the US border policy if 100 million migrants were entering the country?

Ultimately, any solution to illegal immigration is likely to be messy, balancing costs between different groups. But the status quo may present most of the solution: **the net rate of illegal immigration has dropped to zero in the past few years.**[19] The number of total illegal immigrants peaked at about 12.2 million in 2008 and has been slightly dropping since, as illegal immigrants exit the country faster than they enter.

There are millions[20] of citizens in the US who are children born to illegal immigrants. This suggests that mass deportations would leave millions of parent-less American citizens. Eliminating the right to soil (that is, the fact that one becomes a US citizen if born on American territory) could leave millions of stateless children. These solutions leave large new problems in their wake.

But given that the illegal immigration rate has dropped to zero (which may be driven in part by the growing fence[21] along the Mexican border and doubling of border agents),[22] the situation may resolve itself in the long term: new American-born citizens

---

19   The year-over-year change of total illegal immigrants in the United States has either been negative or close to zero since 2008.

20   Philip Bump, *The Washington Post.* "How many American children are 'birthright' citizens born to illegal immigrants?" 8/20/2015. http://www.washingtonpost.com/news/the-fix/wp/2015/08/20/how-many-children-born-to-undocumented-immigrants-are-there-in-the-u-s/, accessed 10/4/2013

21   Frank Clifford, *The American Prospect.* "The Border Effect." 9/18/2012. http://prospect.org/article/border-effect, accessed 10/4/2015

22   Robert Farley, Politifact. "Obama says border patrol has doubled the number of agents since 2004." 5/20/2011. (Politifact rated this as "true.") http://www.politifact.com/truth-o-meter/statements/2011/may/10/barack-obama/obama-says-border-patrol-has-doubled-number-agents/, accessed 10/4/2015

can integrate themselves into the US population and a negligible illegal immigration rate may persist. In the long term, illegal immigration may be a problem that more-or-less goes away.

Even if the problem is not already on the way to being solved, the solution is not going to be found in mass deportation, nor in crying "racist" at those with concerns about amnesty. The solution will require balancing costs and benefits that apply over different groups in uneven ways. Recognizing this complexity will open the way to a conversation that allows us to find a solution that effectively strikes these balances.

Until then people will continue to wedge on!

THE AFFORDABLE CARE ACT

"Healthcare is the cornerstone of the socialist state. It is the crown jewel of the welfare state."

> *-Monica Crowley, political commentator*

"Healthcare should be between the doctor and the patient. And if the doctor says something needs to be done, the government should guarantee it gets paid for."

> *-Michael Moore, political commentator and documentarian*

Healthcare has been consistently a high priority for Americans, frequently rated by 10-20% of the country to be the most important issue the nation faces. The US healthcare system's quality ranks similarly to peer countries, but its costs per person have been about twice as high[23] and are growing at a rate of about 0.25% of GDP per year.[24] Coverage has been low compared to many European countries: throughout the early 2010's, the US adult uninsured rate hovered around 16-17%.[25] These Americans

---

23   The Commonwealth Fund's "Mirror, Mirror" ranking system uses data from the WHO and OECD, ranking countries' health systems by different standards of effectiveness, access, efficiency, equity, etc. 2014 edition: http://www.commonwealthfund.org/publications/fund-reports/2014/jun/mirror-mirror, accessed 10/1/2015

24   US Department of Health and Human Services.

25   Lindsey Sharpe, Gallup. "US Uninsured Rate Rises Before Health Exchanges Open." 10/24/2014. http://www.gallup.com/poll/165557/uninsured-rate-peaks-health-exchanges-open.aspx, accessed 10/1/2015

have access to care, but often must pay out of pocket, which can be very expensive.

About 70% of Americans have believed, since the early 1990s, that the US healthcare system has major problems or is in a crisis[26] and requires fixing. But the US healthcare system is a complex machine: it has a mix of coverage by state and federal government, private employers, and individual plans. Each of the 50 states has different regulations for providers and insurers. Government involvement in the system has changed and grown since the 1960s: as of 2010, Medicare and Medicaid together accounted for over 35% of all national health expenditures.[27] The reasons behind its growing costs are not easily or clearly pinned down to a few causes.

Ideas for national healthcare reform have been part of national and legislative discussions for decades, including proposals for tort and patent reform, regulatory rationalization across the 50 states, a health insurance mandate, a single-payer system, and others.

In 2008, the Affordable Care Act (ACA) entered the national dialogue and quickly became a wedge issue that dominated headlines and campaign stumps for years. The bill is massive, undergoing significant conceptual transformations in the years it was debated and even after it passed. The ACA contains dozens of provisions that most Americans don't know exist,[28] and predictions of the short- and long-term effects of the bill, as estimated by the Congressional Budget Office, are changing continually.[29]

---

26   Frank Newport, Gallup. "Americans' Views of Healthcare Quality, Cost, and Coverage." 11/25/2013. http://www.gallup.com/poll/165998/americans-views-healthcare-quality-cost-coverage.aspx, accessed 10/1/2015

27   Centers for Medicare and Medicaid Services, Office of the Actuary, National Health Statistics Group via cms.gov. Accessed 3/23/2012.

28   Between 20% and 60% of Americans aren't aware of the core building blocks of the ACA, according to Kaiser Foundation: Liz Hamel, et al. "Kaiser Health Tracking Poll: March 2014." 3/26/2014. http://kff.org/health-reform/poll-finding/kaiser-health-tracking-poll-march-2014/, accessed 10/1/2015

29   Comparing quarterly projections of total costs to the federal government, total costs to the national health expenditure, total uninsured rate, coverage by health exchanges, and other reports by quarter, available at the CBO's website: https://www.cbo.gov/taxonomy/term/45/featured, accessed through 10/1/2015

The staggering complexity of the content and ongoing effects of the ACA are threatening to the politicians attempting to turn it to their political advantage, and to political media outlets attempting to communicate about the law and its impact on the US healthcare system. In classic style, the political industry has instead reverted to emotional wedging tactics in order to engage the public, resulting in an all-or-nothing war limiting the ability of the country to nimbly and effectively respond to the strengths and weaknesses of both the bill and the greater system.

The Oversimplification and Battle Lines

The parties drew their battle lines solidly around the ACA: it passed the House and Senate with only Democratic votes. Support and opposition for the ACA among the American public is along partisan lines as well; about 75% of Republicans opposed it and about 70% of Democrats supported it throughout its lifetime:[30] introduction, amendment, passing, and implementation. Even though the contents of the bill changed between 2008 and 2010, and even though its effects did not always match predictions, partisan American support wavered little.

30 Michael F Cannon, Cato Institute. "Partisanship Plays a Larger Role in Support for 'Obamacare' than Opposition to It." *Cato at Liberty*, 6/19/2013. http://www.cato.org/blog/partisanship-plays-larger-role-support-obamacare-opposition-it, accessed 10/1/2015

SUPPORT FOR ACA ALONG PARTISAN LINES

The Washington Post and ABC News Poll

■ Democrats ▨ Independents ■ Republicans

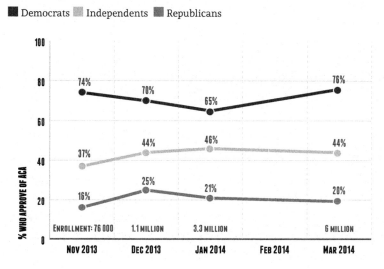

Source: http://www.washingtonpost.com/blogs/the-fix/wp/2014/03/31/democrats-support-for-obamacare-surges/

When the ACA was challenged in the Supreme Court in 2012, Republicans overwhelmingly believed the Court should find the law unconstitutional and Democrats that the Court should uphold it.[31] Americans' interpretations of the Constitution were colored by their desire to have the law be upheld or overturned.

"Most of us know nothing about constitutional law, so it's hardly surprising that we take sides in the Obamacare debate the way we root for the Red Sox or the Yankees. Loyalty to the team is what matters."

-Paul Bloom, Professor of Psychology at Yale University

The partisan divide in approval for the bill, despite the legislation's breadth and complexity, is due in large part to effective oversimplification of the bill into one-line concepts that emotionally resonated with the partisan portions of the American public. The most powerful of these oversimplifications

---

31   Jennifer Agiesta, CNN. "Poll: Majorities back Supreme Court rulings on marriage, Obamacare." 6/30/2015. http://www.cnn.com/2015/06/30/politics/supreme-court-gay-marriage-obamacare-poll/, accessed 10/1/2015

is the reduction of the 1000-page bill into a single word: "Obamacare."

Unlike other wedge issues, the ACA requires only one core moniker that worked equally well for both camps. One camp is for Obamacare and one against it. For one camp, citing the President's name makes the bill infallible; for the other, the President's name makes the bill anathema. One's stance on "Obamacare" is a declaration of one's political loyalty, far more than it is an expression on what one believes about the effectiveness of the bill.

How much does the term "Obamacare" matter? **When the term "Obamacare" is used in polls rather than "The Affordable Care Act," support by Democrats goes up 15% and opposition by Republicans and Independents goes up by 10%.**[32] It's no wonder both camps are happy to revert to this term to describe the bill.

Democratic legislators often simplify their support for the bill into a stand for "human rights." The line, "healthcare is a human right" took over rallies for Obamacare, and opportunistic politicians leapt on it.

"I campaigned on a pledge to make affordable, quality healthcare a right, not a privilege, for all Americans."

> *-Bart Stupak, former member of the House of Representatives (MI-1)*

"Healthcare is a right and we must ensure provision of that right for Americans."

> *-Bernie Sanders, Senator from Vermont and 2016 Presidential Candidate*

Linking the ACA to a fundamental right makes it difficult to disagree with any part of the bill. If access to healthcare is like freedom of religion or freedom of expression, it leaves little

---

32   Michael F Cannon, Cato Institute. "Partisanship Plays a Larger Role in Support for 'Obamacare' than Opposition to It." *Cato at Liberty*, 6/19/2013. http://www.cato.org/blog/partisanship-plays-larger-role-support-obamacare-opposition-it, accessed 10/1/2015

space to ask "how much?" and "at what cost?" or to discuss "by which mechanism?" The ACA is tied to the fulfillment of this fundamental right and can't be questioned.

Republican legislators and pundits, on the other hand, energize their own base by claiming the ACA is a "big government" disaster and a step towards "socialism."

"This is a government takeover of our healthcare system. It is the government basically running the entire healthcare system, turning large insurers into de facto public utilities, depriving people of choice, depriving people of options, raising people's prices, raising taxes when we need new jobs."

   -Paul Ryan, member of the House of Representative (WI-1)

"Obamacare is part of the socialist vision for America... to provide for the have-nots, the far left wants the federal government to seize the assets of solvent Americans. That's what Obamacare is all about."

   – Bill O'Reilly, Political talk show host

"The Stamp Act was a direct tax imposed on the colonies by King George III. This act inevitably led to the American Revolution. Just as the Stamp Act did in 1765, Obamacare should act as a wake-up call."

   -Rand Paul, Senator from Kentucky and 2016 Presidential Candidate

These framings leave no room to support the bill without also supporting "socialism" or a government takeover of a huge part of the economy. The federal government already foots about 1/3 of the total medical bill in the United States, but the wedging tactics from the right leave no room to acknowledge this or consider in any way what is the federal government's role in healthcare.

Both of these oversimplified framings force Americans to choose a side in the same way that the pro-life and pro-choice labels do. One is either "for human rights" or "against socialism," rather than existing anywhere within an ample and very grey spectrum of possible positions about healthcare.

Rallying the Tribe, Calling Out the Enemy

With a false binary established, the camps – both the political industrialists and wedged partisan citizens –pivoted their efforts to the vilification of the well-crafted evil forces in healthcare, and of each other.

Pro-Obamacare politicians and media outlets rally against the greed of the healthcare industry, particularly by insurers. These corporations have become the bogeymen responsible for the high cost of healthcare in the United States.

"The health insurance industry's outrageous greed has been nakedly exposed," says the Huffington Post.[33] Mother Jones[34] elaborates: "Sharp rise in premiums exposes health insurer's greed." Moveon.org is trying to start an online movement with the Twitter hashtag "#ShutItDownPharmaGouging." Alternet bemoans "Big pharma's out-of-control greed which is bankrupting patients."[35]

The Republican Party is framed as a band of fools, cronies, and even racists for their opposition to Obamacare. They are accused of blindly following the whims of special interest groups and manipulators due to their own lack of understanding or good ideas to bring to the table.

"[Referring to the Obamacare debate:] The last time I had to confront something like this was when I voted for the civil rights bill and my opponent voted against it. At that time, we had a lot of Ku Klux Klan folks and white supremacists and folks in white sheets and other things running around causing trouble."

   -Rep. John Dingell (MI)

---

33   Peter Dreier, Huffington Post. "Health Insurance Industry Exposes its Insatiable Greed." 5/25/2011. http://www.huffingtonpost.com/peter-dreier/health-insurance-industry_b_318066.html, accessed 9/8/2015

34   Rick Ungar, "Sharp Rise in Premiums Exposes Health Insurers' Greed." Mother Jones, September 27, 2011. http://www.motherjones.com/mojo/2011/09/sharp-rise-health-insurance-premiums, accessed 10/15/2015

35   Steven Rosenfeld, "Doctors Protest Big Pharma's Out-of-Control Greed Which is Bankrupting Patients." AlterNet, July 24, 2015. http://www.alternet.org/activism/doctors-protest-big-pharmas-out-control-greed-which-bankrupting-patients, accessed 10/15/2015

"These are nothing more than destructive efforts to interrupt a debate that we should have, and are having. They are doing this because they don't have any better ideas ... It's really simple: They're taking their cues from talk-show hosts, Internet rumor-mongers and insurance rackets."

-Senate Majority Leader Harry Reid (NV)

The anti-Obamacare camp accuses the proponents of the law of a deep conspiracy to dupe the American public into handing over their freedoms to a power-hungry state on the false promise of better healthcare that would never be fulfilled. They claim Democrats ultimately sought a malicious control over the American public through the law.

"Obamacare is not about improved health care or cheaper insurance or better treatment or insuring the uninsured, and it never has been about that. It's about statism. It's about expanding the government. It's about control over the population. It is about everything but health care."

- Rush Limbaugh, radio talk show host and political commentator

"If the government controls your health care, the government controls you. Obamacare was never about health care. It was about government power, dependency, and control."

Monica Crowley, radio talk show host and political commentator

This camp claims that the federal government has been handed the power even over your very life, via bureaucratic "death panels."

"One of the things in Obamacare is that for the elderly, is every five years, you must have end-of-life counseling. Translation: 'suicide counseling.'"

Rafael Cruz, father of Senator Ted Cruz

The America I know and love is not one in which my parents or my baby with Down Syndrome will have to stand in front of Obama's

"death panel" so his bureaucrats can decide, based on a subjective judgment of their "level of productivity in society," whether they are worthy of health care. Such a system is downright evil.

    – Sarah Palin, former Governor of Alaska

The political leaders of both camps have turned mutual antipathy and fear into greater election prospects: Obamacare was the crux of the 2010 and 2012 elections: politicians like Pelosi, Boehner, Romney, and Obama emphasized that the election could swing the long-term outcome of the ACA either way. Each camp claimed that a victory by the other side would spell doom for America, that victory was life-and-death essential, and that your vote, donation, and volunteer hours were critical. Obamacare was incredibly emotionally energizing and a highly effective wedge.

Beneath the Rhetoric, Nuance

The emotional engagement of the Obamacare wedge comes at the price of effective policy debate over the provisions of the law: hard-liner Republicans and Democrats fight furiously over a concept called "Obamacare," with intense disregard for the law's sprawling, evolving content.

There are big questions about healthcare in the United States that are important to ask in order to reform the system in a way that meets our joint priorities: improving coverage and quality, and reducing cost for everyone. The US system is a unique patchwork of institutions; exploring it in-depth is necessary to be able to improve it.

But those questions have been pushed to the background of the debate. The story of the ACA may have been very different if the national dialogue focused on some of these questions:

»   Is the employer healthcare subsidy the most efficient way of delivering healthcare?

»   How do we best use co-pays to balance access and patient incentives?

» When should children be considered adults and off their parents' insurance?

» What level of subsidy is "fair," effective, and "enough?"

» Who should pay for healthcare subsidies?

» What are the pros and cons for the government mandating certain kinds of coverage, versus letting these be optional purchases?

» What impact do government regulations, patent law, tort law, market incentives, and American lifestyle behaviors have on prices?

» What policy proposals not included in the ACA—like tort reform, patent reform, and interstate regulatory rationalization—are worth bringing to the table to discuss as additional adjustments to the US healthcare system?

When exploring healthcare in this light, we can adjust our approach to the ACA. Instead of seeing it as a monolith, we can look at the ACA for what it is: a package of many disparate policy changes, all with their own merits and drawbacks. It's likely that any given American would approve of some number of these provisions and disapprove of others. It's likely that Americans of different political ilk would have significant overlap in which policies were most attractive to them or seemed most sensible to them. But there was no space in the national dialogue for Americans to have this conversation: you had to join one camp or another.

Analyzing the Data: The Wedge Obfuscates Real Complexity

The purposeful oversimplification of healthcare involved in wedging tactics leaves us with a largely distorted understanding of what the problems are, what's involved in the ACA, and what its effects are likely to be. The wedge in healthcare pressures our thinking to be limited to what makes us angry: that government is trying to take control of our health, or that corporate greed is the main roadblock to a healthy country.

Such stories are easier to tell than the more accurate, but less satisfying, narrative of immense complexity and general lack of agreement regarding the causes of, and solutions to, the biggest problems in healthcare.

These stories are also simply misleading.

The story that the government is taking over healthcare covers a more complex reality: the insurance mandate of the ACA compels people to buy insurance from businesses, not the government (unless covered by Medicare or Medicaid). The healthcare exchanges are marketplaces through which individual customers can be linked up with private insurers. Medicaid is being expanded, but the proportion of healthcare paid for by Medicaid has been expanding steadily for decades. To call the ACA a "government takeover" or compare it to the French or Canadian systems is inaccurate.

The story of "insurance company greed" at the root of American healthcare costs covers a complex reality: health insurance companies have only 3%-4% average profit rates:[36] far below the US corporate average. The ACA is not designed to eliminate health insurance company involvement or profit. Indeed, Democratic legislators have made clear that health insurance companies will be getting "billions" in new revenues from the increase in health insurance sign-ups.[37]

But the story that the ACA is about "affordability" is also an over-simplification. The relative cost of US healthcare compared to other countries is one of the points often brought up to support the ACA, but CBO and independent estimates project that health-care costs in the US will continue to rise by over 5% per year into the 2030s,[38] without any sign of slowing. In order to subsidize

---

36   PricewaterhouseCoopers, *The Factors Feeding Rising Healthcare Costs*, 2014

37   Robert Lenzer, "ObamaCare Enriches Only the Health Insurance Giants and Their Shareholders." Forbes, Oct 1, 2013. http://www.forbes.com/sites/robertlenzner/2013/10/01/obamacare-enriches-only-the-health-insurance-giants-and-their-shareholders/, accessed 10/15/2015

38   Cynthia Cox, *Kaiser Family Foundation*. "Health spending growth expected to bounce back in coming years." *Peterson-Kaiser Health System Tracker*, 7/28/2015. http://www.healthsystem-tracker.org/2015/07/health-spending-growth-expected-to-bounce-back-in-coming-years/, accessed 10/2/2015

costs for the sick, some Americans will pay higher insurance premiums or higher taxes than they do now.

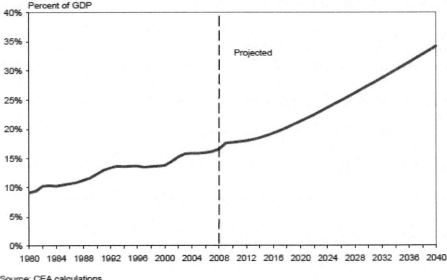

National Health Expenditures as a Share of GDP, 1980-2040

Source: CEA calculations.

Finally, the story that the ACA fulfills the "human right" of healthcare is also an oversimplification. The Congressional Budget Office's estimates of the long-term number of uninsured under the ACA have varied as the law's effects have become better understood. While the uninsured rate has dropped, there are no predictions that the long-term statistic is going to approach zero within the scope of the current law.

Ultimately, the ACA is not a revolution of the US healthcare system, for better or worse: its policies and impact are incremental. It does not represent the most aspirational claims of its most aggressive proponents, nor the direst faults claimed by its greatest detractors. The insistence by political industrialists that Americans stick to "pro-Obamacare" or "anti-Obamacare" camps—and our willingness to do so—robs us of the capacity to have very involved and difficult national conversations about what are the next best steps to take as a country on healthcare. Understanding how this wedge occurred will arm us to deny these forces in the future, when the next policy proposals about healthcare are brought forward.

BLACK LIVES MATTER

"[The Republican] party is full of racists... and the real reason a considerable portion of my party wants President Obama out of the White House has nothing to do with the content of his character, nothing to do with his competence as commander in chief and president, and everything to do with the color of his skin. And that's despicable."

-Col. Lawrence Wilkerson, former Chief of Staff to Secretary of State Colin Powell[39]

"Mr. President, in honor of Martin Luther King, Jr. and all who commit to ending any racial divide, no more playing the race card."

-Sarah Palin, former Governor of Alaska

The Black Lives Matter wedge exists within the aegis of the greater issue of race relations and outcomes in the United States. Americans believe that the umbrella issue of racial inequality is important: 70% of Americans see racism today as a major issue[40] that needs to be fixed. About two-thirds of Americans believe the country needs to make significant changes in order to achieve racial equality.[41]

Today, significant divides in socioeconomic outcomes remain between black Americans and other races, particularly white and Asian Americans. Black Americans are consistently twice as likely to live in poverty and be unemployed as whites.[42] Black

39   Ben Cohen, The Daily Banter. "Yes, the Republican Party is Racist, and here's why." 1/23/2013. http://thedailybanter.com/2013/01/yes-the-republican-party-is-racist-and-heres-why/ , accessed 9/9/2015

40   Sputnik News. "New Poll Sees 7 Out of 10 Americans Rate Racial Tensions as a Major Issue." 1/22/2015. http://sputniknews.com/us/20150122/1017212757.html, accessed 9/9/2015

41   David Lauter and Matt Pearce, The Los Angeles Times. "After a year of high-profile killings by police, Americans' views on race have shifted." 8/5/2015. http://www.latimes.com/nation/la-na-race-poll-20150805-story.html, accessed 9/9/2015

42   American Psychological Association. "Ethnic and Racial Minorities & Socioeconomic Status." 2015. http://www.apa.org/pi/ses/resources/publications/factsheet-erm.aspx, accessed 9/30/2015

Americans are more likely to attend low-performing schools, achieve lower test scores, and complete fewer years of education than whites.[43] Evidence suggests that they face racial discrimination from employers more than other races.[44] Blacks are over six times more likely than whites to be imprisoned, at a rate of over 2% of the adult black population.[45] A significant majority of Americans believe that police treat black and white people differently.[46]

There are many historical and ongoing drivers of this gap in outcomes and a great deal of disagreement over which government policies can most effectively decrease the gap. While most Americans appear to desire a decrease in the racial disparities in social and economic outcomes, many efforts over the past 50 years have made little progress in decreasing that gap. It remains politically dangerous to acknowledge the complexity and ambiguity of the issue, or to express a lack of confidence in the efficacy of many policy options proposed to make the progress that Americans want.

Instead, members of the political industry seize opportunities to strike an emotional chord with voters, donors and viewers by promoting absolutist positions and language about sensational and emotional events. One such wedge emerged during 2014 after the shootings by police of Michael Brown in Ferguson and Freddie Gray in Baltimore.

The rise to prominence of the Black Lives Matter (or BLM) movement in response to the Brown and Gray shootings reveals how quickly a wedge can be lodged into the political dialogue over a sensational incident, drowning out more productive

---

43   Lindsey Cook, US News. "US Education: Still Separate and Unequal." 1/28/2015. http://www.usnews.com/news/blogs/data-mine/2015/01/28/us-education-still-separate-and-unequal, accessed 9/30/2015

44   Farhad Manjoo, *The New York Times*. "Exposing Hidden Bias at Google." 9/24/2014. http://www.nytimes.com/2014/09/25/technology/exposing-hidden-biases-at-google-to-improve-diversity.html?_r=0, accessed 9/9/2015, accessed 9/30/2015

45   Prison Policy Initiative. "United States Incarceration Rates by Race and Ethnicity, 2010." 2012. http://www.prisonpolicy.org/graphs/raceinc.html, accessed 9/30/2015

46   Byron Dobson, USA Today. "Poll: Blacks, whites agree police treat blacks differently." 9/9/2015.http://www.usatoday.com/story/news/nation/2015/09/09/poll-blacks-whites-agree-police-treat-blacks-differently/71918706/, accessed 9/9/2015

discussion around the issues Americans state in polls they most care about.

The Oversimplification

The Black Lives Matter movement and response spawned textbook examples of oversimplified one-liners that are designed to be impossible to disagree with and to shut down any nuanced conversation.

Just as the "pro-life" and "pro-choice" camps beg the question "are you against choice?" or "against life?" in their framings, the Black Lives Matter slogan leaves little room for reasoned argument. No one wants to be heard saying that they think that black lives don't matter. And subtlety just isn't as sexy; imagine a group that disagreed with some of the interpretations or policy demands of BLM, calling themselves, "Yes of Course Black Lives Matter But We Think Sticking to the Big Picture in the Racial Inequality Problem Will Be More Effective."

Opposition monikers emerged: "All Lives Matter," and "Police Lives Matter," or "Blue Lives Matter." These slogans don't solve the problem, of course, they just constrain the discussion in a different direction: signaling that any disagreement with this platform suggests that you value some lives over others, or that you don't value the lives of police in the line of duty.

Political media made the most of this oversimplification, pulling in millions of viewers with articles defending the use of one term over the other.[47] The articles fighting over semantics went viral; those that detailed discussions over the causes of and solutions to racial inequality in the justice system and elsewhere did not.

---

47   Some of the highest-hit articles are the Wall Street Journal's "Black Lives Matter—but Reality, Not So Much" (http://www.wsj.com/articles/black-lives-matterbut-reality-not-so-much-1441755075 by Jason L Riley, 9/8/2015, accessed 10/5/2015) and Huffington Post's "What People Are Really Saying When They Complain About 'Black Lives Matter' Protests." (http://www.huffingtonpost.com/2015/04/15/black-lives-matter-protest-complaints_n_7071788.html?ncid=fcbklnkushpmg00000063, by Nick Wing, 4/15/2015, accessed 10/5/2015.)

Rallying the Tribe, Calling Out the Enemy

Of course, under the surface "Black Lives Matter" and "All Lives Matter" really mean the same thing. Most Americans do not want people being shot and killed by police unnecessarily. Most Americans do not want police being killed. These monikers don't represent meaningful differences in belief or policy: instead, they are simply stand-ins for which tribe one defends, and which tribe one is going to attack.

The Black Lives Matter camp appeals to a left-wing anti-authority cultural sentiment by focusing specifically on the killings of blacks by police, rather than other violent and nonviolent causes of death for black Americans. By focusing specifically on the deaths of blacks rather than the use of violence by police in general (which is less engaging), it appeals to a feeling of righteousness against injustice by making it an issue of racism.

The "All Lives Matter" and "Blue Lives Matter" monikers also served as their own tribal identifiers. The first appeals to a right-wing sense of being part of a silent majority, exhausted by the "race card" and claiming to be above the fray. The second appeals to a traditional respect for and admiration of servicepeople in the line of fire, like "support our troops."

Both labels spoke to the senses of identity of partisan Americans, aligning the issue along already-defined left and right political camps. Like with other wedge issues, each camp focused the bulk of its energy identifying and vilifying enemy groups.

One of the Black Lives Matter movement's co-founders said that "All Lives Matter" is fundamentally "a violent statement."[48] The other co-founder said, "Republicans are using a pattern and practice of violence against black folks to galvanize their base."[49]

48   Jerome Hudson, Breitbart. "Narrative Fail: Majority of Americans, White and Black, Prefer 'All Lives Matter.'" 8/23/2015. http://www.breitbart.com/big-government/2015/08/23/narrative-fail-majority-of-americans-white-and-black-prefer-all-lives-matter/, accessed 9/9/2015

49   Kevin Cirilli, The Hill. "Black Lives Matter Takes On The Right." 9/5/15. http://thehill.com/homenews/campaign/252814-black-lives-matter-takes-on-the-right , accessed 9/10/2015

The Huffington Post[50] and the New York Times[51] have called out the All Lives Matter part of the country as racist, specifically noting that it's a term whites use, ignoring that 64% of black Americans also prefer the term. Traditional and social media called Hillary Clinton a racist for saying that "all lives matter" at a speech she made in a church.[52]

Some of the hard core within BLM also attack the entire police force as an enemy group. Many of the protests have involved screaming at and insulting police officers as they stood nearby. To the most extreme elements of the movement, every police officer is a bad guy.

This anger became especially sensationalized when the violent chants of a very few received hugely disproportionate media attention. Black Lives Matter marchers in Minnesota apparently chanted "pigs in a blanket, fry 'em like bacon!" at the State Fair after two police were murdered,[53] their anger at the police spilling over into violent rhetoric. It seems some protesters in New York chanted, "What do we want? Dead Cops!"[54]

The All Lives Matter camp countered by saying that instead, the racists are in the Black Lives Matter camp. Fox News called it a "hate group."[55] Republican presidential candidate Ben Carson said that the movement is trying to start a race war.[56] Front Page

50   David Bedrick, Huffington Post. "What's the Matter with 'All Lives Matter.'" 8/24/2015. http://www.huffingtonpost.com/david-bedrick/whats-the-matter-with-all-lives-matter_b_7922482.html, accessed 9/10/2015

51   The Editorial Board of The New York Times. "The Truth of 'Black Lives Matter.'" 9/3/2015. http://www.nytimes.com/2015/09/04/opinion/the-truth-of-black-lives-matter.html, accessed 9/10/2015

52   Derek Hunter, The Daily Caller. "Hillary Called 'Racist' for Saying 'All Lives Matter.'" 6/24/2015. http://dailycaller.com/2015/06/24/hillary-called-racist-for-saying-all-lives-matter/, accessed 9/10/2015

53   Lee Stranahan, Breitbart. "Black Lives Matter Activists Chant 'Pigs in a Blanket' After Cop Murder." 8/30/2015. http://www.breitbart.com/big-government/2015/08/30/black-lives-matter-activists-chant-pigs-in-a-blanket-after-cop-murder/, accessed 9/9/2015

54   December 15, 2014, protest in New York City. Phone recording posted on YouTube. https://www.youtube.com/watch?v=dj4ARsxrZh8, accessed 9/10/2015

55   WND. "Black Lives Matter Under Fire as a 'Hate Group.'" 9/6/2015. http://www.wnd.com/2015/09/black-lives-matter-under-fire-as-a-hate-group/, accessed 9/30/2015

56   Charles M Blow, The New York Times. "'Black Lives Matter' and the GOP." 8/9/2015. http://www.nytimes.com/2015/08/10/opinion/charles-m-blow-black-lives-matter-and-the-gop.html?_r=0, accessed 9/10/2015

Mag calls it "profoundly racist."[57] Some mainstream outlets like the Wall Street Journal claim that because most black people are killed by other black people (and not police), the movement's focus on police means it doesn't actually care about black lives.[58] After a Pennsylvania church put "Black Lives Matter" on its front-lawn sign, they began receiving harassing and insulting phone calls from opponents to the movement.[59]

The conservative opposition camp also accuses the Black Lives Matter movement of being part of a "war on cops,"[60] or existing specifically to kill police.[61] These articles pick out a statistically negligible number of isolated incidents from among the hundreds of peace-promoting demonstrations, claiming that the actions of a few represent the underlying motivations of the entire group. Such a claim is as unlikely as the entire American police force being racist. The overexposure of the unacceptable behavior of perhaps a dozen people among tens of millions is used to falsely delegitimize the entire movement.

Beneath the Rhetoric, Nuance and Agreement

The vast majority of Americans see racial inequality as a major problem that requires significant ongoing work to be fixed. Americans don't want institutional racism. They don't want an unfair justice system. They don't want people to be unjustifiably killed by police, regardless of color. They don't want police killed on the line of duty.

---

57   John Perazzo, Frontpage Mag. "The Profound Racism of 'Black Lives Matter.'" 6/1/2015. http://www.frontpagemag.com/fpm/257808/profound-racism-black-lives-matter-john-perazzo, accessed 9/30/2015

58   Jason L Riley, *The Wall Street Journal.* "'Black Lives Matter' – but Reality, Not So Much." 9/8/2015. http://www.wsj.com/articles/black-lives-matterbut-reality-not-so-much-1441755075, accessed 9/10/2015

59   Justin Heinze, *Montgomeryville-Lansdale Patch.* "Lansdale Church's 'Black Lives Matter' Sign Invokes Uproar." 9/8/2015. http://patch.com/pennsylvania/lansdale/lansdale-churchs-black-lives-matter-sign-invokes-uproar, accessed 9/10/2015

60   Dan Gainor, USA Today. "Yes, there is a war on police: Column." 12/29/2014. http://www.usatoday.com/story/opinion/2014/12/23/new-york-police-killing-protesters-war-rhetoric-pigs-al-sharpton-war-column/20821457/, accessed 9/10/2015

61   Katie Pavlich, Townhall. "Exposing the Black Lives Matter Movement For What It Is: Promotion of Cop Killing." 9/2/2015. http://townhall.com/tipsheet/katiepavlich/2015/09/02/exposing-black-lives-matter-for-what-it-is-promotion-of-cop-jilling-n2046941, accessed 9/10//2015

Most Americans even agree in their general sentiment about police killings. 78% of Americans prefer to say "All Lives Matter" rather than "Black Lives Matter," including 64% of black Americans.[62] Americans even seem to agree on a policy package that would directly address the number of people shot and killed by police: about 80% of Americans believe that police should wear body cameras and be prosecuted by independent prosecutors.[63]

Focusing on these concrete ways to increase accountability in police interactions could make rapid progress if directed with an eye to the data, but in the current climate it is politically unprofitable. Despite this broad agreement and set of potentially-available solutions, the political industry at a senior level spends most of its time fighting over the BLM moniker, and the most engaged Americans get sucked in.

Analyzing the Data: The Wedge Obfuscates Real Complexity

The Washington Post points out that as of August 8th, 2015, 24 unarmed black men had been shot and killed by police in the year, and that they are killed at a rate 7x higher than whites.[64] Each of these is of course a tragedy and each should have a thorough, independent investigation and prosecution in order to make sure justice is served.

But the oversimplified reaction to these incidents distracts the country from addressing their root cause or the greater issue of racial inequality in the United States.

---

62   Bradford Richardson, The Hill. "Poll: Most people prefer 'all lives matter.'" 8/21/2015. http://thehill.com/blogs/blog-briefing-room/251667-poll-most-black-people-prefer-all-lives-matter, accessed 9/9/2015

63   For clarity: "independent" prosecutors are those that don't otherwise work with the police force on other cases. Requiring police assistance in prosecutorial cases is believed by some to make it politically difficult for most prosecutors to effectively prosecute police. Aaron Blake, The Washington Post. 12/29/2014. "Republicans and Democrats have vastly different views on race and police. But they agree on solutions." http://www.washingtonpost.com/news/the-fix/wp/2014/12/29/republicans-and-democrats-have-vastly-different-views-on-race-and-police-but-they-agree-on-solutions/, accessed 9/9/2015

64   Sandhya Somashekhar, et al, The Washington Post. "Black and Unarmed." 8/8/2015. http://www.washingtonpost.com/sf/national/2015/08/08/black-and-unarmed/, accessed 10/1/2015

For example: blacks are killed by police at a rate 2x higher than whites,[65] and black men are killed by police at a rate 2.5x higher than white men.[66] It can be easy to conclude that police are more trigger-happy when interacting with black men. But the arrest rate (by population) for black men is about 4x that of white men.[67] It's difficult to track the simple "interaction rate" across the nation, but these statistics suggest that per incident with police, blacks and black men are less likely to be killed than whites.

This changes when black men are unarmed, in which case they're killed at a frequency 7x that of white men, or a little less than 2x as likely per interaction. But the sample size is so small (27 black men and 20 white men in the first 9 months of 2015) that basic statistical analyses say we don't have strong confidence in that number.

Should we conclude that black men are actually generally safer than white men per arrest-worthy incident? Or perhaps black men are just targeted for arrest more often than whites for trivial reasons, and therefore most police interactions with black men are less likely to escalate? It's tough to say.[68]

Knowing these statistics can lead us to more complex and messy, but more useful, questions: what is causing the higher rate of arrests for blacks and black men in the US? How much of it is related to poverty, to the war on drugs, to population density, or to criminal activity? Blacks are convicted of violent crime at a rate five times higher than that of whites: how much of that is due to higher criminal activity and how much due to racial prejudice in the justice system? How much might be due to the poverty rate among blacks resulting in on average less

---

65   Between January 1 and October 1, 2015, the date this section was written. Using The Guardian's statistics from "The Counted: People killed by police in the US:" http://www.theguardian.com/us-news/ng-interactive/2015/jun/01/the-counted-police-killings-us-database#, accessed 10/1/2015

66   Ibid.

67   Brad Heath, USA Today. "Racial gap in US arrest rates: 'staggering disparity.'" 11/19/2014 http://www.usatoday.com/story/news/nation/2014/11/18/ferguson-black-arrest-rates/19043207/, accessed 10/1/2015

68   This is an area that seems to lack a popular, rigorous study. We look forward to finding a rigorous study on this topic.

competent lawyers working in their defense? Can that question be accurately answered? Probably not with the average attention span of a modern media outlet.

Quickly, the issue becomes murky and complicated. Such an analysis does not provide an obvious enemy group or a simple solution, so it does not receive the same kind of media and political attention as one-line slogans.

The "Blue Lives Matter" framing is also overly simple. This response to Black Lives Matter suggests that police are at a disproportionate or growing risk of violent death or murder than other people. But the data suggests otherwise. 2015 has seen a decrease in killings[69] from 2014,[70] and with the exception of spikes in 2010 and 2011, the number of police killed per year has been on a steady decline since 2000.[71] In 2013, 27 police officers were feloniously killed; in 2014, the number was 51 (a temporary spike in an otherwise-steady decline).[72] This puts them at an average victimization rate of about 4.3[73] per 100,000 officers per year, which is slightly lower than the overall US murder rate of 4.7. In other words, it's slightly safer to be a police officer than a regular citizen. This seems unexpected, as police are in harm's way far more often. But it appears that any seeming crisis in the safety of police officers is overstated.

---

69 We're specifically tracking police killed by civilians, rather than dying of heart attacks, car accidents, etc. These are called "felonious deaths" by the FBI.

70 Michael Tarm, Associated Press. "Are More Police Getting Killed? A look at law enforcement deaths across the US." 9/2/2015. http://www.usnews.com/news/us/articles/2015/09/02/a-look-at-recent-law-enforcement-deaths-across-the-us, accessed 9/10/2015

71 National Law Enforcement Officers Memorial Fund. "Officer Deaths by Year." http://www.nleomf.org/facts/officer-fatalities-data/year.html?referrer=https://www.google.com/, accessed 9/10/2015

72 FBI National Press Office. "FBI Releases 2014 Preliminary Statistics for Law Enforcement Officers Killed in the Line of Duty." 5/11/2015. https://www.fbi.gov/news/pressrel/press-releases/fbi-releases-2014-preliminary-statistics-for-law-enforcement-officers-killed-in-the-line-of-duty, accessed 10/9/2015

73 This is based on an estimate of about 900,000 federal, state, and local police from the FBI Bureau of Justice Statistics: Brian A Reaves. "Federal Law Enforcement Officers, 2008," June 2012. http://www.bjs.gov/content/pub/pdf/fleo08.pdf; and Brian A Reaves, "Census of State and Local Law Enforcement Agencies, 2008." July 2011. http://www.bjs.gov/content/pub/pdf/csllea08.pdf, accessed 10/9/2015

We must also note that black men are about 23 times more likely to be murdered by a citizen than killed by a police officer.[74] It's likely that most Americans would agree that every time a black man is killed, or anyone else for that matter, the country should strive to conduct a full investigation and provide justice. For the preservation of the lives of black men, the data suggests that the bigger impact will come outside of police reform. But a dispassionate examination of the data does not engage an audience the same way that sensational incidents do, and thus the former takes a back seat to the latter in the political discourse.

The wedge tactics that make us focus so exclusively on the deaths of black men at the hands of police, and police at the hands of citizens, distract the country from having the important conversations around the state of racial inequality and race relations that the majority of us want to tackle. The Black Lives Matter movement is just one of several wedge sub-issues in the umbrella of race relations. But taking notice of the tactics being used in the national dialogue helps us take a step back and focus on the bigger issue at hand.

Getting Back to the Big Issues

Either by emotionally charging low-priority issues like abortion and guns, or by focusing attention on simplistic, soundbite-ready components of large complex national issues like immigration, healthcare, and race relations, partisan camps continuously take over the public discussion and remove nuance from it.

In hugely complicated policy questions like immigration and healthcare, support and opposition represent something closer to team loyalty than real policy preferences. On issues like race and gender, Americans deeply share core values, but the emotional nature of these issues has been exploited into the formation of unnecessary camps that focus primarily on controlling the narrative of events to paint the other side as

---

74   Comparing the number of black men killed by police from the Guardian's "The Counted" to the total number of homicides of black men, using the FBI Uniform Crime Reports' "Crime in the United States 2013: Expanded Homicide Data Table 1.": https://www.fbi.gov/about-us/cjis/ucr/crime-in-the-u.s/2013/crime-in-the-u.s.-2013/offenses-known-to-law-enforcement/expanded-homicide/expanded_homicide_data_table_1_murder_victims_by_race_and_sex_2013.xls, accessed 10/1/2015

evil. This wedge effect drives political power to the fringes of American politics, drives votes to the politicians that exploit it best, and drives viewers to the media outlets that sensationalize it most completely. It hollows out the middle ground of American politics and stifles any productive investigation of these problems that could lead to a constructive solution.

Unlike the cases of abortion and guns, these issues cannot be easily compromised away or simply deprioritized. They have real substance and often represent a need to balance costs and benefits, different priorities and values we hold. If the wedge was removed from these issues, a long discussion would likely continue, with new proposals and sometimes even bitter fights over different constituencies with something to gain or lose in the debate.

Removing the wedge won't end debate, but it will open the path to making progress. It will free the minds of Americans to think independently about the real implications of different policy proposals. It will enable us to hold our representatives accountable for results, rather than simply hold them accountable for opposing the other party. It might also give life to politicians that are not simply voting along party lines.

And in the end, taking the wedge out of these more substantial issues works the same way as taking it out of the classic wedge issues.

PART III
HOW WEDGE ISSUES DIE

"Human progress is neither automatic nor inevitable... Every step toward the goal of justice requires sacrifice, suffering, and struggle; the tireless exertions and passionate concern of dedicated individuals."

-Martin Luther King, Jr.

Wedge issues don't have to be permanent sores on the nation's dialogue. We are accustomed to cases like abortion in which very little has changed in American opinions or the tenor of dialogue, and it seems like we will be stuck with it as a wedge issue for many years to come. And we've seen other issues like inequality and taxation flaring into becoming wedge issues after lying dormant for some time.

But wedge issues can die. Examining how they do may provide us with a model for resolving the wedge issues that the country continues to face. The following recent case study gives us hope that things can change.

Chapter Seven:
Gay Marriage: A Case Study

"Gay rights is just a matter of time. Look at the polls. Worrying about gay marriage, let alone gay civil unions or gay employment rights, is a middle-age issue. Young people just can't see the problem. At worst, gays are going to win this one just by waiting until the opposition dies off."

> -Gail Collins, journalist and columnist

Gay marriage is probably the best recent example of a once-powerful wedge issue that is quickly dying out. It was the dominant wedge issue in the United States for about 15 years, but suddenly fizzled in the early 2010's. How did this happen?

A Brief History of Gay Marriage

In the United States, up through the 1960s, the gay community lived largely in the shadows: being gay was something kept private. Homosexuality was illegal in 49 states.[1] The question of

---

1   Illinois was the only state that did not outlaw homosexuality. As a historical footnote, "sodomy" was illegal in 14 states until 2003, when a supreme court decision found such bans unconstitutional.

whether gay people should be allowed to marry simply did not cross the minds of most people. It was common to believe that being gay was a form of sexual perversion. A 1966 CBS report said that "the average homosexual, if there be such, is promiscuous. He is not interested in, nor capable of, a lasting relationship like that of a heterosexual marriage."[2]

After the Stonewall Riots of 1969,[3] the national discussion about gay rights caught traction. More gay people started to "come out" in public, and the United States had to confront the fact that gay people really existed. National exposure to LGBT people increased as the storied history of gay rights unfolded.

But opposition to gay marriage remained so complete that it remained out of the national dialogue for decades. Gallup, for example, didn't even begin polling Americans about their positions until 1996. At that time, a 27% minority favored gay marriage.

As exposure to gays in America outpaced acceptance, a stiff opposition rose to gay marriage. In 1993, President Clinton enacted "Don't Ask, Don't Tell," (DADT) which banned openly gay members of the military. In 1994, Hawaii became the first state to ban gay marriage. In 1996, Congress passed with over 85% approval[4] the Defense of Marriage Act (DOMA), which barred federal recognition of gay marriage. By 1997, 27 states had banned gay marriage.[5]

We see the wedge beginning here: more than half of the union banned gay marriages even though they weren't occurring. The increasingly public presence of gay culture in America was taken advantage of by largely conservative politicians in order to stoke fear in voters of a collapse of traditional mores and values. Their voters reacted by demanding bans in their states

2   Stephen Holden, *The New York Times*. "June 28, 1969: Turning Point in Gay Rights History." 6/15/2010. http://www.nytimes.com/2010/06/16/movies/16stone.html, accessed 9/10/2015

3   These riots were a series of violent demonstrations by the LGBT community and its supporters after a police raid at the Stonewall Inn in New York City.

4   224 Republicans (all but one) and 118 Democrats (vs 65 nay) voted for HR 3396 DOMA. Govtrack.us. https://www.govtrack.us/congress/votes/104-1996/h316, accessed 10/22/2015

5   Procon.org. "50 States with Legal Gay Marriage." http://gaymarriage.procon.org/view.resource.php?resourceID=004857#timeline, accessed 8/21/2015

and demanding that the federal government pass DOMA. The issue of gay marriage had been painted as a threat to the identity and values of conservative Americans, so it suddenly became a critically important political issue.

Like in the case of other wedge issues, the emotional partisanship of one side created its own opposition. In the late 1990s, support for gay marriage reached 35% and advocates began serious efforts to make gay marriage legal in friendly states. As an anti-gay marriage camp solidified, a pro-gay marriage camp emerged, also suddenly convinced that gay marriage was a critically important issue. In 2000, a lawsuit in Vermont resulted in the state Supreme Court declaring that the Vermont constitution already protected gay marriage.

RAPID TURNAROUND IN SAME-SEX MARRIAGE LAWS

- ■ States where same-sex marriage is banned
- ■ States where same-sex marriage is legal

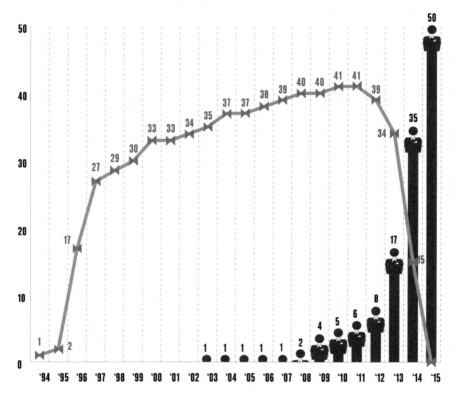

This graph shows us the very rapid turnaround in the legal status of gay marriage in the United States. Gay marriage only reached national policy attention in the mid-1990s, when states like Hawaii and North Carolina started passing laws banning it. By 1997, the majority of states had outlawed gay marriage. In 2003, Massachusetts became the first state to allow gay marriage, but any momentum did not pick up until the late 2000s. From 2008, when Connecticut legalized gay marriage, only six years passed before 35 states in the union had legalized it. It took only 21 years from the first ban to the complete national legalization.

A flurry of activity began. Funding for pro-gay marriage organizations like the Human Rights Campaign and anti-gay marriage organizations like the National Organization for Marriage exploded. Gay marriage became an issue at the top of national and state candidates' list of talking points. Conservative state legislatures scrambled to pass legislative or constitutional bans. Marriage equality advocates began to challenge these state-level bans in courts across the country.

It's here that we see the kind of activity that we associate with traditional wedge issues: camps formed with identifying, simple monikers: "pro marriage equality" and "pro marriage" or "defending marriage," and protests and demonstrations around every legislative or court decision. Each camp focused on denouncing the other as "bigots" or "attacking traditional families." Over the history of Gallup's polling, never more than 1% of respondents said gay marriage was the most important issue facing the country. The emotion and effort poured into the gay marriage war far outweighed its relative importance to most Americans.

But unlike the other wedge issues we've seen, gay marriage reached resolution, and quickly. By the late 2000s, state supreme courts began overturning gay marriage bans and support for gay marriage reached parity with its opposition. Before the 2015 Supreme Court ruling that made gay marriage legal throughout the United States,[6] 37 states legalized gay marriage on their own; 29 of those legalizations occurred in 2012 and 2013 alone. It was one of the most rapidly reversed social policies in the history of the US.

If we look at polling over time, we see a pretty steady trend. The fairly consistent growth of support for gay marriage[7] (and the fact that voters under 30 support gay marriage with a whopping 78% majority)[8] may be convincing many politicians hoping for future election that the time to abandon opposition to gay marriage is yesterday. President Obama, for example, switched his stance on gay marriage from being opposed to being in favor in 2012.

---

6   This announcement reverberated across the world, heard at gay pride rallies in dozens of countries.

7   Justin McCarthy, Gallup. "Same-Sex Marriage Supported Reaches New High at 55%." 5/21/2014. http://www.gallup.com/poll/169640/sex-marriage-support-reaches-new-high.aspx

8   Ibid

STEADY MOMENTUM IN SUPPORT FOR SAME-SEX MARRIAGE

Do you think marriages between same-sex couples should or should not be recognized by the law as valid, with the same rights as traditional marriages?

■ % should be valid   ■ % should not be valid

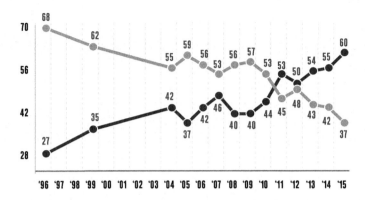

Note: Trend shown for polls in which same-sex marriage question followed questions on gay/lesbian right and relations. 1996-2005 wording "Do you think marriages between homosexuals..."

GALLUP

Even before the gay marriage question was resolved, the sense of crisis had abated; it adopted an air of inevitability. By 2012, gay marriage was at the very bottom of Pew's poll of most important issues in America[9] and in 2015 marriage simply doesn't register on the charts when Americans are asked to identify their top priorities. Most Americans have moved on to other issues, no matter which side of the question we took. It's not that nobody cares any more, but simply that it seems "settled" to most Americans and not as important as everything else that the country needs to face.

Just before the 2015 Supreme Court ruling on gay marriage, between 60%[10] and 63% of Americans supported it, with 36% opposing.[11] Enough opposition remains that it could remain an effective wedge issue if the conditions were right. But the

---

9   Pew Research. "Social Issues Low on Voters' Minds in 2012." 4/26/2012. http://www.pewre-search.org/daily-number/social-issues-low-on-voters-minds-in-2012/, accessed 9/10/2015

10   Justin McCarthy, Gallup. "Record-High 60% of Americans Support Same-Sex Marriage." 5/19/2015. http://www.gallup.com/poll/183272/record-high-americans-support-sex-marriage.aspx, accessed 8/21/2015

11   Freedom to Marry. "Polling Tracks Growing and Increasingly Diverse Support for the Freedom to Marry." 6/8/2015. http://www.freedomtomarry.org/resources/entry/marriage-polling, accessed 8/21/2015

opposition has been crushed. Three in four Americans see gay marriage legality as "inevitable"[12] – something that hasn't happened in other wedge issues like guns and abortion.

WHAT KILLED THE ISSUE?

Support for gay marriage continues an uninterrupted climb and its importance has dropped in the minds of most Americans: contrast this to abortion, where Americans' opinions have been almost completely unchanged since *Roe v. Wade*.[13] What drove the wedge out of the question of gay marriage? We know a few of the factors involved, and can make educated guesses at others.

Some of what has removed the teeth from this issue might be that support is visible among almost every demographic group (conservatives support gay marriage at 31%; 37% of Republicans support it; Southerners show 48% support and Midwesterners 53%;[14] Blacks, Hispanics, Republicans, Catholics, and even young Evangelicals show significant support),[15] so even those who oppose gay marriage probably know plenty of people (even those they like) that support it. Much of this may be driven by the fact that whether one is gay likely has very little to do with one's political affiliation, race, etc. As more Americans came out as gay, more Americans began to know personally people that were gay.

The gay community has also focused patiently on outreach – rather than outrage – in order to win allies. The community focused on demonstrating that they and other Americans were

---

12   Pew Research. "Support for Same-Sex Marriage at Record High, but Key Segments Remain Opposed." 6/8/2015. http://www.people-press.org/2015/06/08/support-for-same-sex-marriage-at-record-high-but-key-segments-remain-opposed/#most-americans-say-legal-same-sex-marriage-is-inevitable, accessed 9/10/2015

13   Karlyn Bowman and Jennifer Marsico, *The Atlantic*. "Opinions About Abortion Haven't Changed Since Roe v Wade." 1/22/2014. http://www.theatlantic.com/politics/archive/2014/01/opinions-about-abortion-havent-changed-since-em-roe-v-wade-em/283226/, accessed 8/21/2015.

14   Ibid

15   Peyton M Craighill and Scott Clement. "Support for same-sex marriage hits new high; half say Constitution guarantees right." 3/5/2014. http://www.washingtonpost.com/politics/support-for-same-sex-marriage-hits-new-high-half-say-constitution-guarantees-right/2014/03/04/f737e87e-a3e5-11e3-a5fa-55f0c77bf39c_story.html?hpid=z4, accessed 8/1/2015.

similar, with the same core values. If the LGBTQ community had focused primarily on vilifying those that disagreed with gay marriage rather than having focused on creating empathy, the outcome might have been different.

Taking Power Away From Politicians

But by far the biggest factor in the rapid legal victory for gay marriage was the legal strategy of gay marriage advocates. By focusing on seeking legalization through the state supreme courts (and their interpretations of the state constitutions), gay marriage advocates were able to take the power of the decision out of politicians and into the hands of lawyers and judges, who do not have the same need to pander to partisans.

The push for legalization of gay marriage has focused mostly in courtrooms (26 of 37 states) rather than the legislature (8 of 37) or popular referendum (4 of 37).[16] Those latter 12 states are all reliably Democratic (so it was less of a contentious issue during the vote) and held most of the votes in the past 2 years, where the movement had already had serious momentum and a majority of support across the country. The turning of gay marriage from "nonexistent" to "inevitable" occurred in the courtroom.

The only major nation-wide actions on gay marriage since the 1996 legislative passing of the Defense of Marriage Act (DOMA) were its repeal in 2013 and the 2015 nationwide legalization of gay marriage. Both of these came from the Supreme Court, rather than legislature. This means that congressional and presidential candidates have largely had the wind taken out of their sails as they have very few policy positions they could take in order to take advantage of passion about gay marriage. This limits the amount of wedging they can do.

Court action has a good track record in granting legitimacy to a law or policy (however unintentionally), often by invoking the US Constitution (or state Constitutions) as the justification of a certain law or liberty. These kinds of rulings differ greatly from the heated debates of "good and bad," "right and

---

16   Procon.org. "50 States with Legal Gay Marriage." 7/1/2015. http://gaymarriage.procon.org/view.resource.php?resourceID=004857#timeline, accessed 8/21/2015

wrong" in legislatures and referendums. Citing the Constitution often makes it easier to accept what we might otherwise find appalling, like the right for the KKK or Westboro Baptist Church to have public rallies.

Furthermore, many judges are far less subject to the whims of public support and need not use wedging, grandstanding, or other "fire-up" tactics in order to win support to continue at their post. This relative immunity from the ugly business of electoral politics removes the incentive to manipulate the American public and keeps rhetoric focused on policy rather than sweeping statements of good and evil (often to the disappointment of even the supporters of the ruling).

Because politicians' primary motivations are to get re-elected, their primary incentives are to keep their supporters excited. This means elected politicians have a greater incentive to keep an issue alive than to resolve it. Skipping elected politicians entirely was key in the rapid ascendancy and victory of the gay marriage movement.

WHAT CAN WE LEARN FOR OTHER WEDGE ISSUES?

Ultimately, when policy questions are decisively resolved, their potential to be used as wedges withers significantly. For a politician to be re-elected, it's more valuable to have an existential enemy than it is to have a track record of success. Going through courtrooms rather than through legislatures is an effective way to get decisive decisions rather than endless grandstanding.

How can we learn from the resolution of gay marriage in the US? A few possible ingredients for success:

» When an issue is crafted such that politicians gain more by fighting about it than resolving it, they're unlikely to seek resolution, and alternative paths may be more effective: courts, referendums, etc.

» "Charm offensives" are likely more effective than war-fighting: issues are best resolved when public opinion changes, and that requires going through the patient process of changing minds, rather than trying to crush the enemy.

» Creating appeal and exposure across different demographic and political groups will erode hard-core partisan camps: when someone knows and respects a lot of people that disagree with them, it becomes harder to vilify the entire set of people who hold that opinion.

PART IV
OVERCOMING THE WEDGE

"As you navigate through the rest of your life, be open to collaboration. Other people and other people's ideas are often better than your own. Find a group of people who challenge and inspire you, spend a lot of time with them, and it will change your life."

-Amy Poehler, American comedian

The middle ground in American politics has been slowly dissolved by the tactics political professionals use to manipulate us into reliably viewing and voting. Most of those issues we become most angry about are not our highest priorities. Our anger is fueled by repeated exposure to oversimplified messaging designed specifically to elicit intense emotion.

We now understand how wedging works and why it is so powerful. We know it's at the root of political dysfunction in the US, and if nothing is done gridlock and hyperpartisanship are only going to get worse.

And we know that it's not in the interest of the politicians or media to drive this change. The political industry has very powerful incentives to maintain the status quo, and demanding change from the industry is a waste of time.

When problem solving, the first step is always to rigorously define the problem. We know now that the current American political climate is highly fertile for wedging: Americans are effectively manipulated by, and contribute to, these emotional tactics. We buy into and reinforce these oversimplified, hostile narratives because they exploit the tribal parts of our brains.

It's too late to simply demand that others change. We ourselves, the American public, are a fertile soil of political climate in which wedging tactics now blossom.

For those that wish to fight back against the forces of the wedge, the winning strategy is to change the soil in which the flowers of wedging bloom – that is, to **build a new mindset for ourselves and those around us that makes wedging tactics ineffective**, and turn our culture instead towards one that ignores and condemns such tactics, favoring instead an effective discourse between different perspectives.

This process starts by changing ourselves. By allying with partisan camps or dropping out of politics, we feed their power and neutralize our own effectiveness. We must instead change our own mindsets and behavior: by doing this, we start to fight back against the wedge, and become once again powerful agents in US politics.

There are three new mindsets that, when cultivated in ourselves, will turn us into agents for positive change:

1. **"Hey, wait a minute."**
   Recognize when you're being wedged. Because wedging tactics effectively tap into our natural instincts, if we make no conscious effort to notice that it's happening, we will contribute to the wedge and propagate it. Noticing when we're being wedged allows us to reject the attempt to manipulate us and gives us the awareness we need to stop contributing to the problem.

2. **"I want to learn more."**
   Choose to educate yourself about the political issues of our time. Wedging tactics paint an issue as a false, extreme binary. We've seen that diving deeper reveals incredible nuance and complexity behind these issues: the simplicity of the conventional story is either deceptive

or simply incorrect. Developing a deep sense of curiosity about issues – wedgey or otherwise – enables us to develop our own sophisticated viewpoints that better reflect reality and lead to better solutions for the country.

3. **"This is unacceptable."**

   Use your voice to make clear that wedging behavior is unacceptable around you. When politicians do it, we need to call them out. When media does it, we need to vote with our feet and change the channel. When our well-intentioned friends participate in it, we need to gently help them understand that their warfighting approach is politically ineffective and puts them in a pigeon-hole. We can help them see that there is more nuance than they're stating, and that they share many values with their perceived enemies.

Chapter Eight:
Starting With
Ourselves

"You must be the change you wish to see in the world."

   -Mahatma Gandhi

Recognizing when we're being wedged requires alertness. We must be looking for the signs of wedge issues as we encounter others talking about them, whether they are politicians, media, or our friends. We need to look into ourselves for the emotional reactions that we're manipulated into feeling. When we become aware of these reactions, we can start to overcome them.

We know the 7 tactics used in wedging and should refresh ourselves on them from time to time to make sure we know how to identify the elements of a discussion that make it destructive. With knowledge of these tactics at your side, you can become highly attuned to wedging. When listening to political speeches or media commentary, when reading comments and memes online, look for the tell-tale signs of wedging tactics. This is most easily done when observing the people that disagree with you:

the brain is naturally more skeptical when exposed to opinions that don't resonate.

Then look to yourself: What other issues are you passionate about that might be causing you to think of other Americans as political enemies? Do you find yourself talking with your friends about politics in a way that indicates you see the opposition as a monolithic enemy? As dumb, or malicious? Do you find yourself falling back into the trap of hoping certain data is true, and rejecting certain data that doesn't agree with what you already think?

Look for when you divide people into two camps. Look for when you pretend that the worst part of the opposition represents the whole thing. Look for when you leave no room for question, debate, and nuance in an issue.

CULTIVATING CURIOSITY

Consider these kinds of questions going forward as you speak about politics to your friends, coworkers, and others around you. When we notice and reject the wedging tactics around us and the reactive emotions within us, we will naturally become curious to understand the issue better: we need only take that curiosity and run with it to become better citizens.

It is important to research these issues independently, but it's just as important to open our ears to Americans around us with opinions that don't match ours.

When we only talk politics with those that agree with us, we create echo chambers that reinforce false assumptions and beliefs founded on only half the picture. We learn nothing and begin to believe there are no other legitimate points of view. We make the chasm greater and contribute to the broken system.

We can re-create the environment where it's enjoyable and effective to discuss how to make the country and world a better place. But to do that, we need an inviting, productive way of talking that's different from our current norm.

As we've seen reviewing the wedge issues, Americans have a deep core of shared values and are capable of a great deal of capacity to reach agreement on seemingly-intractable issues. By finding those shared values first, at the beginning of the conversation, we establish that we're on the same team, rather than each other's enemies. It's a small change, but we may be surprised at how much more pleasant political conversation can be.

In these new kinds of conversations, curiosity dominates and competitiveness takes a back seat. In these kinds of conversations, we can mine the depths of what others truly think and why. This will not only give us a better base by which to work together, but might actually cause us to refine our own thinking.

CHAPTER NINE:
CHANGING THE SOIL

"If we want to live freely and privately in the interconnected world of the twenty-first century – and surely we do – perhaps above all we need a revival of the small-town civility of the nineteenth century."

-James Gleick, author and historian

Taking the power away from wedging is a daunting task: it requires changing the soil of political culture in the United States such that it is no longer fertile to the seeds of these tactics.

The history of cultural change in the United States offers us a blueprint for success. If we study how racism, sexism, and other toxic cultural behaviors have lost power in the country, a common ingredient becomes apparent: people that believed the behavior was wrong had the courage to tell others that the behavior was unacceptable when they saw it happening.

Many years ago, it was acceptable to say, "I'm not going to go to that party because there are black people there," or, "I don't want Jews in my club." It was once acceptable to think of women as inferior to men, and once crazy to say that political speech should be free. In all of these, it was the convictions of individuals on the right side of history that turned the tide. They not only had the guts to say that these old ways of thinking were no longer acceptable, but they had patient and compelling arguments that inspired others to change. The mindsets around these issues changed slowly, over decades, even if the outward, visible signs of public perception changed quickly. It took millions of people engaged in billions of interactions to move forward.

The process of changing American political culture could take a generation if we do nothing and allow these habits to persist in ourselves: change would occur only when political dysfunction becomes so precarious that younger generations reject our ways. But imagine what we can do if instead each of us creates a pocket of excellence in our friends, where political discussion is civil, engaging, and productive. Imagine if millions chose to turn off the media that amplifies wedging. Imagine if tens of thousands wrote letters to the editor of their newspapers that call out the invalidity of politicians' framing of a false binary.

BEGINNING THE CHANGE

Changing mindsets is more easily done with friends than enemies: this is where an agent for change should start.

Find a friend that has some different political opinions, and explore together wedging that you see in day-to-day life. Share what you find across the political spectrum. Start to alert each other to when each of you is engaging in these wedging habits, and be open to hearing the honest feedback from your friend. Help each other think hard about where you really stand on an issue, embracing the complexities and complications of your position, the benefits and drawbacks of yours and others.

After some practice, try choosing to not engage in the false binaries posed by others. Don't be sucked into agreeing completely or fighting: this powers the system. Instead, gently head towards the nuanced ground of your true position. You might say that you largely agree, but have a few questions. You might say that you see some of the arguments from different angles. Perhaps you recognize that there's more to explore and you don't have all the perspectives. You don't need to pick a fight, or to challenge someone's identity: you can simply refuse to engage with the framing of "with me or against me." By doing this, you deny some of the energy that propagates the wedge in American politics.

In time, you may be able to spread this new thinking. If you help your closest friends and family members to begin to see that participating in the wedge is unacceptable and politically ineffective, a small pocket of excellence will grow. Within it, a social convention can dominate: "here, no wedging allowed."

In these groups we can intervene when we hear something that amounts to, "if you don't agree with me 100%, you're a bad person." Others that begin wedging tactics will be gently shut down by the group and walk away wondering: "what's changing in my world?" They might get curious in time and start to ask questions. In time they, too, will begin to understand why their participation in the wedge is bad for themselves and others. Rinse, lather, repeat.

This will probably take a long time to change, but it does not have to. With the right effort, we can shorten that time to reclaim the American political dialogue, end our dysfunction, and solve together the problems that most need solving.

This effort starts with each of us. To take our power back, we – each individually – need to be aware of the wedging that's going on around us, challenge our own assumptions and emotional responses, and have the courage to inspire change in those around us in order to fill the artificial chasm that appears to separate us.

ABOUT THE AUTHORS

ERIK FOGG

Erik attended MIT, where he studied Mechanical Engineering and Political Science and fell in love with American politics. He earned his Masters of Science, co-authoring a number of academic papers on international relations and security before working with MIT, Harvard, the United Nations, and other NGOs on conflict resolution. He then spent four years as an operations and management consultant, improving organizational effectiveness and culture for a number of clients across North America.

He's been blogging and writing essays on improving American democracy since he was young, but his greatest influence for working on Wedged was his realization that those that disagree with him had much more to teach him than those that already agree. He believes everyone can adopt this mindset and become hungry to learn from each other in political dialogue.

Erik lives in Cambridge, Massachusetts, and is the CEO of MidTide Media and co-founder of Something to Consider, focused on improving American political dialogue by undermining the destructive mindsets that ail politics in the US.

NATHANIEL GREENE

Nat has a background in Engineering and Business management. He has studied at Oxford University, Cambridge University and Harvard Business School. He is the CEO of Stroud International, using data to solve the problems that clients believe are impossible.

Nat's political views have evolved significantly over the years through discussions with the many great people that he has been fortunate enough to encounter while living in Asia, Europe, and North America and during his travels to over 50 countries and territories.

Nat has noticed that people will often get upset or shut down when engaged in political or policy discussion: in many circles if you fail to fully and completely identify with an entire suite of dogmatic policy positions then you are headed for social trouble. It is rare to find people who are curious about a situation, are actually open minded, and are willing to dig into primary sources for data.

Frustrated at this state of affairs Nat figured there were two options open to him: give up completely or look to apply his analytical and problem solving skills to help change how we conduct political dialogue. Thus Wedged was born.

Nat is the Chairman of MidTide Media, and co-Founder of Something to Consider. He lives in Marblehead, Massachusetts with his wife and four children.

GLOSSARY

Wedge Issue (Noun):

Wedge issues are political issues used deliberately by politicians to mobilize their base through anger and fear, and by media outlets to capture devoted customers through the same emotions. The unintended and dangerous consequence is that reliance upon these issues "wedges" the electorate into two very different, distant, emotional camps. But because the wedging tactic is effective in an individual election, it continues to be relied upon.

We define wedge issues as having a few particular characteristics. They're often highly emotional, difficult to debate with facts, and linked strongly to a sense of personal and group identity. Often, but not always, they're ultimately low on the list of voters' total priorities in government. Sometimes they're not even relevant to the job description of the politician using them to potential voters: for example, individual states had jurisdiction over same-sex marriage law, but national politicians used it as an issue to energize their base supporters.

Generally, think of wedge issues as those about which we'll spend a lot of time carrying banners and shouting at each other, but where slow or little progress towards consensus or solution is made.

Some good examples of wedge issues:

- » Abortion & birth control
- » Gay marriage
- » Gun control
- » Religious expression
- » Moral "decay" / behavior, pornography, etc

Wedging (Verb):

The deliberate process of pushing wedge issues to the front of the national dialogue in order to increase emotional engagement. Most often performed by politicians seeking votes and campaign contributions for elections, political media outlets seeking loyal viewers, or highly partisan political groups seeking followers or donations.

Wedge Tactics (Noun):

Seven common tactics are used in order to create, reinforce, and take advantage of a wedge issue. These tactics are used by politicians, media outlets, advocacy groups, and ideologically extreme Americans to take control of the national dialogue.

1. **Inflated Issues.** The issue is made out to be world-stoppingly important: a matter of fundamental human rights, of our core values as Americans, of a very deep right-and-wrong. The stakes are made out to be very high, and any incremental movement or compromise is painted to be total loss on the issue, as it would create a slippery slope or domino effect towards defeat. Though we don't rank wedge issues as most important when forced to choose between them and other issues, they are made to feel highly important when we discuss them, and we are made to feel that we cannot give any ground, even on the parts of the issue we do not care as much about.

   Examples: Even though government functionality, the economy, and healthcare are the top priorities for Americans, it is most common to hear that disagreement issues like abortion and guns are those that will prevent someone from voting for a candidate. Abortion is a matter of murder vs. the fundamental rights of women. Guns policy is a matter of inalienable constitutional freedoms vs. the lives of children.

2. **Tribe Rallies.** Simple arguments, bumper-sticker one-liners, and team identifiers dominate messaging. These are not intended to change the minds of others that disagree, but to create a sense of group identity among

supporters. The issue is tied to the cultural identity of the demographic group that's being courted for the vote. This reinforces the emotional commitment of supporters and maintains social pressure not to break rank.

Examples: Camps pick simple identifiers for themselves that don't allow for any nuance, like being "pro human rights" and "fighting oppression," or being "pro freedom" or advocating for "responsibility."

3. **Cherry-Picked Data.** Because complexity and nuance are a threat to a highly emotional narrative, wedging relies on the manipulation and careful selection of data to create so called "analyses" that support one side of the argument. Highly complex phenomena are broken down into simple graphs that claim to fully explain the problem with a single, simple variable. This provokes our natural confirmation bias and makes us more certain that anyone disagreeing with us is a fool.

Examples: Events in the US are often compared to those in other countries, without controlling for the size of the American population. A correlation is presumed to be causation. Variables are deceptively defined and labeled. An event like a school shooting is used to show that we should ban all guns; a person stopping a robbery with a gun is used to show that we should all carry concealed weapons.

4. **Symbolic Battles.** Legislative or court battles over ultimately trivial, low-impact, or tangentially-related sub-issues are touted by supporters as great victories or grave defeats. Such battles reinforce a sense of progress, threat, and pride among supporters, and give politicians activity that they can point to during campaign season when they have not made substantial progress in other fields.

Examples: The battle over whether abortion should be restricted to 20 or 24 weeks encapsulates only 1.2% of abortions, many of which are "health of the mother" exceptions, and would be allowed in either case.

5. **Enemy Groups.** The opposition to each camp's position on the issue is painted as stupid, evil, or both. They are made out to be enemies with bad intent that must be defeated and painted to share none of our core values to prevent the temptation to work towards consensus. This taps into our sense of righteousness, fear, and natural human tendency to be motivated by having an enemy to fight against. When the opposition is evil, one does not require curious investigation.

   Examples: With gay marriage, the sides are painted as oppressing fundamental civil rights or attacking the moral foundations of our society. With economic inequality, the sides are painted as either corporate fat-cats stealing from hard-working Americans or government stealing from hard-working Americans to buy votes with welfare.

6. **Sensationalized Events.** Specific events in the news are pounced upon and editorialized in order to reinforce messaging. Each camp in a wedge issue wages a war of narrative, trying to successfully frame the event in the eyes of their camp as an example of the truth of their position. Though they are quickly forgotten, each event leads to a surge of energy and emotion for the camp. Rather than looking at a big picture, politicians and media can cherry-pick isolated events that stoke senses of fear, violation, and injustice.

   Examples: Despite the small number of victims compared to other violence in the US, highly visible shootings (like those in schools) garner massive attention and cause each side of the guns issue to release a flurry of messaging. Every proposed change in taxes, no matter how small, sparks a fight. Amid the Confederate flag controversy, quite suddenly private indi- viduals or institutions choosing to sell or not sell it, wave it or take it down, made enemies.

7. **Permanence.** Perhaps most importantly, the most successful wedge issues are those that are framed to be unresolvable. With demands that are intentionally vague

and designed to not be fully addressed by new legislation, each camp is able to keep wedge issues at the forefront of the minds of their supporters.

Examples: An issue like abortion will never be fully resolved unless there are 0 abortions, or unless there are no barriers at all – between those two extremes, there is always room to fight. Taxes can be fought over endlessly unless the government is dissolved. Inequality can be fought over until everyone has the exact same amount of money. None of these will ever truly go away on its own.

The Wedge in American Politics (noun):

The outcome of wedging tactics, The Wedge is the current state of American political polarization. Partisan extremes have a highly disproportionate share of voice and attention. The tenor of American dialogue has moved nearly exclusively to war-fighting. Politicians are unable to work together and have come to work along party lines on every issue due to their mutual antipathy. A sensible middle ground has dropped out of politics entirely, disenfranchising itself from being able to influence politics.

The Political Industry (noun):

The elements and organizations in the United States that depend on emotional political engagement to succeed, and use wedging tactics to engage citizens. This industry primarily includes politicians, political media and pundits, and advocacy organizations. Politicians depend on emotional engagement in order to cultivate votes, campaign contributions, and volunteer hours. Political media need readers/viewers that are loyal and advertise for them by sharing emotional articles or videos on social media. Advocacy organizations need volunteers and donors.

Wedged Partisans (noun):

American citizens that have succumbed to the false binary of American politics, as painted by wedge tactics. These people are highly engaged and emotional, and are unwilling to explore issues with others that disagree with them. Their emotional fervor pressures others in their social groups to be "with us or against us." They end up using the same wedge tactics as the political industry, and unwittingly propagate and exacerbate the wedge in American politics.

SELECTED BIBLIOGRAPHY AND RECOMMENDED READING

"Andris, Clio, et al. "The Rise of Partisanship and Super-Cooperators in the US House of Representatives." PLOS One, April 21, 2015.

Boatrright, Robert C. *Getting Primaried: The Changing Politics of Congressional Primary Challenges.* University of Michigan Press, 2014.

Ellis, Christopher, and Stinson, James A. *Ideology in America.* Cambridge University Press, 2012.

Greene, Joshua. *Moral Tribes: Emotion, Reason, and the Gap Between Us.* Penguin Books, 2014.

Haidt, Jonathan. *The Righteous Mind: Why Good People Are Divided by Politics and Religion.* Vintage, 2013.

Hibbing, John R., and Smith Kevin B., *Predisposed: Liberals, Conservatives, and the Biology of Political Differences.* Routledge, 2013.

Lanthrop, Douglas. *The Campaign Continues: How Political Consultants and Campaign Tactics Affect Public Policy.* Praeger Publishers: Westport, CT, 2003.

Layman, Geoffrey, et al. "Party Polarization in American Politics: Characteristics, Causes, and Consequences." Annual Review of Political Science, 2006, issue 9, pgs 83-110.

Pew Research Center: US Politics & Policy. "Political Polarization in the American Public." June 12, 2014. Available at: http://www.people-press.org/2014/06/12/political-polarization-in-the-american-public/. Accessed 10/15/2015.

Prinz, Jesse J. *The Emotional Construction of Morals*. Oxford University Press, 2009.

Weeden, Jason, and Kurzban, Robert. *The Hidden Agenda of the Political Mind: How Self-Interest Shapes Our Opinions and Why We Won't Admit It.* Princeton University Press, 2014.

Westen, Drew. *The Political Brain: The Role of Emotion in Deciding the Fate of the Nation.* Public Affairs, 2008.